SUCCESSFUL SHOTGUNNING

How to Build Skill in the Field and Take More Birds in Competition

PETER F. BLAKELEY

STACKPOLE
BOOKS

Copyright © 2003 by Stackpole Books

Published by
STACKPOLE BOOKS
5067 Ritter Road
Mechanicsburg, PA 17055
www.stackpolebooks.com

Printed in the United States

First edition

10 9 8 7 6 5 4 3 2 1

Illustrations by Linda Rogers

Library of Congress Cataloging-in-Publication Data
Blakeley, Peter F.
 Successful shotgunning : how to build skill in the field and take more
birds in competition / by Peter F. Blakeley.— 1st ed.
    p. cm.
Includes index.
 ISBN 0–8117–0042–9 (hardcover)
 1. Trapshooting. I. Title.
 GV1181 .B52 2003
 799.3'132—dc21
                                                              2003003848

To Alison,
my eternally patient
and supportive wife

CONTENTS

FOREWORD

Peter Blakeley is one of the most involved, enthusiastic, and animated shotgunning aficionados I have known in my thirty years plus of competing. Since I do most of my practicing at the Dallas Gun Club, I have experienced a few years of the "Peter Blakeley experience." Peter gives about 150 percent all the time. If he is not teaching on the field, he is discussing shooting theory with other shotgunners, or is changing the sporting clays course, or is writing an article for a shooting magazine, or is looking for someone with whom to discuss the finer points of shotgunning. I have rarely seen him stand still. And as I see it, all his efforts are in an attempt to achieve his ultimate goal: the tireless pursuit of the art of shotgunning.

At first, communications with Peter were not crystal clear. When a heavily accented Scot tries to carry on a conversation with a native Texan, one would have a very difficult time believing that both are speaking the same language. I have adjusted, however, and now know that "shotgoon" means shotgun.

As we come from different backgrounds, we were often wary of each other's philosophy regarding certain shotgunning theories. But after many discussions, I can honestly say that I have benefited greatly from Peter's philosophy and his unique presentation. He has given this old skeet shooter a fresh perspective on shooting theory.

Peter has compiled a treasure of great information and shooting theory, along with some great shotgunning tales. Pay attention to what he has to say.

Robert Paxton is a thirty-two-time all-American skeet shooter, two-time high overall world champion, and nine-time Texas state champion, and he has set numerous world records throughout his shooting career. Robert was inducted into the National Skeet Shooting Association Hall of Fame in 1995.

PREFACE

This book is based on my personal knowledge of shooting methods, including over forty years of wingshooting, over thirty years of sporting clays experience, and over twenty-four years as a full-time shooting instructor in the United Kingdom and here in the States. During those years, I have written many instructional letters and articles. I currently write articles for *Sporting Clays* magazine. I have a genuine enthusiasm and willingness to communicate all this accrued knowledge to you, the shooter. However, the contents of this book should never be considered a substitute for shooting lessons. Quality shooting instruction is a worth-while commodity, and long-term involvement with a good coach should improve anyone's game tremendously. Nor is this book for beginners, although it contains material that is beneficial to the beginner. I hope you will come to think of *Shotgunning* as a reference book, one that offers a better understanding of the shooting process as a whole—a guide to the evaluation of targets in wingshooting situations either in the field or a competitive environment, such as on a sporting clays course or skeet field.

Some guys will tell you that their success with a shotgun is unimportant to them. You know, the "I don't care if I hit anything, I just like to see the dogs working, feel the wind in my hair, and be at one with nature" guys. Really? I don't believe any of it. Nobody likes to miss, and with good instruction, everyone can improve. Nobody hits them all, either, and a bad day's shooting is often more enjoyable than a good day of doing some of the more menial tasks that take up large chunks of our lives, but make no mistake, the enjoyment of the shooting experience as a whole is defined ultimately by the proficiency with which we use a shotgun. So here's something to think about. The aspiring shotgunner has absolutely no control over any airborne target. Once he triggers the shot, it's over. It would make sense, therefore, to pay more attention to the things that he can control—gun fit, stance, mount, swing, and most important of all, visual ability to accurately evaluate all the variables involved. This book will show you how.

ACKNOWLEDGMENTS

During the course of my shooting life, many people have influenced my decision to write this book. Many of them are valued personal friends and acquaintances who contributed in some way with their vast accumulations of knowledge of the sport of shotgunning. (This isn't to say that, on various shooting-related topics, we are always in agreement.) They include Andy McCloud, head keeper on Lord Edgerton's estate in Cheshire; Bob Brister, *Shot-Gunning: the Art and the Science;* Cyril S. Adams, *Lock, Stock & Barrel;* Michael Yardley, *Gun Fitting: the Quest for Perfection;* Sam Shiller, ZZ bird (Helice) champion; Roger Silcox, Clay Pigeon Shooting Associaton (CPSA) staff tutor; Mick Howells, former 1996 Sporting Clay World Champion; Robert Paxton, thirty-two-time all-American skeet champion; Brian Mitchell, head grouse keeper on the Duke of Buccleuch's estate in Langholm; John Baxter, head keeper at Westerhall Estate; Patrick Hope-Johnstone, his Grace the Earl of Annandale; David Hope-Johnstone, the young Earl; and Thomas Florey, estate manager, Earl of Annandale's estate, Southwest Scotland. I thank Barbara Dickson, Mace McCain, Martin F. "Bubba" Wood, and Bob Troutt for their advice and help with photographs. Last but not least, I give special thanks to my friend Ralph "Cush" Cushman from Anchorage, Alaska, who dedicated many hours of his spare time to edit the manuscript. Cush is a rare find; editors with his combination of literary skills and expert knowledge of the art of shotgunning are few and far between. He did an admirable job.

INTRODUCTION

It has been my pleasure and privilege, over the last thirty-five years or so, to meet many shooting men who are skilled and accomplished with a shotgun. During most of those years, I lived in an ideal location, with some of the best sporting estates in the world within view of my doorstep. I've seen shots that can pull a stratospheric, soaring archangel cock pheasant from the clouds high above a wooded glen at Westerhall Estate, and others that can successfully decipher all the directional changes and intercept a heather-hugging red grouse as it rides the wind over the misty, purple hills of the Roan Fell. I've seen the guys who can stroke a white-wing dove, cruising the thermals of a hot Texas breeze out of the sky, and the quail hunters who can snap-shoot a bobwhite with the speed of a striking rattler—quicker than most of us can blink an eye. I've seen Robert Paxton, thirty-two-time all-American skeet champion and one of the best skeet shooters in the world, systematically pulverize targets with enviable precision. I've watched former World Sporting Clays Champion Mick Howells pause for a moment before taking a second, successful shot at a target that defeated him on the first. The parameters are the same; all these guys have something in common—they don't succeed by accident. They are all specialists in their own particular way. They have honed their skills and refined their techniques to the point where there is no guess-work involved. They have developed the ability to evaluate moving targets and put their shot pattern precisely where it is needed. Anyone who believes that these men have the ability to do this because of some inherent trait, and that they have become expert shots by relying on instinct alone, should think again; it just doesn't happen. The so-called "natural shot" is as mythical as the unicorn.

Years ago, in the days of my youth, fish, fowl, furry animals, and especially firearms were a distraction for me. Firearms? Ah yes, seductive and enticing. My parents were apprehensive about firearms, but for me, they held an overwhelming fascination. I was attracted to them like a moth to a light. Even before these, more humble means of *armes du chasse*—in fact anything that would heave some sort of projectile—was considered: bows and arrows, catapults, and a blowpipe made from one of my mother's tubular brass curtain rods. The blowpipe fired darning needles with suitably fashioned tufts of wool for flights. These were wicked looking, surprisingly accurate, and potentially quite deadly, as my older sister and the cat next door often found out to their discomfort.

As is usually the case with any fledgling hunter, these early targets were stationary, but as I eventually aspired to moving ones, I soon found out that it was necessary to "lead" them in order to connect. I would practice this by firing rocks at my father's tin army plate with a catapult (slingshot). A friend would throw it into the air or roll it down a hill at the local golf course (the original bolting rabbit?). We would do that for hours. Later, I progressed to a "Diana" pellet gun and, eventually, when I was ten, my first shotgun—a bolt-action Webley & Scott .410. With a gun tucked under my arm and few Eley Fourlong shells in my pocket, my spirits would soar and I was in paradise. I would wander the fields and woods of the surrounding countryside, oblivious of time, hoping to get a shot at a rabbit or pigeon.

My enthusiasm was shared by like-minded others, and we would fish and hunt to the exclusion of everything else. During the summer holidays, it became a lucrative business. We could get three pence each for a rabbit or pigeon and six pence for a hare. We were grubby, unruly individuals with unkempt hair and permanently skinned knees, as wild as the heather, and we would spend all our daylight hours on these *forays du chasse*. We were probably ten or eleven years old. Guns and anything with explosive capabilities were our passion, and our *piece de resistance* was a cannon with a two-inch bore, which we engineered from a steel scaffolding tube fixed to a set of pram wheels. The crude propellant for the shot charge was a deadly concoction of sodium chlorate weed killer, sugar, and potassium permanganate, and it was certainly productive. An enticing bait trail of potato peelings and old, blackened bananas, which we would beg from the green grocers' shops, would be put down in the shallow waters around the edges of the local disused gravel pits. Concentrations of teal and mallard would be in abundance during the winter

months, and we would ambush them with the cannon as they unsus-
pectingly wafted in at dusk. Sportsmanship and hunting ethics were not
an issue in those days, and a dead duck was, well, quite simply a dead
duck. Business was business, and although rabbits and pigeons were
good, ducks were even better. We would wander along the cobbled
streets and sell them door to door, cleaned and oven-ready, for six pence
each. Diana, the goddess of hunting, must have smiled down upon us all.
How we managed to survive through this pyrotechnical period without
a loss of a finger, eye, or other part of our anatomy, I have no idea. My
poor mother worried incessantly about the next unscheduled appearance
from the local constabulary, but I was unperturbed and undeterred by
her scolding.

In these early days, I lived in the north of England, but I later
moved to Scotland. Cartridges were expensive, and out of necessity, anything that I could shoot was eaten. A lucky shot at something edible was
a welcome weekend treat. Despite this, my grandmother would call me
unpleasant names, and I could never fully understand why. On one
occasion, as I proudly appeared at the kitchen door with a cock pheasant, his resplendent plumage glowing amber and black like campfire
coals, she referred to me as a bloodthirsty child. Meal times were a family affair, and the next weekend, as we gathered for the feast, I watched
in silence as Grandma took great pride and pleasure in ceremoniously
carving the Sunday lunch, an anemic-looking supermarket chicken.
Comparisons with the pheasant were futile, and I soon learned to accept
the situation. Hunters are often the targets of unfettered emotionalism,
and certain areas of our society sometimes disapprove of our actions for
the flimsiest of reasons. But I was inescapably a predatory animal, and as
soon as the backs of my critics turned, I would search for other things to
shoot. A kindred spirit to the elements, with passions residual from some
ancient hunting ancestry, I would strive to put something in the bag on
my hunting trips, time being immaterial.

I enjoyed an advantageous location. I was slap-bang in the middle of
some of the best sporting estates in the world, with no shortage of
gamekeepers to give me free advice. One man helped me more than any
other—Andy McCloud, the head keeper on Lord Edgerton's estate at
Tatton Hall in Cheshire. I can hear his booming voice ringing in my
ears even today, after an uncoordinated poke at a cock pheasant, "Don't
shoot *at* him, laddie. Put t' shot where he's *going*!" Very good advice.
Years later, I had the pleasure of shooting on some of the best estates in
Scotland, including the Earl of Annandale's estate, where I was the chief

shooting instructor until I moved to the States, and the Duke of Buc-
cleuchs estate in Langholm, where I owned my gun shop, Border Tackle
& Guns. The Earl of Dalkeith's grouse moors in Langholm were at one
time considered by many to be the best in the world. In fact, the Scottish record stands at 1,261^{1}/$_{2}$ brace, which was shot off the Roan Fell on
August 30, 1911. The head keeper, Brian Mitchell, is a friend of mine,
and I have walked the purple, hallowed heather surrounding Langholm
many times. Until recently, the historic Langholm grouse moors made a
significant economic contribution to an area that hitherto was incapable
of supporting anything else, apart from the occasional sheep. Sadly, the
days of the big bags are gone, but not forever, I hope. All this was many
years ago. And now? I am proud to be the resident shooting coach and
club professional at what is considered by many to be one of the most
elaborate and prestigious shooting facilities in the world, the Dallas Gun
Club in Lewisville, Texas.

Shooting's a funny game, and owning a gun shop is a bit like the
proverbial curate's egg—good in parts. Shooters befriend you sometimes
for the wrong reasons: discounts on shooting paraphernalia and good
deals on shells and guns immediately spring to mind. On the upside, you
get a lot of invitations to shoot, but I was never really sure why that was.
I would like to believe that it was because people thought that I was a
nice guy, or that I had a couple of well-trained Labradors that were
sought after to pick the birds on the pheasant shoots, or that I was a
shooting instructor. The downside? When the chips are down, shooting
instructors aren't allowed to miss or have a bad day under any circumstances. There is always one stratospheric cock pheasant that, at the end
of a drive, tries hard to emulate the actions of a kamikaze pilot and commit suicide just before the final whistle sounds. This usually happens
when everyone else is unloaded, looking in the wrong direction, or at
least pretending to be. "Your bird, Peter!" someone (usually with a grin
on his face) bellows. When this happens, I am instantly plunged into a
dilemma, a certain lose–lose situation. If I make the shot, the comments
will be equally divided.

"You see that shot Peter made? Brilliant! That bird must have been
fifty yards at least. Folded him up like a pack of cards, he did!"

"Yeah, but don't forget he *is* a shooting instructor. If he can't hit
'em, who can?"

And if I missed? Same result.

"I thought you said that Peter was a shooting instructor? How did
he miss that shot? Don't think I'll be taking a lesson with him!"

So what's the answer? Make sure I don't attempt any "pressure" shots that are too far and hope I don't miss any that I couldn't possibly avoid. As I said, shooting's a funny game.

True shooting instructors are a breed apart. They are sucked into this profession gradually over a period of time, during which there is a natural progression of learning, a lifetime's accumulation of technical and practical knowledge. Although I shot competitively for many years and was the equivalent rank of a state champion, a top shot doesn't necessarily make a good coach. Ken Davies, the chief instructor at Holland & Holland, is probably the best-known shooting coach in the world. He has never really shot competitively, but his success as a coach is legendary. Genuine enthusiasm, a sense of humor, good communication skills, patience, and the ability to read the client and recognize when your methods aren't working are far more important than shooting ability. Regardless of what they say, everyone who picks up a shotgun for the first time is apprehensive. A good coach should have the ability to establish a rapport quickly and make a client feel at ease, and as a result, the lesson will be more enjoyable for both parties. The look on the face of someone who has always wanted to shoot but doesn't try it for fear of failure, as he learns to break targets, gives me a feeling of elation that is hard to describe.

For many years I have considered writing a clear, concise, definitive book on the art of shotgunning, or more precisely, wingshooting and sporting clays. So why, after such a long involvement in the sport, would I suddenly feel the urge to do it now? Although we have had shooting schools for a hundred years or so in the United Kingdom, they are a fairly recent addition in the United States. Mainly due to the explosive interest in sporting clays and double-guns over the past fifteen years, shooting schools are currently springing up all over like flowers in a roadside ditch. There are more shooting instructors out there than fleas on a hedgehog's back. Some are good and some not so good, but make no mistake, all of them are determined to persuade you, the shooter, to part with your hard-earned dollar. People with far less experience than I are climbing aboard the shooting bandwagon and either producing how-to videos or writing a book on the subject, so I might as well throw my two pence in!

So, mainly in an attempt to help all the guys (and gals) out there who are thirsting for knowledge about how to become a better shot, here goes.

CHAPTER 1

The Shotgun: A Brief History

It is a widely held belief that it was the Chinese and Hindus who started it all with their crude cannons and ceremonial firecracker parades, as far back as 500 A.D., even though there is no concrete evidence of this. Gunpowder (or something with similar explosive capabilities) was used in the siege of Constantinople in 688, and there are records that show that the Arabs and Saracens used it at the siege of Mecca in 690. The original formula is vague, and the actual composition of the explosive was of doubtful quantities of saltpeter, charcoal, and sulfur. We know from early manuscripts that the Greeks had "fire tubes" fixed on the bows of their ships as early as 1098, and in 1218, artillery was used in battles at Toulouse. So who actually invented gunpowder?

The first man to write about the actual composition of gunpowder was undoubtedly Roger Bacon, of Oxford, but his writings were always shrouded in mystery. There is evidence that by 1280 early firearms were already belching out death and destruction in Spain and North Africa. Little did any of these early artillerymen realize that the discovery of the explosive properties of saltpeter would, over the next several hundred years, lead to the development of the weapons of destruction and complex instruments of recreation that we have today.

The first semiportable guns were made from two pieces of hard wood, each with a groove down the center, fastened together with iron hoops to strengthen them. Evidence suggests that these were in use in China and other Far Eastern countries. Foot soldiers on the battlefields (staggering under the weight no doubt) would carry these cannons to the front line and attempt to wreak havoc on the opposition. When in position, these primitive firearms were wedged between forked sticks

1

A semiportable gun of around 1370–1450. These were usually constructed from two pieces of hard wood, each grooved down the middle, joined together and then reinforced with iron hoops. The crude projectiles were round stones.

and pointed in the general direction of the approaching enemy. The other end of these crude guns was stuck in the ground just before firing, to give some resistance to the force of the recoil. The usual projectiles hurled from the end were roughly round stones.

Gunpowder eventually made its way to Europe, and there is no doubt that in England during the fourteenth century crude cannons or "hand gonnes" were used as weapons of war but with little effect. These early cannons consisted of simple iron tubes, primitively fire-forged around a central former or "mandrill" and welded shut at one end. These crude tubes were mounted on wooden shafts to give some sort of control as they were aimed at the enemy. There was no lock mechanism; the soldiers had the unenviable task of sticking a match (a smoldering piece of rope soaked in saltpeter) into the crude touchhole at the end of the weapon at exactly the most opportune moment. The idea was to surprise and temporarily subdue the enemy with the noise of the explosion, and it was this element of surprise that was the main advantage over the bow and arrow. Unfortunately, the disadvantages often outweighed the advantages. If the powder was damp or, even worse, it started to rain, the opportune moment sometimes didn't present itself. This doubtful reliability, combined with the visual distraction of dozens of blood-strained, battle-ax-wielding adversaries bearing rapidly down on them, was usually enough to deter all but the bravest of these early artillerymen. Small wonder that most of these guys opted for the reliability and vastly superior range of the crossbow or longbow!

The superiority of the bow continued well into the eighteenth century, and there were many contests between the musket and the

Hand "cannoneers" of about 1390–1450. The "gun" was ignited by means of a handheld smoldering match soaked in saltpeter. Woodcut from the *Rudimentum Noviciorum, Lübeck, 1475.*

longbow. One at Pacton Green in Cumberland in 1792 proved "conclusively" that the bow was superior both in range and accuracy, placing sixteen arrows in the target, while the musket placed only twelve balls. The result was hailed as a triumph for the longbow, but there was also evidence that the archer in the contest was an expert in his field, and although the result was impressive, the bow was already as efficient as it could be, whereas the gun would continue to improve.

By the early sixteenth century, the "hand gonne" had evolved sufficiently to enable it to be used with more success, and by this time a crude lock, known as the matchlock, was employed. This was a simple devise that carried the "match" in a "serpentine" shaped like a striking snake's head. As the trigger was pulled, the serpentine struck forward to ignite the powder in the flash pan, which was located on the side of the gun next to the touchhole where the main charge was. The slow-burning match needed to be moved forward manually during use, which must have been a problem if the enemy decided to press home a surprise

The crude matchlock of about 1450 was the first lock. This was nothing more than a handheld cannon with a primitive S-shaped trigger, the top of which held a smoldering match. Both hands could now be used to steady and aim the handgun as the shot was triggered.

attack, but at least it was an improvement. The serpentine lock allowed the user to have both hands free (at times) to support and maneuver the weapon. More accurate and powerful than both the longbow and crossbow, the matchlock and its advantages were quickly appreciated, and it became the weapon of choice for the aristocracy of the era. Matchlock rifles, loaded with a single lead ball, were used to hunt the large animals that were plentiful in the forests of Europe, and these same guns could also be loaded with small pieces of lead to give a useful shotgun pattern. This early lead shot was known as a Hayle shot, and it was made by clipping pieces of lead from a sheet. These small pieces were then placed in a "rattler" or "tumbler," which resembled a small butter churn and turned over and over to knock the corners off. The resulting patterns, due to the primitive aerodynamic qualities of this shot, must have been of considerable size. It was during the reign of Henry VIII that the use of these early scatterguns for fowling was first mentioned.

Up to the reign of King Henry, all battles were fought with the royal archers, and the English longbow reigned supreme on the battlefield at extended ranges, cutting down the enemy with barrages of arrows. Although there are exaggerated reports of the potency of the longbow, there is no doubt that the arrows would pierce armor as easily as a musket ball would, and it could be reloaded much quicker in the heat of battle. There are authenticated cases where the bows used by the North American Indians would send arrows completely through the buffalo they hunted. The longbow won many battles, and the English retained it as a weapon of war even though the early firearms were rapidly gaining ground. The use of guns for either military use or hunting was forbidden by the king except by special license, but by 1537, the superiority of the matchlock over the longbow was being proven. About this time a "crack" artillery regiment, the Guild of St. George, was formed. The gun it used was known as the matchlock arquebus.

At first this permitted use of firearms was restricted to this regiment, who were also known as the Honorable Artillery Company of London, but by 1545, landowners and certain citizens who were in favor with the king were permitted to hunt under royal license. This license was granted only on the deposit of a bond of £20 into the royal coffers, and this money was to be forfeited if any of the complicated hunting laws was abused. The illegal use of firearms was frowned upon, and to enforce these rules, royal forest keepers were employed, each armed with a matchlock. There were stiff penalties for shooting the king's deer and fowl. Despite these harsh penalties, official measures had little effect on the poor country folk, and throughout the harsh winter months, they had no choice but to attempt to supplement their meager diet with a potshot at anything that came within range of their guns. Hungry mouths to feed and a rumbling belly would eventually always override fear of the consequences. There was a huge demand for black market guns, much to the delight of local blacksmiths, who would forge the barrels in the same way as the medieval cannons of the earlier era. There was a downside for these desperate poachers, however. The longbow had been silent, but the audible report of the more efficient matchlock would often betray the hunter's position to the king's keepers. Many of these early poachers paid the price of ignoring the stringent royal laws with their life. Public beheading was fashionable in those days, and as a royal disciplinary example, it was unsurpassed.

These restrictions would remain in force in England for some time. Birds for the elaborate banquets of the aristocracy were either hunted from horseback with hawks or falcons or netted in large numbers with the aid of hunting dogs. Birdlime and snares were also used. However, the invention of rifling in barrels and the development of the wheel lock made stalking with the gun much easier throughout Europe for two reasons. The rifling greatly improved accuracy, and with the wheel lock there was no need to carry a smoldering match to fire the gun. The inventor of the wheel lock is apparently unknown, but because it was considered in those days to be a complex and intricate mechanism, it was thought to originate from the clock-making areas of Germany or Italy. In the wheel lock there was a serrated steel wheel, as its name implies, which was powered by a small, coiled mainspring, similar to a clock. A small, square-ended key or spanner wound up this spring. The

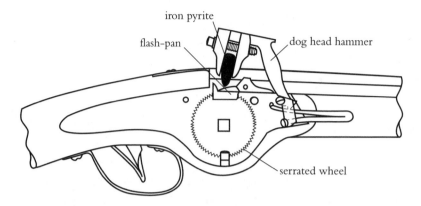

The wheel lock mechanism was a wheel device powered by a circular spring, rather like a clock spring. The serrated wheel was wound with a square-ended key, and as the trigger was pulled, the wheel revolved against the iron pyrite, which produced the sparks to ignite the priming powder in the flash pan.

hammer (or cock) of the gun was lowered against this wheel if there was the chance of a shot, and as the trigger was pulled, the wheel would then rotate against this, similar to the disposable cigarette lighter of today. The sparks were produced by a piece of iron pyrite, which was held in the jaws of the dog-head hammer. Pot hunting with these early rifles and shotguns was common throughout Europe by the mid-sixteenth century.

The earliest reference work I can find on the subject of bird hunting in England is contained in *The Merry Wives of Windsor,* which was written in 1597 by Master Ford. He refers to "going out a' birding" in the book, but unfortunately, there is no reference to the type of weapon or how it was used to shoot these birds. The earliest records of the art of shotgunning were made in the classic treatise *Hunger's Prevention or the Whole Arte of Fowling by Water and Land,* by Gervase Markham, written in 1621. At that time, bird hunting was popular as a necessary method of supplementing the thin winter diet, but there was no sport or sentiment involved. The idea was to approach as near as possible to flocks of ducks, geese, pheasants, or anything else that looked as though it might be edible. All the guns were long barreled, necessary to allow the pressure to build up and push the shot charge out of the end with enough velocity to kill and maim as many birds as possible. Markham suggested that a fowling piece should be at least 5½ to 6 feet long and of 16-bore gauge, which was about .662 of an inch. Because the birds were shot on the

A stalking horse, any suitable old farmyard nag that was past its sell-by date, was sometimes used to approach feeding flocks of water fowl without being seen. Due to the extremely inefficient powder and the resultant slow buildup of pressure during ignition, "fowling pieces" were usually anywhere between 5^1/$_2$ and 6 feet long. Engraving from *The Gentleman's Recreation,* 1686.

ground, there was no incentive to modify the barrel length. Markham also mentions the use of a stalking horse. This was exactly as the name suggests, an old farm nag that had seen better days and was long past its sell-by date for useful farm labor. Any old horse would do, providing it was reasonably quiet and presumably fairly deaf. The intrepid hunter would use this old nag as a moving screen to creep up on his quarry and blast away, until any fowl that remained realized that the horse had lethal qualities.

THE EARLY FLINTLOCKS

In about the middle of the sixteenth century, a simple version of the flintlock was produced in Europe, possibly Scandinavia. This type of lock was called a snaphaunce, an aptly descriptive word derived from Dutch meaning "pecking hen." A flint was gripped firmly in the jaws of the cock by means of a turn screw. The cock snapped forward upon the trigger-pull to hit the flash pan cover, which then exposed the priming powder to the sparks. These snaphaunce locks rapidly became more popular across Europe and remained popular until the early eighteenth century.

It was in the early seventeenth century that the English, or "dog-lock," mechanism was perfected. All the weapons of this period were still muzzleloaders, and although many of the European gun makers had attempted to produce a weapon that could be loaded more efficiently, these efforts had failed because of the massive exchange of gas at the junction of the breech and action face. There was no satisfactory way of inspecting the status of the barrels of these muzzleloaders, except by unscrewing the breech plug, which was a tedious operation for the avid bird hunter. Consequently, carelessly loading too much powder and shot in the heat of the moment could have disastrous, sometimes fatal results. How those primitive barrels must have stretched at times, and I dread to think how many fowlers lost a few fingers here and there due to a burst barrel, or an eye due to the inevitable flashbacks that must have occurred. More and more fowling pieces were imported from the continent, notably France and Italy, and in 1637 a charter was granted by King Charles I that required that all imported guns be "proofed" by subjecting them to greater stress than they would receive under normal use. The barrels that passed these tests were stamped with proof marks. These were the letters *GP* under a crown, which stood for gun makers proof.

King Charles II had spent many years in exile on the continent, and upon his return to reclaim his throne with the restoration of the monarchy in 1660, he brought with him French flintlocks of the best quality. During his exile, the king and his followers had developed a taste for shooting flying game, which was already popular on the continent. Lighter and more pointable fowling pieces were imported, mainly from France and Italy, and the English gun makers were quick to respond to

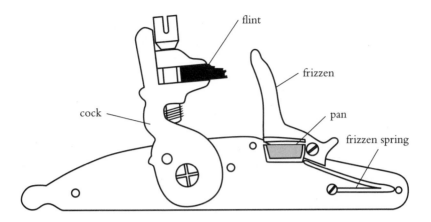

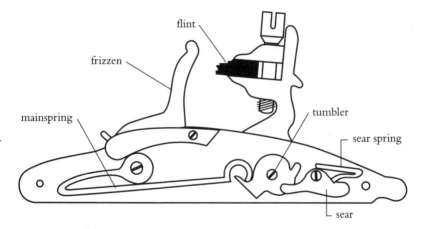

The flintlock mechanism. The earliest form of flintlock was called a snaphaunce, derived from the Dutch word meaning "pecking hen." From the snaphaunce, the true flintlocks evolved.

these with their own designs in an effort to overtake their French rivals. These guns had single barrels, usually about four feet long, and were still cumbersome by today's standards, but they were certainly better balanced and a distinct improvement on the fowling pieces of the previous century. Theoretically, it was now possible to attempt shots at flying targets by keeping the gun out in front of the bird (the origins of sustained lead?), until the shotcharge had left the barrels. In his book on shooting flying game, *The Gentleman's Recreation,* published in 1686, Richard

Blome relates that shooting from horseback was popular, with servants and dogs standing by to retrieve the birds.

The flintlock mechanism continued to undergo several minor improvements over the next 150 years or so. This was a period of consolidation for the gun-making industry in England, and the English craftsmen in the late eighteenth and early nineteenth centuries continued to produce guns of increasingly better design and efficiency. Until the late 1700s, all barrels were made by forge welding around a mandrel, but some ingenious barrel maker hit on the idea of welding strips of horseshoe nails, which were coiled around the mandrel in a spiral fashion to produce a circumferential seam. This method produced a barrel that was stronger and thinner than the early barrels where the seam was longitudinal. The method was the basic principal of the Damascus barrel, which was further developed by Rigby of Dublin.

This was a period of rapid change, and there was fierce rivalry between gun makers to bring their guns up to date with the latest inventions. Patents were ten a penny, and although many of these innovations were insignificant, three would have a major impact and lasting effect. The first was the discovery of how to form lead shot by dropping it from a tower. Story has it that in 1782, enterprising Bristol plumber William Watts was repairing a church roof. In those days, lead, because of its low cost and excellent malleability, was used in sheet form to repair roofs. These sheets were "welded" together with a kerosene blowtorch to produce a watertight seal. Watts, after finishing work for the day, climbed down from a church roof that he had been repairing. He noticed that some of the molten lead droplets had solidified on the way down and landed in a puddle of water. He was perplexed to find that many of these solidified molten droplets were nearly perfectly cylindrical. Luckily, Watts was blessed with a lively and inquiring mind. He was so much intrigued that he hardly slept that night. The next day, he returned to the church roof with two of his wife's prized kitchen utensils, a kettle and a sieve. Watts heated some lead in the kettle and instructed his wife to pour the molten lead through the sieve. Lo and behold, the first dropped shot, as it came to be called, was produced. Rumor has it that Watts took out a patent on the process (patent no. 1347) and later sold the rights to this patent for the princely sum of ten thousand pounds. No doubt that was a lot of money in those days, but over the next four hundred years or so, no one has found a better way to produce lead shot, and it is still produced in "shot towers" like this today. I am inclined to think that Watts sold himself short on the deal.

Gentlemen are shooting flying game from horseback, a pastime that was fashionable in the eighteenth century. Servants were employed to load the guns and retrieve the birds with dogs. Reproduction of an engraving from *The Gentleman's Recreation,* 1686.

The second important innovation was described in a patent issued in 1815 to Sir William Congreve for the standardization of gunpowder. Now the quality of the powder could be controlled to give a more calculable efficiency.

The third innovation, and probably one of the most significant for the gun trade, was Henry Nock's (1772–1804) patented breech that appeared in 1787. Until this invention, the powder charge had been ignited through the touchhole in the side of the barrel. As the flint ignited the primer in the flash pan, the main charge was ignited at the side, which gave the effect of an uneven, slow burn of main propellant. Nock's breech eliminated this; now the propellant powder burned quicker and more efficiently, and guns shot harder and quicker. More importantly, however, there was no need for long barrels to allow the explosive gas pressure to develop. It was now possible to reduce barrel length to about thirty inches, which gave a much more pointable, better-balanced weapon. The English craftsmen were quick to see the opportunity, and the result was the production of the double-barrel flintlock, a final triumph and the culmination of centuries of effort—the perfection of the flintlock. During the next two decades, prominent London gun-making houses; the Manton brothers, Joseph (1795–1853) and John (1780–1834); Durs Egg (1785–1834); and James Purdey (1784–1863) elevated the muzzleloader system, which had remained stagnant for almost two hundred years, to the next level. The game gun

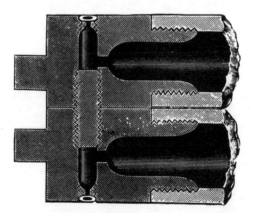

Henry Nock's patent breech resulted in a faster burn. As a result, the ignition time was considerably quicker, pressures were increased, and flintlock guns shot harder.

Joseph Manton and Colonel Peter Hawker partridge shooting at Longparish, 1827.

was about to evolve from a primitive weapon to the classic modern shot-gun, with the elegance and graceful lines that we still appreciate today.

There were many prominent names in the gun-making industry at this time, but most people are in agreement that the Manton brothers' contribution to the art of gun making was incalculable. There were many other fine gun makers of the period, but there is no doubt that the two brothers were the masters. John Manton, the elder brother, set up on his own after working for one of the more celebrated double-gun makers of the era, John Twigg. John's younger brother Joseph was an apprentice to John until he left to start his own business in 1789. Joseph had an inventive mind, and his patented elevated rib had the effect of raising point of impact (relative to point of aim) so that the birds could remain in view as the trigger was pulled. Manton guns were elegant and stylish, the Rolls-Royces of the gun trade, and within a few years, all the gun makers were producing similar double-guns with only slight variations.

THE EVOLUTION OF PERCUSSION IGNITION
As the flintlock was reaching perfection, an alternative method of ignition was sneaking in the back door that would eventually make the flint

obsolete. The Reverend Alexander John Forsyth, a church minister from Belhelvie in Aberdeenshire, Scotland, was perfecting the percussion ignition system. This system used a fulminate-based detonating charge that was exploded by a spring-loaded firing pin, which was hit by the hammer as the trigger was pulled. Percussion ignition was fast and more reliable, and Forsyth's invention opened the floodgates for dozens of ingenious ways for gun makers to apply it. Detonating powder was used in caps, tubes, and small pellets (called pills), but the most popular form to emerge was a small, copper cup filled with a noncorrosive fulminate. These caps were placed over a small nozzle with a hole bored through it and called a nipple. The nipple was screwed into the breech of the gun, and as the hammer hit the cap, the fulminate exploded to ignite the main charge. The debate over the merits of the flint versus the new percussion system raged for years and was the source of heated controversy among the sportsmen of the early 1820s. Slowly but surely the percussion guns gained ground, and by 1830, the flintlock conceded defeat to the superiority of the percussion weapon. One of the main reasons for this was the fact that the sport of pigeon trapshooting, where birds were released from box traps, was becoming highly competitive. This attracted many "professional" pigeon shooters, and now valuable prizes were an attraction, with large sums of money changing hands in wagers on the outcome of the event. The birds were released by pulling a cord on the signal from the shooter, and they had to be dispatched before they reached the boundary fence. Speed was now a critical factor, and since there was money at stake, this was no time for trivialities! The faster ignition time of the percussion gun was preferred, and the flintlock began to lose popularity. Many flintlocks were converted to percussion guns. One cheap and cheerful way of doing this was to simply screw a side plug into the touchhole and replace the cock with a percussion-type hammer, known as a hen-toed hammer. The next stage of the percussion era was the breechloader.

EARLY BREECHLOADERS

Gun makers had strived for many years to produce a weapon that could be loaded more efficiently than the muzzleloader, but they had always failed to find a way to successfully lock the barrels. Samuel Johannes Pauly, who was Swiss, produced and patented one of the first breechloaders in 1812. Inextricably caught up in the development of the breechloader was the necessity of a self-contained cartridge to go with it. Clement Pottet took out a patent on a self-contained cartridge in 1829.

It was further developed by Paris gun maker Houllier in about 1850, and consisted of a paper-cased cartridge with a brass base. The cartridge was fired by a brass pin, which was struck by one of the hammers to fire the gun. The other end of the brass pin was embedded in an internal percussion cap.

The invention of the breechloader was an improvement, although not everyone was quick to accept it. The muzzleloader appeared to be more robust in construction, because the barrels were only open at one end, the other closed by a steel plug, which was screwed securely into the breech. It wasn't easy to put confidence in something loaded into a paper and brass cartridge, and then sealed in place in the breech by a method that appeared to be flimsy by comparison. There were many skeptics, and the breechloader was not an instant success by any means.

One man who had a huge influence on the development of the sporting shotgun was Casimir Lefaucheax. At the Great Exhibition of London in 1851, he introduced a breechloader with a drop-down barrel that used pin-fire ammunition. The idea appealed to London gun maker Joseph Lang, who was quick to see the potential of this latest development and copied the idea with his own version. Other gun makers were soon jumping on the bandwagon, each applying his own personal ingenuity and imagination to make subtle improvements. James Purdey, Robert Adams, and John Dickson and Son, Edinburgh, Scotland, all produced their own variants. One patented by James Dougall of Glasgow was known as the lock-fast action. The principle was the simple, sliding round bolt, which engaged into a hole in the back of the action to lock it.

The only drawback of these drop-down barrel guns was the method of closing the action. Although it was reasonably strong and efficient, it was a manual operation, by means of either a side- or underlever. What was needed was a snap action that closed with a spring-loaded bolt, and in 1858 Westley Richards produced the first. Around the same time, George Daw introduced to England a cartridge that was in effect a crude version of the cartridge that we know today. It was invented by Clement Pottet of Paris and was an ideal complement to these new drop-down, snap-action guns. But the pin-fire cartridge had disadvantages. Loaded with highly unstable black powder, a sudden knock on one of the pins could transform a pocketful into an incendiary device—certainly not recommended for the successful pheasant hunt.

But still this new cartridge was a big improvement. Guns were designed with the firing pin fitted through the standing breech, but there was a problem in normal use. As the firing pins struck the primer, they were held in place against the cartridge with the pressure of the mainspring, preventing the gun from opening. In 1866, Thomas Stanton invented the rebounding lock, which did exactly as the name suggests. With Stanton's invention, the hammers rebounded as the gun was fired, allowing the strikers to return to half cock so that they were flush or behind the face of the standing breech. This action also reduced the possibility of the cartridges being detonated as the gun was closed, which before was definitely possible.

The hammers were neater on these guns, and the early snap actions were steadily improved until the introduction of the Purdey bolt in about 1863. This locking system, which was opened and closed by the top lever, was a significant breakthrough. The strength of this mechanism was unsurpassed, and it became the dominant lock for both double-barreled shotguns and rifles. Even today, most top-lever side-by-side shotguns are secured by means of a Purdey bolt. Elegant hammer guns were in production at this time by many famous gun makers, among them Greener, Grant, Holland & Holland, Rigby, and others who are all still in existence today.

The first hammerless gun, which cocked the action by opening, was the Anson & Deeley, patented in 1875. W. Anson and J. Deeley both worked for the Birmingham company of Westley Richards. This was an ingenious mechanism. The components of the lock were simplified to such an extent that there were only three main components. The result was legendary reliability, and the revolutionary action they developed is still used today in some form or other by many English, Spanish, Italian, German, and American gun manufacturers. Parker Brothers made their first shotgun with an Anson & Deeley action in 1879. A hammerless version was available by 1889.

Perhaps the only other true shotgun we should consider is the over-and-under. Early attempts to build a shotgun with this principle were unsuccessful in Britain for two reasons. First, the barrels were stacked

Opposite page: The Anson and Deeley side-by-side action is still virtually unchanged from its invention in 1879. Most countries have produced these sidelock actions in some shape or form with only minor modifications. At the top, the gun is shown in the closed and fired position. In the middle illustration, as the gun is opened, the cocking lever compresses the mainspring, which cocks the hammer. The sear engages in the slot at the base of the hammer and is held in position by the sear spring. At the bottom, the gun is closed and ready to fire. As the trigger is pressed, the sear disengages and the hammer falls.

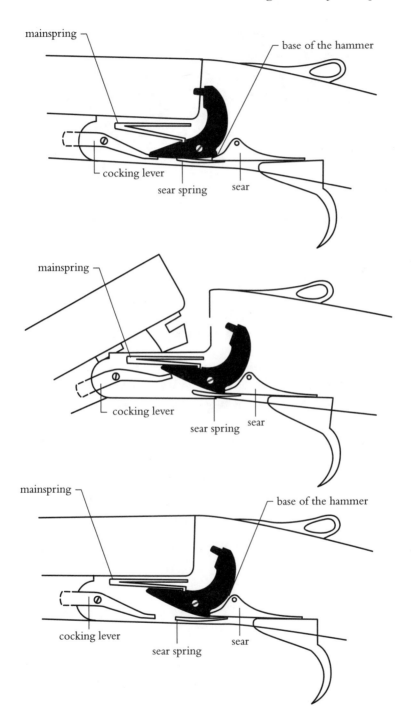

The Browning action is easily one of the most famous over-and-under actions. The design of the trigger mechanism completely disconnects between shots, which prevents a double discharge. All Brownings have automatic ejectors.

above one another; conventional locking systems available at the time produced a bulky depth of action. Second, this large and somewhat cumbersome action lacked the grace and lines of the traditional side-by-side, which until then had been a trademark of the British manufacturers. Two manufacturers produced an alternative locking mechanism to overcome this. These were Thomas Boss, who patented the design in 1909, and James Woodward, who followed with his in 1911. But there is no doubt that the most famous over-and-under shotgun is the Browning, the brainchild of John Moses Browning. Unfortunately, he never really saw the full potential of his invention, as the gun went into production at the same time as the inventor's death, in 1926. Commercially, it is the most popular over-and-under, and the design, like many British designs, is still widely copied today.

Early Westley Richards 14 bore muzzleloader. The Westley Richards company was established in 1812. The barrels for these early muzzleloading guns were wound on a mandrill and often fitted with "blow out" breech plugs in case the pressure build up was too severe due to the dubious consistency of the powder in those days. Apart from the half-cock feature, this gun has the added luxury of a trigger-blocking, hand-grip safety feature.

Single-barreled Henry Nock 16 bore muzzleloader. Judging by the shape of the hammer and the flat at the side of the breech, this gun was probably converted from flint to percussion. Note the blow-out plug safety device at the side of the breech.

The Mantons, John (1780–1834) and brother Joseph (1795–1835), without a doubt refined and influenced the development of the sporting gun more than any others. Here is a superb example of a gun that epitomizes the style, grace, and characteristic elegant lines, which are basically still unchanged with modern side-by-sides today.

Percussion back-action rifle, made in Kilmarnock, Scotland, for Lord Kennedy. The gun clearly shows the high, percussion fences that were to prevent a "flashback" as the percussion cap exploded. The weapon has slow twist rifling grooves of 1:72 inches, to give greater accuracy. It was possibly made for military use in India.

Steven Grant, back-action, Damascus double-barreled 16 bore. Grant was in partnership with Thomas Boss in St. James Street, London, 1866. This gun has an early Jones Rotary underlever and the locking device on the fore-end dates the gun to around 1875.

Damascus-barreled hammer gun by Charles Boswell. Boswell was in business in 1869 in Edmonton but moved to larger premises at 124 The Strand, London, in 1884. There is little doubt that this gun was originally intended for live pigeon shooting, which was popular in England at that time.

English Icon, American classic. Two nice examples of classic side-by-side shotguns, the Holland & Holland box-lock in 12 gauge and a reproduction Parker in 20 gauge. The Parker was first manufactured at Meridian, Connecticut, from 1868 until 1937. Most American doubles were box-locks with Anson and Deeley actions.

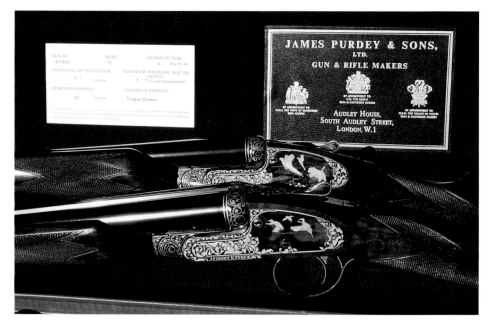

For some side by-side devotees, the choice is not one of affectation, but the immensely pleasurable enjoyment of shooting something that oozes elegance and unsurpassed workmanship. *Picture by kind permission of Jesse Kirk, Dallas.*

CHAPTER 2

Gun Safety and
Shotgun Etiquette

Discussions of gun safety are considered by some shooters to be "old hat," a sort of complacent, "Oh no, here we go again (yawn, yawn)— not the old gun safety stuff *again;* let's turn the pages and get to the more important stuff." Well, be that as it may. You may be familiar with the rules of gun safety, but it doesn't hurt, no matter how experienced you may be, to read about them again. You never know, it may save you someday from injury or perhaps even something more permanent. So before you skip this section and decide you know all about gun safety, let me tell you a couple of stories. Some years ago, I had the misfortune to witness a nasty accident. During a grouse shoot on a Scottish moor, the loader in the next grouse butt was peppered with shot from a distance of about forty yards. Seventeen pellets were removed from the unfortunate man's face, and one of these was less than an inch above his right eye. Thankfully, there was no permanent damage, but it was a gamekeeper with over forty years of gun-handling experience who discharged the gun!

The second story involves a novice shooter. Many years ago, my wife and I managed a large shooting facility, which included holiday accommodation, in the south of England. Each week, as the new guests arrived, we would insist that new shooters spend at least an hour on one of the skeet fields with me so that they could learn or demonstrate the basics of safe gun handling. The cost of this was about $40. It would always amaze me that the new guests would nod approvingly in agreement to this suggestion, but as soon as there was a mention of cost involved, the previously "never held a shotgun in their life before" guys miraculously became competent, safe gun handlers. To cut a long story short, one of these young fellows, unfamiliar with a single-trigger shotgun and under the guidance of his "experienced" father, almost shot some-one's leg off. All for the princely sum of $40. These are just two exam-ples of what could have easily been fatal accidents involving dangerous gun handling at both ends of the spectrum. I have many more that I could tell you. People make mistakes, but they can be taught to make a lot fewer mistakes.

I have two primary aims as a shooting instructor. The first is to pro-duce a safe shot; the second is to produce a competent shooter. The first is by far the more important. Treat all guns as loaded until proved other-wise. A loaded gun pointed carelessly in the wrong direction has no respect for anything and will quickly do what it was intended to do, destroy things. It does not matter if it is a clay target on a sporting clays course or skeet field, live quarry, or a human being. Many people have a complacent, almost foolhardy attitude toward gun handling for some reason—almost a resentment to being shown the basics. This is a mis-take, in some cases with dire consequences.

I teach over twelve hundred clients a year to shoot, and it is an inevitable consequence of gun handling on a daily basis that over the last twenty years or so, despite being extremely vigilant, I have experienced my share of close calls. Shooting instructors *must* display constant vigilance. Never turn your back on a beginner with a gun. The time interval between a safe situation and an accidental discharge is a bloodcurdling millisecond. A good instructor must anticipate his student's actions and be ready to block them when necessary. Switch off for a split second during a lesson, and you have created a situation that is as dangerous as if you were a drunk driver. Don't forget, the new student is *your* responsibility, no one else's. Never leave anything to chance; all guns should be treated as loaded and viewed with suspicion. I now try to make a habit of either carrying the client's gun from the clubhouse or being present when he takes it from the trunk of his car. I have on numerous occasions witnessed the look of surprise on the client's face when the snap caps turned out to be live ammunition from last year's duck hunt.

Experienced shooters develop muzzle awareness. They *never*, under any circumstances, allow the muzzles of a closed gun to be pointed in a dangerous direction, even if they know the gun is unloaded. Novice shooters don't have this awareness, and time and time again during a shooting lesson it must be reinforced so that it eventually becomes per-manent. With any new shooter, *constant* vigilance must be displayed, until he becomes a safe gun handler. People who are in constant contact with firearms are often so safety conscious that it verges on paranoia. I owned a gun shop for many years, and when taking a gun from the rack, I would always open it to make a visual check that it was empty, even though I may have already done so only minutes before. Better safe than sorry, and a big part of gun safety is developing good habits. Never forget that the shotgun was designed primarily for killing things.

LOADING

When instructing, I always load each round into the client's gun until he demonstrates that he is competent. "I've been shooting for over twenty years" unfortunately isn't proof that the client is safe. The proper procedure for loading a break-barrel (over-and-under, side-by-side) gun is to first look down the barrels to check for obstructions before you use it. This is particularly important if the gun has been in storage for several months or if there is otherwise any chance the muzzles might have become blocked by anything. I once had a client who almost loaded and fired his favorite side-by-side at the start of a lesson, but luckily discovered an obstruction just in time. It turned out to be an unfortunate mouse that had crawled up there during the closed season, became lodged, and subsequently died! Firing the gun would have had disastrous results.

Any shell that has an abnormal sound as it goes off must be investigated to make sure the wad is not lodged in the barrel. It is also a good idea, in the field, to periodically check the barrels for obstruction. It isn't unusual for a duck or dove hunter to climb a fence and, in the heat of the moment, unwittingly stick his muzzles in the ground, blocking them with mud or snow, and you might be amazed at how little snow in a barrel it takes to cause a rupture. The gun should be closed smoothly when the shells have been placed in the chamber, not snapped shut with excessive force. Why? A sticking firing pin is capable of firing the gun. The trigger finger should be off the trigger, preferably along the trigger guard. The muzzles should be pointed at the ground as the gun is closed.

One of the things that I always ask my clients is if they know why 20-gauge shells are (almost) always yellow. Do *you* know? The reason for this is, of course, recognition, but how many shooters know that a 20-gauge shell easily drops through the chamber of a 12-gauge until the rim gets caught by the forcing cone, making it possible to load a 12-gauge shell on top of it and close the action? You have then produced a very efficient pipe bomb, because not only will the 12-gauge shell be detonated by the strike of the firing pin, but the 20-gauge shell will also be fired by the shot charge from the 12-gauge, producing a double detonation effect and enormous pressure spike. The gun will almost certainly

Left: Not many people know this, but for recognition purposes, 20-gauge shells are always yellow. A 20-gauge shell will drop neatly into the chamber of a 12 gauge and when the rim of the shell reaches the end of the chamber, it will lodge there. In exactly the same way, the 28-gauge shell will drop into the chamber of the 20 gauge.
Right: The shell drops out of sight. The result is a very efficient pipe bomb. Both shells will detonate as the shot is triggered.

blow up in the unfortunate shooter's face! Husband and wife shooting partners take note. Don't ever mix her 20-gauge shells with his 12 gauge. Disastrous!

Loading in Competition Situations

With skeet, trap, and sporting clays, the gun should be loaded only *after* the shooter is standing in the designated shooting position. Despite having a safety notice displaying this rule (which all shooters have to walk past) at the Dallas Gun Club, I regularly see shooters loading as they walk from station to station. These shooters should *always* be reprimanded. With sporting clays when loading the gun, the barrels should be *over* the front bar of the safety cage. I often see shooters loading with the gun inside the safety cage, and then lifting the barrels over the front bar. This is a dangerous practice and should be avoided. Sometimes this "lift" is accompanied with an unsafe "flourish" of the gun in an unsafe

Don't stand behind these guys! They are carrying their guns in a dangerous manner. If one of them turns around quickly, an innocent bystander could lose his front teeth, or worse still, the sight of an eye. The correct way to carry a gun from station to station is either in a gun sleeve or, in the case of a semiauto, with the muzzles pointing at the ground. Side-by-sides and over-and-unders must be carried with the action open. All guns, semiautos, over-and-unders, and side-by-sides, should have the action open and empty except when on the station waiting to shoot. *Picture posed by actors for demonstration purposes.*

Don't load the gun and then lift it over the front bar. The muzzles should be over the front of the safety bar *before* the gun is loaded. *This picture was intentionally posed for demonstration purposes.*

direction. I have on two occasions seen, as the competitor attempted to lift the gun over the front rail of the safety cage, the muzzles of the gun hit the rail and the gun discharge. Of course the guys who did this were apologetic, but it might have been too late. The gun should be open and empty as the shooter comes out of the safety cage; semiautos and pumps should have the action open. Only two shells should be loaded in target situations, never three.

Loading in the Field

New shooters and youngsters should be allowed only one shell in hunting situations until they have proven that they are trustworthy and capable of handling the gun. Why? Because novices and kids, especially when they hit what they are supposed to with the first shot, forget that they may have more than one shell in the gun and that it is ready to fire again. Excitement and overenthusiasm can sometimes result in a split second of carelessness, and the early success at the first dove or quail can be short-lived, as the error may have disastrous consequences.

Also, don't forget that extra vigilance is necessary when in wing-hunting situations, because the added excitement wild birds create can

This dove hunter doesn't bother to unload or open his gun as he negotiates the fence. His safety may be on, but a sudden slip could cause the gun to fall, which in turn could jar the safety catch and cause the gun to discharge. The safety catch is a mechanical device. Unfortunately, there is no such thing as a foolproof mechanical device.

Always unload before crossing fencelines or ditches, climbing over gates, or moving to a more productive area; it only takes seconds. This gun has been unloaded and opened before negotiating the fence. *Picture posed for demonstration purposes.*

cause unconscious carelessness, and most of this will be carried out in remote areas with no immediate access to medical or hospital facilities. A bad accident can quickly turn into a fatal one in these situations. Load only when there is a possibility of seeing the quarry. Always unload when negotiating ditches or fences, stopping to tie a shoelace, or returning to the vehicle to move to a different or more productive spot. Develop the habit of *double-checking* your chambers before putting a gun into a vehicle. A high percentage of shooting accidents occur when supposedly unloaded guns are removed from vehicles.

Merely applying the safety catch in such situations is *not* acceptable. Don't shoot when you can't identify your quarry clearly, or if you are not positive that there isn't anything in that direction that you don't mind shooting, either in the foreground or background. Although I have seen people attempt to shoot quail through bushes, I believe this is a dangerous

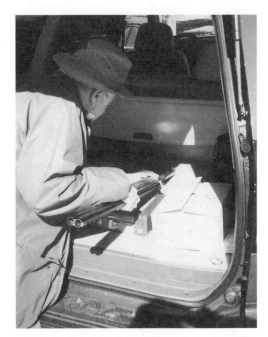

This gun should be empty, but it may not be. Taking a gun from a vehicle in this way is asking for trouble. Guns should be unloaded and replaced in their sleeves for transportation. I once gave a lesson to a lady who drove from the center of Dallas with two live shells from her husband's last dove hunt in the chambers of a 20-gauge gun. The gun was uncased, on the back seat of her suburban next to her ten-year-old daughter.

A low shot at a dove. Of course there's no one behind the mesquite trees on the left, is there? Are you sure? In hunting situations, make sure you know where your companions are, and make sure you don't shoot where you can't see. One more bird in the bag isn't worth the risk of the eye of a good dog, or worse, a shooting companion. *Picture posed by the author for demonstration purposes.*

practice. It is too late when a hurried shot at a quail in thick cover results in the loss of an eye of a faithful companion or shooting partner, all for the sake of one more bird in the bag. It is not worth the risk. Always know the position of other shooters, and when using dogs, be ever aware of where they are. In the United Kingdom we have an area, when walking up game, which we call the safety zone.

SAFETY CATCHES

There is no such thing as a foolproof safety catch. That small *S* that appears above the safety catch is a trap for the unwary and must not be relied on. The safety catch is a mechanical device, and *all* mechanical devices can fail without warning. The general principal of a safety catch is a spring-loaded hammer, which is held back by a sear. In normal use, pulling the trigger will not fire the gun when the safety is on, but the contact between the hammer and the sear is only slight. In an old gun, the sear can become worn over the years and any sharp impact, dropping the gun, for example, can easily fire it. I have actually seen this happen when a loaded gun was carelessly leaned against the side of a vehicle. A sudden

Look at the position of this quail hunter's gun. A sudden stumble would result in a reflex action that would momentarily tighten the grip on the gun, which may in turn trigger the shot. The result could be the loss or injury of a faithful companion. *Picture posed for demonstration purposes.*

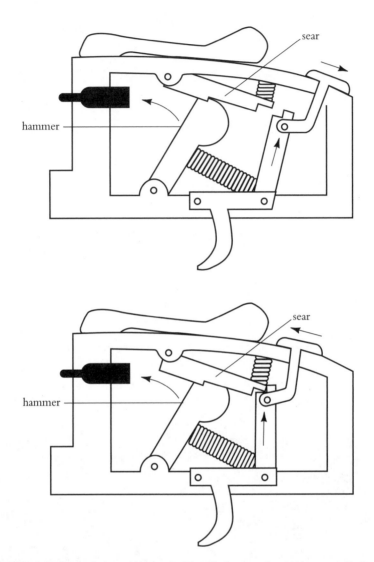

Top: With the gun on safe, it would be impossible to fire because the sear is engaged in the slot at the top of the hammer. This contact area is subject to wear over a period of time. The spring pressure is all that holds the safety in the "on" position.
Bottom: Any sudden impact (the gun being dropped, for example) could cause the sear to bounce upward, which would disengage the safety, and the gun would fire.

gust of wind rocked the vehicle, and the gun hit the ground and went off. Thankfully, no one was hurt, but it was a tense situation. It created an unpleasant atmosphere among the shooters for the rest of the day.

A safety catch has no practical use on a competition gun, as either you should be shooting or the gun should be open and empty. No exceptions. In wingshooting situations, when the gun is loaded in antic- ipation of a dove or duck, the safety should remain on until the gun is mounted with the intention to fire it. This should be when the birds have actually flushed, not before. How long does it take to do this—to actually flick the safety catch off? A tenth of a second? This procedure

Don't ever lean a loaded gun against the side of a vehicle, even for a second. I once actually witnessed what could have been a nasty accident. An old side-by-side gun (obviously with a worn sear) was momentarily placed against the side of a Land Rover. A sudden gust of wind rocked the vehicle and the gun discharged both barrels as it hit the ground. Luckily, no one was injured, but the outcome could have been worse.

should become an integral part of the gun-mounting technique and be practiced thoroughly. Novice shooters should be made to practice this with snap caps until they become proficient.

Finally, between the time that I started to write this chapter and the time I completed it, for the first time in over twenty-four years as a shooting instructor I was involved in a very unpleasant argument with a White Flyer biodegradable target. This is a true and accurate account of what happened. During a shooting lesson with a young client, as the target was hit, a large piece broke off and hit me squarely in the left eye. I never saw it coming. The broken target hit me with such force that one of the detachable plastic lenses of my shooting glasses was knocked out, and as the target disintegrated, fragments were showered into my left eye. The pain was excruciating. I was admitted to the local emergency hospital, and within an hour, the eye was completely closed. Here I had to endure a process known as eye-ball irrigation, which involved fitting something like a large contact lens with a small water hose attached over the eyeball and flushing water through for about 15 minutes to remove the debris.

All this was a very unpleasant experience. Four hours later, after several doses of pain-killing eyedrops, I was allowed to go home. Apparently the surface of the eye heals rapidly, and a week later, apart from slightly blurred vision, I had completely recovered. The point I make is this: there is no doubt in my mind that without the shooting glasses, I would have lost the eye, or at least suffered some serious, permanent damage. I was shaken by the experience. *Accidents can and do happen when you least expect them.* Always remember, safe shooting is no accident; you don't always get a second chance.

CHAPTER 3

Which Gun?

A WHIFF OF NOSTALGIA

From as far back as I can remember, I loved guns. My mother still has a photograph of me at four or five years old, in my backyard with my trusty companion Spot, the dog, wearing a cowboy outfit and toting two six-guns. Many kids, as part of childhood's progressive process, tread this imaginative path, and just as most little girls play with dolls, boys delight in dressing up in soldier or cowboy outfits to play with guns. I loved them all: guns that were replicas of western Colts, loaded with a roll of paper caps and making a loud crack as they were fired; spud guns that fired small pieces of potato; dart guns that fired projectiles with rubber suckers on the end that would stick to glass; and, in fact, anything that would actually fire something out the end. I menaced the local cat and sparrow population incessantly. Shooting and the desire to hunt were my deeply seated passions, but they weren't genetically engineered traits. My father wasn't a shooting man and, in fact, possessed a strong distaste for firearms.

I have no idea where my first real gun actually came from (I probably traded a bag of marbles or a collection of bird's eggs for it), but even now, I can vividly remember the fun I had with it. It was a .177 Diana air weapon. There can be few shooters out there who do not remember, with a certain degree of misty-eyed nostalgia, their first gun. This particular gun was ridiculously inaccurate, only slightly better than a slingshot, and it was possible to follow the trajectory of the pellets' passage through the air—it was that slow. (Perhaps this was an early lesson on seeing the shot as it exits the barrel of a client's gun, as I do today.) The gun didn't emit a business-like crack as the pellets became airborne; it was more

A whiff of nostalgia. The author, age 5.

like an asthmatic chug as the gun spat the projectile out. But it was still a gun—my first gun, and I shot rats, sparrows, starlings, and, in fact, almost anything that dared to venture within range, which I suspect was only about thirty feet or so.

I soon progressed to a Webley & Scott Mark III .22-caliber under-lever air rifle, which was a different animal altogether. Now rabbits, pigeons, crows, and jackdaws were my quarry. This new toy was powerful, so much so that at twenty yards the pellets would go through both sides of a baked bean can. It was deadly accurate, and it was easy to place a group of pellets in a small circle at twenty yards. Once, on impulse, I shot a tiny brown wren, which was creeping busily in and out of the ivy-clad wall at the back of the house. As I looked at the bloodied, smashed body, I was ashamed at what I had done. Although I had taken careful aim at the wren and it had been my intention to hit it, the outcome wasn't as I expected. There was no feeling of elation, just one of remorse, and even now I'm ashamed when I think about it. I was inescapably a predatory animal even then, and I loved to hunt, but shooting the wren wasn't hunting; it was senseless killing. There was no logical reason for it, and that is where the difference lies. I vowed never again to commit such a meaningless act, and to this day, several decades later, I have not.

The air rifle stage was short-lived. I was anxious to progress to bigger and better things, and the opportunity soon presented itself. Out of the blue I became the proud owner of a single-barreled Webley & Scott bolt action .410. A benevolent uncle, who joined the merchant navy and no longer had a use for it, gave it to me. I couldn't believe it. The other guns were the toys of childhood, and they paled in significance beside it. Somehow it was just different. The unmistakable smell of Hoppes gun oil would assail my nostrils as I took the gun from its canvas sleeve to admire it, which was often. I marveled at the smoothness of the action and loved to hear the satisfying clunk as the bolt pushed home. It was bewitching. It was my first shotgun proper, and I couldn't wait for the initiation ceremony.

The gun was heavy, resembling a rifle, and at first, I had no choice but to use it to shoot only at stationary targets, resting the fore-end on something as I triggered the shot. It was almost impossible for me to control the wildly swinging barrel enough to hit a moving target. Rabbits and the occasional pigeon were hit more from luck than anything else, but I was a wiry twelve-year-old. But before too long my adolescent muscles developed, my coordination improved, and I became capable of handling and pointing the rifle. Now I could aspire to moving targets, and every weekend seemed like Christmas or a birthday to me. The gun fired Eley Fourlong shells, and I would wander for hours, oblivious of time, in the hope of getting a shot off at a rabbit or pigeon. One notable foray produced two pigeons, a cock pheasant, and a mallard drake—four shots, four birds—and my chest was puffed out proudly for a week. The barrel was full choke, and I soon learned to "let things get out a bit" to avoid blowing them to pieces at close range. Ah yes, the acquisition of a first shotgun is a moment to be savored.

SAFE SEX

For some illogical reason, most males, regardless of whether they possess genetically engineered hunting instincts, are hopelessly drawn to weapons of any sort, like iron filings to a magnet. They will drool as unashamedly over sporting firearms as they would over the current *Playboy* magazine centerfold. A glass-fronted gun cabinet and the eye-catching aesthetics of the contents are an undeniable topic of conversation, even in a room full

It is so easy for the new shooter, when faced with such a tempting display of mouth-watering goodies with a "just looking, thanks" intention, to emerge sometime later in a trancelike state, heart pounding wildly with excitement. Underneath one arm is a newly acquired shotgun, underneath the other, his now severely depleted wallet.

of strangers. It will always induce a warm, fuzzy feeling, attract attention, and hold the gaze of curious onlookers more than any beautiful woman. Similar words are used to compliment both female form and firearms. *Pretty, elegant, sleek,* and *sexy* are just some of the suitably descriptive adjectives that spring to mind. Stroking the smooth contours of a thoroughbred sporting shotgun will, for some men, induce the warm feeling of desire as easily as most women can. Because of this fatal attraction, it is easy for the new shooter, absolutely determined to enter the premise of that even more tempting display of mouth-watering goodies— the gun shop—with a "just looking, thanks" intention, to emerge sometime later in a trancelike state, heart pounding wildly with excitement. Underneath one arm is a newly acquired shotgun, and underneath the other is his now severely depleted wallet. Sometimes this first purchase is a wise choice, based on good advice from a helpful salesman, and the proud new owner eventually learns to use the gun successfully. More often than not, though, the opposite happens, and he doesn't. Most of us don't have the financial resources necessary to buy several guns, and we must consider all our options if we are to choose wisely. Below is some guidance.

The New Recruit

Let's look at the gauges first. We all know that the humble .410 is the ideal choice for a lightly built beginner, right? Choice, yes. Ideal, no. Contrary to popular belief, although it is often the choice of the ill-informed, the .410 is best suited to the capabilities of the expert. The rapid shot dispersal of the .410 at close ranges is used to advantage by some, and the little gun is often the choice of gamekeepers in the United Kingdom for rabbits in thick cover. The reason? Three-inch magnum .410 shells generate more pressure than either a 12 gauge or 20 gauge, and because there is only a small amount of shot in each cartridge, somewhere between ½ and to ⅝ of an ounce, the initial high pressure of the detonation of the .410 cartridge (around five tons) means that a bigger percentage of the pellets in the shot charge are subjected to more bore scrub and abrasion as they travel up the barrel. This is because this deformation is proportional to the layers of pellets in the cartridge and the size of the bore diameter.

Contrary to many beliefs, the .410 is an expert's gun. Dallas Gun Club member and accomplished shot La Roque Johnson uses the diminutive .410 to shoot a round of skeet.

Quite simply, more pellets deform with the .410 as a result of this bore scrub, and at close range the pattern is larger than a 12 gauge. Over here, bird hunters use them with success on quail and doves at medium ranges, up to twenty-five yards. At thirty yards plus, the gun is inadequate and birds will be pricked and lost. An expert shot knows this, and he can center his pattern accurately at reasonable ranges and kill cleanly, just as in the .410 event at a skeet shoot, where the targets are ink-balled into puffs of dust since they are centered with the pattern. I repeat, the guys that can do this with quiet confidence are *experts*. In the hands of the beginner, the .410 is often the opposite—a source of disappointment and frustration. The inadequate shot load, the resulting exaggerated, elongated shot string, and the patchy pattern density, as full of holes as Swiss cheese, all add up to an exasperating number of missed targets, and all these combined ingredients add up to failure.

Make no mistake—the two things that are most attractive to a new shooter are early success and the absence of recoil, in that order. Breaking targets inspires confidence, and this is indispensable in the early stages. Missed targets are symbolic of failure, and repetitive failure is a certain deterrent, something that a new shooter needs about as much as a bad toothache. A new recruit will often tolerate a *small* amount of discomfort as the gun recoils. In fact, most expect it, and their tolerance of recoil will improve as shotgun technique improves. However, failure to break the target is different. Beginners must be able to break a reasonable number of targets in the early stages to keep the spark of enthusiasm burning brightly. Repeated failure eventually erodes desire to participate. For this reason, a much better choice for a youngster is the 28 gauge (better still, the 20 gauge), because the difference in weight between the .410 and the 28 or 20 is minimal, and yet both the 28 gauge and 20 gauge are classed as "adult" guns.

My personal preference for a new shooter is the 20 gauge. Why? A massive range of ammunition is available for the 20 gauge, from $3/4$ to $1\frac{1}{8}$ ounces, all of which is reasonably priced. With a youngster, as confidence and muscle strength grow and coordination improves, the shot load can be increased proportionately, without the necessity to move up in guns. A standard 1-ounce load of $7\frac{1}{2}$ shot through a 20 gauge will produce a pattern very similar to that of a 1-ounce load of no. 6 through a 12 gauge, although the killing range will be a few yards less because of the reduction in penetrative energy with the $7\frac{1}{2}$ pellets.

Now what about the 28 gauge? There is a growing trend over here at the moment for light, side-by-side 28-gauge guns, usually Damascus

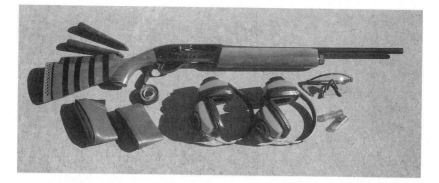

This is a Remington 20-gauge semiautomatic that the author uses for teaching women and all young students. All new shooters are apprehensive about recoil, even though they don't like to admit it. With light ¾-ounce loads, the felt recoil of this gun is negligible, the shooting experience is more enjoyable as a whole, and the student will gain confidence quickly. By using rubber comb raisers and electrical tape, this gun can be quickly and simply adjusted for comb height to accommodate the physical requirements of any student. A slip-on rubber or leather pad can be used to temporarily lengthen the stock if necessary.

barreled and of English origin. Why? A hundred years ago on the great sporting estates in the United Kingdom, the 28 gauge (as opposed to the 20 gauge) was the ideal choice for the new shooter in the family, and the gun could be handed down to each youngster until he was old enough to use a 12 gauge. The standard British 28 gauge in those days would be chambered for 2½-inch cartridges and would fire a charge of ⁹⁄₁₆ of an ounce of shot. There was minimal perceived recoil with this modest load, and the 28 gauge was light enough to be handled comfortably by most twelve-year-olds.

In adult hands, the 28 gauge is useful for doves and quail at modest ranges, perhaps, but let's not get carried away. At ranges in excess of thirty yards, it is inadequate, because pellet deformation is directly proportional to pressure buildup. One-ounce magnum shells are available for the 28 gauge, but if we compare the pressure required to achieve this increase in payload to the equivalent pressures in a 12 gauge, there is a huge increase, in some cases up to 20 percent, which is at the eventual expense of a blown pattern at extended range. This is explained in great detail in *The Mysteries of Shotgun Patterns,* written by Dr. George G. Oberfell and Charles E. Thompson, two professors from Oklahoma. These two enterprising fellows carried out many exhaustive and elaborate tests over several years. They eventually concluded that it is the eventual shot load that reaches the target as cohesively as possible, not the gauge, that ensures clean kills. Although this excellent book is long out of print, published by the Oklahoma State University Press in 1960, I was lucky enough to be able to borrow a copy from one of the members of the Dallas Gun Club, Dr. Van Telford. It makes compelling reading, if you can find a copy.

Size Is Everything

Beware of the inherited or hand-me-down shotgun. I was lucky; the .410 I started with was on the fringe of my capabilities, but many shooting men, with obviously good intentions, pass on some totally inadequate holy-relic-of-a-shotgun far too early for the recipient. In my many years as a shooting coach, one question has been asked more than any other; how old must someone be before they are capable of using a shotgun? There is no easy answer. Timing can be crucial; there is no ideal age to start a youngster on the road to shotgun success; the paths are never that clearly marked.

Youngsters come in all shapes and sizes, temperaments, and physical capabilities. To the experienced coach, it is quickly obvious whether the new recruit is capable of moving the gun smoothly or not. Common sense should prevail here, but I have on many occasions given unwelcome advice to a parent who attempts to start his young son too early with an unsuitable gun. In some cases, parents don't like to hear my advice. Others ignore it completely and take their youngster to some other shooting coach who is more than happy to take their money and may eventually destroy any latent talent that the youngster may have. "You'll soon grow into it, lad" isn't much consolation for the seventy-pound twelve-year-old that, because of an overenthusiastic parent, is persuaded to struggle with the long-barreled 12-gauge side-by-side that is impossible to point and kicks him like a mule. Cutting a lump off the stock is not the answer in this case. All that will happen is that the balance of the gun will be destroyed and excess weight will be distributed forward of the hinge pin, producing too much forward inertia. This will make the gun feel heavy during use, and this weight-forward situation will result in the gun starting with a jerk as the new recruit attempts to swing it.

Overall handling dynamics and feel are apparent only after the shooter has done a reasonable amount of shooting and acquired a healthy dose of shotgun technique. Amateurish attempts to coach the underdeveloped new recruit with an unsuitable gun may result in a flinch developing or, even worse, apprehension at the very thought of firing the gun ever again. This is true for both youngsters and lightly built ladies. The gun should always be matched to the physical capabilities of the user and to the purpose for which he intends to use it. There is an old Hindu saying: "Softly, softly, catchee monkee." Very true. With any beginner, it is better to progress slowly and always well within their physical capabilities. Someone who is thrown in at the deep end and forced to use an unsuitable gun just because it belonged to Uncle Joe is not on the way forward.

Side-by-Side or Over-and-Under?
The side-by-side is the oldest form of multishot shotgun and rifle. For decades the English side-by-side has been the traditional, fashionable choice of gun for driven game shooting in the United Kingdom. Driven game shoots were something of a novelty until around 1861 when the Prince of Wales bought the Sandringham estate purely to satiate his growing appetite for the sport. Almost instantly, game shooting became more than a sport. There was a certain ritual etiquette involved, a flavor of pomp and pageantry to which the participants would conform, and the traditional best English sidelock was soon to become an icon of this golden era.

The shooting society became the hub of the well-to-do, and the great sporting estates would compete with one another for the biggest and best bags. Lord de Gray, the second marquis of Ripon, shot an astonishing 556,813 head of game in his long and eventful shooting career, which spanned from 1867 to 1923. The marquis certainly loved his

A pair of Purdey side-by-sides, almost one hundred years old and still reliable today.

shooting; he dropped dead at the age of seventy-one during a grouse shoot on his beloved moor at Dallowgill, in Yorkshire, on September 22, 1923. What a way to go! On some of the great estates upwards of 3,000 birds would be shot in a single day, such was the insatiable appetite of these Victorian and Edwardian sportsmen. The affluent society of the period demanded guns that were capable of handling this incredible volume, and there was no doubt that the reliability of the traditional side-by-side could certainly fit the bill. Cost was immaterial, and these guns were made to exacting standards from the very best materials available. Quality side-by-sides were not made to become familiar with the inside of the gunsmith's shop; they were made to endure. Today there is a massive resurgence of interest in quality side-by-sides, many of which are just as serviceable and reliable now as when they were produced over a hundred years ago.

What about the advantages and disadvantages of the side-by-side versus the over-and-under? Some people will tell you that the side-by-side swings better and cuts through the air easier on crossing shot, especially if there is a strong crosswind. Others will tell you that the side-by-side opens easier than the over-and-under to facilitate loading and that the narrow gape of the barrels allows both shells to be dropped quickly into the chambers. By contrast, the over-and-under needs to be opened fully to drop a shell into the lower chamber. Side-by-sides are usually lighter than an over-and-under and are much "whippier," with faster handling properties, a trait that I suspect is residual from the twenty-five-inch-barrel Churchill days. Is this an advantage with driven birds, which can be seen well in advance of the shot being triggered? At the risk of being hung, drawn, and quartered by some of the more prejudiced side-by-side devotees, in my opinion the answer is an emphatic no. It does mean that the gun swings quicker and barrels will get on the target faster, but it also means that they can pull off line just as easily too.

With birds that change direction quickly, such as quail, woodcock, snipe, and the like, this isn't a problem, and in fact, it is a distinct advantage. With other targets that don't require rapid directional adjustments, like pheasants, geese, and clays, it is not an advantage. Most men of average build will find that they overpower a traditional light, short-barreled side-by-side, and it will feel far too "whippy" and "wave-about-y" on driven pheasants. I have used both types of guns for many years on driven pheasant shoots, and I feel that I am qualified to comment on this. High driven birds require a smooth, progressive swing, which is more

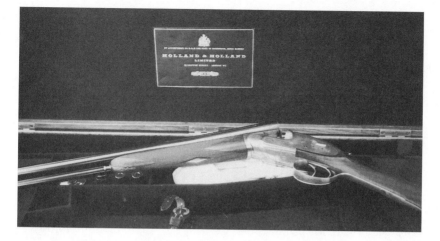

Quality 28-gauge side-by-side by Holland & Holland. Quail are small birds, never moving as fast as the illusion their wing beats give. A wild bobwhite will average only 5 to 6 ounces and most are shot at modest ranges. Even under full power, the birds will be doing only twenty miles per hour, which is about ten to twelve yards per second. On a covey rise, most shots will be taken in the first second or two, in other words, within twenty yards. The fast-handling dynamics and wide sighting plane of this 28 gauge would make it a more than adequate gun (as well as a delight to use) on quail, or even doves at modest ranges.

suited to the superior pointability and stability of the over-and-under. Side-by-side purists insist that they point better because of the broad sighting plane, but this is dependent on the type of shooting it is intended for.

I believe that the broad sighting plane can very definitely influence visual fixation and acquisition of the target as the gun is brought to point of aim, but on pure, driven incoming pheasant and partridge shoots, there is no doubt in my mind that the broad sighting plane of the barrels is restrictive. It is more difficult to see "through" or around the gun with the other eye when shooting high birds with the side-by-side. Nevertheless, it is traditionally the number one choice of gun for this type of shooting in the United Kingdom. Although single triggers are available, most traditional sides-by-sides have double triggers, and of course, this does give instant barrel/choke selection, an advantage for many, without the need to fumble with the barrel selector, which is, of course, necessary with the over-and-under. In cold weather, however, double triggers (for some people) can be a disadvantage. Most driven birds in the United Kingdom are shot from November to February, and all the duck and goose hunting both over there and in the United States is carried out during the winter months. There is little enough space between the triggers on some side-by-sides and in cold weather that a finger inside a shooting glove can be a problem. I have witnessed (on particularly cold days on driven pheasant shoots) gloves being discarded at the expense of a frozen trigger finger. With the over-and-under, the selector mechanism is usually within reach of a gloved thumb or finger. Once the barrel selection is made, the shots can then be fired in quicker succession with a single-trigger gun, without the need to relax the grip so that the finger can locate the second trigger. A small point, perhaps, but one worth mentioning nonetheless.

Where multiple shots are required in quick succession, driven birds, for example, the side-by-side is at a distinct disadvantage. On some driven pheasant or partridge shoots, two thousand to three thousand birds will be pushed over the guns on each drive, and there may well be five or six drives on the day. The splinter fore-end of the side-by-side gives very little to hold, and as the barrels become hot, muzzle control may become a problem. The better heat dissipation and larger surface area of the over-and-under will compensate for this.

Side-by-sides are usually lighter than over-and-unders and are much "whippier" with faster handling properties. These fast-to-point characteristics can sometimes be an advantage in thick cover, for woodcock and quail, for example. For competition and for situations where a smooth, progressive swing is required, the handling dynamics of over-and-under is vastly superior.

Why is felt recoil lessened with the over-and-under? The over-and-under barrel configuration means that the recoil of the lower barrel is transferred more evenly to the center of the shoulder. With the side-by-side both barrels are above the line of the stock, and this creates more felt recoil. In addition, with the over-and-under, when either barrel is fired, the recoil is straight back. This means that even though there may be a certain amount of muzzle flip, it will always be on a vertical plane in relation to the axis of the barrels. The barrels will therefore return to the intended target line, which gives a faster recovery time for the second shot. With the side-by-side barrel configuration, recoil is always at an angle, which creates torque, producing a flip in a sideways direction depending on which barrel is fired; this can have the effect of pulling the gun off-line. Not exactly recommended for many high driven shots where the gun movement is on a vertical plane! The handling dynamics of the over-and-under are more suited to sporting clays because the weight is distributed more evenly over the gun as a whole. This means that although the gun is slower to start than a fast-handling side-by-side, it is also slower to stop. In situations where there is a fast left-to-right followed by a fast right-to-left target, many shooters will subconsciously stop their gun so that they can get on the second target quicker. A muzzle-heavy gun reduces this tendency.

By the way, what's the difference between a sidelock and a boxlock? Boxlocks, as the name suggests, have all the working parts of the lock mechanism built into a box-shaped casting. With the sidelock, the "guts" of the lock, hammers, and sears are mounted on a removable plate called a side plate. The hammers are powered by coil springs with most over-and-unders. With the side-by-side, they are powered by V springs.

TIME FOR A CHANGE?
Changes are on the way, but what factors influenced this change? By the late 1970s, the demographics of shooting were changing. People had more leisure time and disposable income. Clay pigeon shooting was already popular, but the game of sporting clays really took off in the late 1950s and 1960s. The superior balance and stability of the over-and-under against the side-by-side was quickly recognized, and Winchester, Browning, and Beretta were quick to jump into the breech to meet the growing demand in the United Kingdom. Shooting schools were also flourishing to cope with this increase in interest, and most of these new recruits were introduced to the sport via an over-and-under. It is easier

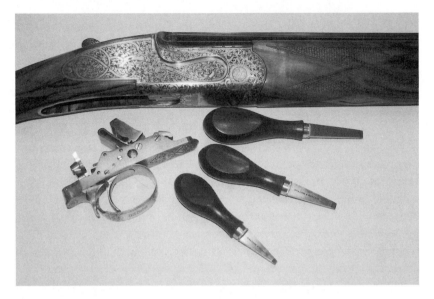

Today, the market is responding to the call. Many of the best English, Italian, and Spanish side-by-side gun makers are now producing over-and-unders that are just as elegant and as pleasing to the eye as the traditional side-by-side. Here is an example of a quality Holland & Holland over-and-under with detachable locks.

to teach a beginner to shoot with an over-and-under, and there is also less felt recoil; this is very important in the initial stages.

Today, the market is responding to the call. Many of the best Italian and Spanish side-by-side gun makers are now producing over-and-unders that are just as elegant and pleasing to the eye as the traditional side-by-side. British gun makers are also now producing one over-and-under for every two side-by-sides produced. If price isn't an option, perhaps an over-and-under will fill the bill, and in some cases, the superior handling and pointability qualities of the over-and-under are all too apparent even to the hardened purist.

In the 1990s Holland & Holland produced a superb over-and-under with detachable locks specifically for the game and clay target shooting market. Scottish gun maker David McKay Brown produces one of the most delicious-looking round action versions of an over-and-under—for around $50,000. It's expensive, but then that isn't a surprise, is it? Think H & H. Think Purdey. In fact, I recently gave a lesson to an extremely wealthy gentleman who had just two days before taken delivery of a new pair of side-by-sides by Purdey, and the price was in excess of $200,000.

They were exquisite, and I was drooling for days. Side-by-sides have commanded top dollar for decades, so it won't be surprising that with the increase in popularity, the over-and-under will eventually follow suit.

So just where does the side-by-side fit into the shooting equation? Weight for weight, a side-by-side is livelier and more responsive than a well-balanced over-and-under. There is an immediate benefit with the lighter weight of the side-by-side for walked-up game. A reduction of a pound or two at the start of the day may seem irrelevant, but after twenty miles, it can make quite a difference. Most walked-up hunting over dogs, for example, is instinctive, reflexive shooting when the birds flush, and although the side-by-side is less precise, in these circumstances, the low profile of the barrels can be an advantage, as they can be quickly brought to point of aim. Where narrow angles and straightaway shots are the norm, it is ideal. Short barrels are quick to point, and in thick cover, the small-gauge, short-barreled side-by-side with its wide sighting plane can be the ideal choice, especially against a backdrop of undergrowth. Think about bobwhite quail, hurriedly extricating themselves from the hostile environment of cactus and mesquite. You need to be on them fast. Then what about the fast-flushing woodcock and ruffed grouse, threading their imaginary needles through the aspens and pine trees? You need to be on them even faster. But long shots crossing shots at extended ranges? I favor something that is more steady and not quite as "whippy," but this is purely a matter of personal choice.

Although there have never been, to my knowledge, any conclusive tests showing that the side-by-side cannot be pointed just as well as any other type of shotgun, *in my experience,* many competent shots who switch from a traditional side-by-side to an over-and-under for the first time see an immediate improvement (sometimes reluctantly) in their shooting and rarely go back to the side-by-side. With regard to the superior sighting plane of the over-and-under, by exactly the same rule that the side-by-side can be restrictive on certain incoming shots, an over-and-under can, under certain circumstances, depending on the degree of eye dominance of the individual, persuade the wrong eye to take over. This point is important. A shotgun is directed in front of the target by a subconscious awareness of the barrels as seen in the peripheral vision, but make no mistake, there is definite visual awareness. Chapter 12 explains this in detail.

The argument of the over-and-under versus the side-by-side has always been a hotly debated subject. Personally, I think that far too many people abandon objectivity and base their opinion of the so-called superior handling capabilities of the side-by-side on traditional prejudices and sentiment rather than reason. The choice is not one of affectation for some side-by-side devotees, but the immensely pleasurable enjoyment of shooting something that exudes elegance and unsurpassed workmanship. The most pragmatic among us will readily admit that there is more to the shooting experience than unwavering accuracy, and the side-by-side fits this particular bill admirably. However, the truth is that the over-and-under is going through exactly the same transitional phase as the side-by-side hammerless gun went through about a century ago as the traditional hammer gun was phased out. There is no doubt in my mind that by the end of the next decade, the over-and-under will be the most popular double-barreled gun.

Finally, side-by-side live pigeon guns have different handling dynamics altogether, and I have often watched Cyril Adams systematically pulverize ZZ birds with enviable precision at Westside Sporting Grounds in Houston. He used a thirty-two-inch Damascus-barreled Grant hammer gun and could hit the targets a lot better than I could using my Miroku MK 38 trap gun. I once made the mistake of asking Cyril, when I first moved to the States, why he didn't use a traditional trap gun for shooting ZZ birds. He replied that in his opinion, since ZZ birds were usually rising targets, he preferred the vertical precision of the side-by-side's sighting plane and added that the over-and-under was more suitable for holding up a convenience store. I later found out that he was a former world champion at the difficult game. If you are in a hole, sometimes it's best to stop digging.

ONE OR TWO BARRELS?

The pump gun is the oldest type of repeating shotgun, and in the United States, it is often the inexpensive first choice as a starter gun for an aspiring bird hunter. It never really managed to get a grip on the British and European markets; however, I did manage to sell a number of Mossberg pumps as cheap wildfowling repeaters in my shop in Scotland. Pumps have since been banned in the United Kingdom for many years, and although out of curiosity I did once try to shoot a pump, I always felt as though they would be more suited to robbing banks and grocery stores than hunting. The do-it-yourself "sawn-off" variety became far too popular in the inner cities for exactly that reason. Once, as a bet, it was suggested to me that I should turn up with a 12-gauge pump on the keeper's day at Westerhall estate. Needless to say, this would have caused more than a few raised eyebrows and I didn't dare try it, but I have often wondered what the outcome would have been if I had. Pumps and semiautos have always been frowned upon in the United Kingdom and in formal, driven shoots; in the eyes of many, repeating guns and driven birds just don't mix.

Why? Tradition, for one thing; evolution of the shotgun, for another. Nothing displays such sleek, graceful elegance of a properly balanced best English side-by-side or a quality over-and-under. As a personal choice, I would never use anything else on a formal shoot. This does not mean that I would insist, as some prejudiced purists do, that the side-by-side double-game gun is the only gun that should be considered for everything, and that the repeater doesn't deserve a place in shooting society. This blinkered attitude is unnecessary, because in my mind these guns do have a legitimate place—as an inexpensive but serviceable wild-fowling gun on the coastal mud flats and marshes, for example.

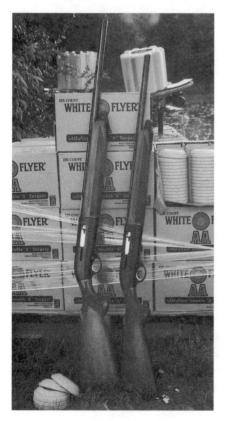

The cycling mechanics of the semiauto softens recoil and lightly built women and fledgling shooters can benefit dramatically from this reduction in felt recoil. The gun on the left is a Beretta 391 in 12 gauge. The gun on the right is an exact scaled down "youth model" version in 20 gauge.

On the skeet field, this sixteen-year-old young lady can easily point and swing this semiautomatic. This gun has the benefit of a Monte Carlo "small radius" grip stock. With 1-ounce loads, the recoil is almost unnoticeable, and, as a result, the shooting experience is more fun.

A step up from the pump is the slightly more expensive gas–operated autoloading shotgun. Its main advantage is reduction in felt recoil. The cycling mechanics of the semiauto soften recoil, and lightly built ladies and fledgling shooters can benefit dramatically from this. The effect of recoil is spread over a longer period with the semiauto, as the breech bolt is driven backwards, and as a result, the felt recoil is more like an extended push rather than a sharp blow. Semiautomatics can also be loaded without opening while there is a shell in the chamber, which is an obvious advantage when doves are coming in to the water hole, pigeons are flighting to the roost, or in the sometimes cramped confines of the duck blind. From the safety aspect, the autoloader can present a problem for the less–experienced shooter. With the bolt forward, it is not readily apparent whether the gun is loaded. An extra shell may be present in the magazine and go unnoticed by the novice hunter. A good safety exercise in the field, when moving from one place to another, is to place a shell at right angles to the action in the chamber, allowing the bolt to slide forward and trap this shell. With the shell trapped in this way, visibly sticking out of the side of the chamber, it is readily apparent that the gun is safe.

The autoloader is also now established as a firm favorite for sporting clays. Most sporting clay presentations prefer a gun with its weight well forward, producing a smooth, progressive swing, and this is where the autoloader shines. On the negative side, autoloaders can be unreliable at the most inopportune moment, they litter their spent shells all over the place, and the shooter is restricted to one choke choice. In certain hunting situations, and very definitely on the sporting clays course, this single choke can be a problem. Also, in the Kansas cornfield, a pheasant may flush near or far. Full choke at a ten-yard rooster will smash him to pieces. A two-barreled gun with cylinder choke is much better for dropping him close, and there should be something left to put on the table.

What about on the sporting clays course under tournament conditions? Any multiple-target presentation that combines variable range, for example, a close rabbit target with a forty-yard crossing midi, will leave the competitive shooter with a single choke in a head-scratching dilemma, trying to choose the right choke to break both targets. His ultimate choice of choke may not be the best medicine for either of them, much less both of them. I know that by now some of the competitive shooters out there will be shaking their heads in disagreement, perfectly happy with their semiauto in spite of its one choke, and that is fine by me. But I will leave you with food for thought: four-time sporting clays world champion George Digweed, three-time world champion John Bidwell, and current or recent U.S. champions Jon Kruger, Doug Fuller, and Andy Duffy all use an over-and-under with its choice of choke combination.

WHAT ABOUT WOODWORK?
Fancy wood is fine for driven pheasants, partridges, and the like, but anything that will be dragged in and out of the duck blind or used for upland game will get a certain amount of abuse. The very nature of this style of hunting (rough shooting, as we call it in the United Kingdom) means that there will be a more-than-occasional ding as the inevitable fences and ditches are negotiated. These guns will suffer more in the way of normal wear and tear in a week than the driven game or competition clay gun may in a year, even though they may have substantially less shells put through them. Of course, if you have bottomless pockets, it is no big deal, but in these circumstances, my personal choice is that function, not fancy, should be the ultimate choice.

Also available in camouflage. For the aspiring duck hunter, this Bennelli autoloader fits the bill admirably. In hunting situations, where the sudden flash of sunlight on the barrels would deter the quarry from dropping in to the decoys, a gun like this can be a distinct advantage.

Finally, a word of caution. A new shooter must allow himself time to acquire some shotgun technique, which will eventually allow him to be more definitive in his requirements. All shooters, providing they have had enough time to acquire this, can learn to shoot well with a gun that fits and feels right to them, and it doesn't matter if the gun is a side-by-side, over-and-under, semiautomatic, or pump. The more you shoot, the more you will learn to recognize if a gun's handling dynamics are compatible with your physical capabilities, and a gun that feels right should not be abandoned in favor of a whim.

For example, the legendary Percy Stanbury, with a shooting career that spanned over fifty years, used a Webley & Scott side-by-side for everything. The gun was choked full and full, and he used it for skeet, trap, and all his live bird shooting. He won everything there was to be won in the world of competitive clay target shooting. There is an old saying in shooting: "Beware of the one-gun man." Percy was an excellent example of this. Unfortunately for some of us, the story does not end there. The grass is always greener on the other side of the fence, or

A rare beast. This amazing contraption is a LJUTICK "space gun." It was invented in the late 1970s by Al Ljutick from Washington state and made its debut at the Grand American trapshoot in Vandalia, Ohio, in 1980. It is a single-shot, bolt-action mechanism that contains a spring-loaded, 6-ounce "hammer bar" in the butt stock. When released, it strikes the back of the bolt to trigger the shot. This almost completely neutralizes the effect of recoil by using the principles of Newton's third law of motion, which states that for every action, there is an equal and opposite reaction.

in our case, the gun shop. We may become afflicted with that most contagious of the deadly diseases—new gun bug—and any one of us can become infected.

For many of us, once bitten, gun choice can develop swiftly into an unfortunate, incurable illness dictating that any new gun that shows up in the marketplace and guarantees to turn us into a world champion must be worthy of a place in our (sometimes already crowded) gun cabinet. Unfortunately, most of these whims gather dust for years, as we only use the "old faithful" for our hunting trips, because it is what works.

CHAPTER 4

Recoil and How to Tame It

Recently a client booked a lesson for his twelve-year-old son.

"Has he got a gun?" I inquired.

The rear door of the suburban opened to reveal the shiny new gun case in which was a pristine replica 20-gauge side-by-side.

"Bought him a nice, light 20 gauge for his birthday. My father had one similar," came the proud reply. "It'll soon be dove season and there seem to be plenty about this year. My brother has a ranch in south Texas, and the Milo fields are thick with them."

The boy beamed from ear to ear, Dad proudly puffed his chest out, and off we went to one of the skeet fields for the first lesson.

First the safety talk, and then gun-mounting procedure. After a few preliminary swings, a station 7 low-house bird was powdered. Then another. Things were looking good. Father watched his son with glowing admiration, and my tip was in the bag. Then, as I have seen so many times before, slowly but surely the wheels came off and targets began to whistle by untouched. The preliminary success was short-lived. After just twenty shots, the youngster was flinching badly. There was absolutely nothing wrong with the gun, but it was totally inadequate for the purpose for which it was intended—as a starter gun for young Robert. He weighed somewhere around seventy pounds with soaking wet clothes on. The recoil was just too much for him. Robert's introduction to shotgun shooting and what should have been an enjoyable experience was fast turning into a nightmare. Although he was reluctant to admit it in front of Dad, the act of shooting wasn't fun anymore. There was a noticeable reluctance to pull the trigger, and he was jerking the gun off-line in anticipation of the recoil.

I have witnessed this scenario a thousand times. Light side-by-sides are often the favorite choice of fathers for their sons in the United Kingdom, and of course, we all know the reason—shooting a smaller gun with smaller shells reduces recoil, doesn't it? No, I'm afraid not, unless the weight of the gun is in proportion to the size of the shot load that is to be pushed through it. There is no point in buying a light 20 gauge, for example, if you intend to put 1-ounce hunting loads through it and expect your twelve-year-old son to enjoy his duck-hunting trips. The double whammy of recoil discomfort and the dimming enthusiasm that always follows isn't exactly conducive to good results. A 20 gauge that weighs six or seven pounds and that shoots a shot charge of $^7/_8$-ounce with a velocity of 1,250 feet per second produces exactly the same recoil as a 12 gauge weighing seven to eight pounds firing 1 ounce of shot at the same velocity.

Unfortunately, once the commitment to a light gun is made, in many cases it is not easy to change the gun because of the expense involved. But continued use in the hope that the youngster will "grow into it" is a big mistake. Punishing recoil at this stage is also a surefire way of developing a flinch that can destroy any latent talent and ability that the new recruit may have. A flinch is very difficult to rectify and may continue long after a more suitable gun is found.

Wingshooters' wives are also often victims of recoil in the "have a go" situation. Common sense should prevail here, but let's be honest, how many times have we witnessed the well-meaning hunter thrusting a shotgun into his wife's reluctant hands? A look of surprise usually follows when the poor lady experiences the recoil that the unsuitable gun delivers and wonders what planet she is on. Unfortunately, guns for hunters' wives aren't exactly top priority on the checklist of hunting gear and usually fall somewhere between spare rubber boots and dog kennels.

Suitable guns can be divided into two categories. The first consists of cheap and nasty pieces of junk found hidden away in the dark recesses of the local pawnshop. This gun is usually accompanied with the hollow promise of "learn to shoot with it, and we'll get you something better." The gun is so totally incompatible in every way with the unfortunate lady, of course, that even if she puts on a brave face and tries to ignore the punishment the gun delivers, she never manages to hit anything with it and is happy to fade into obscurity on the shooting scene. The second category, at the other end of the spectrum, is that nice, light, exquisitely engraved Wesley Richards 16 gauge with the detachable locks that you just *knew* she would love for Christmas! The price almost gave your bank manager a heart attack, and maybe it will kick her like the proverbial mule, but what the heck, you can always suffer and use it yourself if she doesn't like it, right? Exactly! She can stand meekly by, watching with adoration as you confidently stroke everything out of the sky with it.

Make no mistake, excessive recoil either hurts or causes fatigue, or both. In some cases, the introduction to the shooting experience via an unsuitable gun can leave a mental scar that will remain for a long time after the bruises have gone. Even worse, it is sometimes enough to deter the would-be-shooter forever. So just what is recoil and how can we minimize its effect to maximize our performance? Very simply, anything that pushes one way creates an equal and opposite effect the other way. Sir Isaac Newton said that. His third law of motion states that for every action, there is an equal and opposite reaction.

As soon as we pull the trigger and the propellant in the cartridge ignites, the resultant gasses accelerate the wad and the shot charge from rest to around 1,200 feet per second or more. This exerts a force of well over a ton per square inch on the base of the wad, which in turn pushes the shot forward through the crimp and into the chamber. As this initial explosion occurs, the resultant internal pressures cause the barrel to temporarily distort slightly. This sounds ominous, but it isn't. The steel of the barrels is elastic and returns to normal dimensions quickly. The shot charge, which exits the barrel at 1,200 feet per second, exerts the same amount of energy backwards through the gun. This is recoil. It is this acceleration of the shot and wad that produces the recoil, and this is directly proportional to the size (weight) of the shot charge. For example, a 1,200-feet-per-second 1⅛-ounce load of no. 8 shot produces about 20 foot-pounds of recoil; a 1-ounce load will produce approximately 16 foot-pounds of recoil; and a ⅞-ounce load will produce about 12 foot-pounds. That's a big difference in felt recoil. Even mild doses of recoil can have a cumulative effect. After each box or two of shells that the shooter triggers, the flesh of the cheek and shoulder may start to protest, and the repetitive blows begin to register on your neurological system.

In order to understand the effects of recoil better, the actual process can be divided into two periods. The center of gravity of a shotgun is lower than the axis of the barrels, and because of this, the initial movement as the gun is fired is to rotate around this center of gravity and then push rearward onto the shoulder. The gun thus rotates in an upward direction using the shoulder as a pivot, and at the same time the

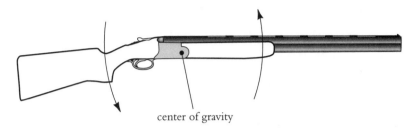

center of gravity

Most shotguns' center of gravity is below the barrels. As the gun is fired, during the first phase of recoil, the gun will move back and rotate around the center of gravity.

head snaps forward, which pushes the sensitive area just under the cheekbone down onto the gun. This is known as the second phase of recoil. This rotation is always greater with a side-by-side shotgun than with an over-and-under because the axis of both the barrels is well above the center of gravity. With the over-and-under, the bottom barrel transmits less felt recoil than when the top barrel is fired because the bottom barrel is nearer to the center of gravity. This is why the bottom barrel usually always fires first on over-and-under shotguns without selective triggers.

If the gun is a bad fit, the effect of this rearward travel is magnified; for example, if only the bottom half of the butt plate is in contact with the shoulder to absorb as much of the first phase of recoil as possible, or if there is too much pitch allowing the butt to slide upwards, this recoil can cause massive discomfort. The amount of rearward travel is directly proportional to the weight of the gun. The heavier the gun, the greater the inertia (or resistance to movement) and the less the recoil that is felt. If the gun fits, the shooter's stance is firm and unyielding, and the type

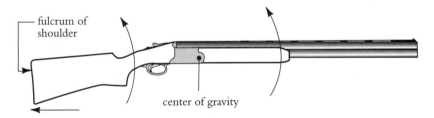

fulcrum of shoulder

center of gravity

As the butt of the gun then meets the resistance of the shooters shoulder, the gun will rotate around this pivot, which may cause "muzzle flip," and the gun will shoot high. This is known as the second phase of recoil.

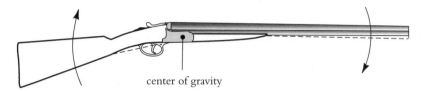

center of gravity

As a general rule, the shot leaves the gun during the first phase of recoil. However, some light side-by-sides have barrel walls that are so thin that during the first phase of recoil the muzzles will flex down, causing the gun to shoot low. This low shooting tendency can be exaggerated even further with side-by-side guns with stocks that are thin in the "hand" portion or when using high velocity loads. This is a characteristic that applies only to the side-by-side shotgun. The barrels of most over-and-under shotguns support each other more efficiently so that there is negligible down-flex, and these guns have a tendency to shoot high as a result. The dotted lines represent the flexing of the stock wrist and barrels.

of cartridge used is compatible with the weight of the gun, all is well. But alter any of these, and you can have a problem.

Small guns and big shells just don't work. Super Xtra and Magnum Duck loads are an emphatic no-no for lightly built beginners. If the gun doesn't absorb the bulk of the rearward energy, the shooter gets it in the face and shoulder. If you're really unlucky, that long day hunting the gray speedsters will leave you with spots before your eyes and an aching head. Believe me, I speak from personal experience. I once owned a pretty little Thomas Bland boxlock, which was a joy to behold. The gun was very finely made with twenty-eight-inch, almost paper-thin barrels and a fine, elegant stock, but it down-flipped badly during recoil and whacked me without mercy every time I used it on the grouse moor. We eventually reluctantly parted company, and I found out later that it did exactly the same to its new owner even though he was of a much heavier build than me. This down-flip of the barrels (which is common with the light English side-by-side) can also produce side-flip due to the bending of the grip, especially with guns that have some degree of cast at heel and toe. This will cause the gun to shoot to the right with a gun with a cast-off stock and to the left with a cast-on stock. With the over-and-under, the upper barrel will throw a pattern marginally high because there is slightly more leverage against the shoulder (during recoil) to flip the muzzles up.

Bruising to the face and shoulder can be positively reduced by proper gun fit and good gun-mounting technique. Discomfort to the side of the jaw is a result of incorrect cast or a bad mount, bringing the face to the gun and not the gun to the face. Long-necked ladies are particularly susceptible to this. Bruising to the face and cheekbone is due to too much down angle at comb, too short a stock, or too much down pitch.

Sometimes the shooter's physique requires some pitch adjustment. Pitch is one of the variables of stock dimension that is often overlooked, and even small pitch adjustments can have a dramatic effect on the point of impact of a shotgun. Pitch is the angle of the butt plate relative to the barrels of the gun, and the correct pitch ensures that the butt fits the shooter's shoulder properly. Large-chested men (and well-endowed ladies) will benefit from a dose of down pitch, but too much will make the gun shoot low, and the recoil can drive the comb up into the shooter's cheek. A parallel or even reverse Monte Carlo may be the answer. There is nothing new in this; as early as 1850 William Greener invented the "rationale" or hogsback stock. The top was humped, as the name suggests, so that the angle of the comb underneath the jaw was the reverse of a conventional stock. An experienced gun fitter should be able to help you figure out what is best for you.

So for hunters who are impatient for a shooting companion on their next trip, here are some useful tips. The ultimate decision regarding choice of gun is ours, and we are (or should be) capable of choosing a gun of a suitable weight that will keep recoil at an acceptable level. The physical strength of the user is also a criterion. There is no point in giving a youngster a light gun if cartridges of moderate power are unavailable to put through it. The stock should be as long and as straight as the new shooter can manage, and this applies to both bend and cast. A narrow comb can cause bruising to the front of the cheekbone when combined with a bad mount, where the shooter brings his face to the

Some competition guns now come with an adjustable comb and built-in recoil reducer.

gun instead of the gun to his face. The farther forward the face is tipped, the more likely this is to occur. A stock with excessive drop is likely to produce bruising of the cheekbone, especially if the shooter has a small amount of flesh covering it.

Most beginners fail to pull the gun into the shoulder properly due to poor instruction on mounting technique. As a result, the gun rotates upward excessively and into the cheekbone. Pain can be experienced from the first shot if this happens, and this often results in the shooter holding his head up off the stock to prevent it from happening again. This makes the situation worse, and a second pop in the cheek is the result. A long stock is usually pulled more firmly into the shoulder and helps to control recoil better. Two inches between the back of the hand and the shooter's nose is about right. Too long, and the gun will tend to jump out of the shoulder on the first shot, especially on a right-to-left crossing shot (right-shouldered shooter). A bruised upper arm will be the result when the next shot is taken.

Bruising to the face and nose is also the usual result, as the recoil is transferred, if the stock is too short. An over-and-under, because of the configuration of the barrels, will transfer recoil better and more evenly to the shooter's shoulder than a side-by-side. A semi- or full-pistol grip stock will help to control recoil better than a straight (English) grip stock, because the hand has more to hang on to, enabling that arm to absorb more of the recoil.

An old gun that has seen a large amount of service may have a worn hinge pin and be slightly "off the face." This means that there is excessive clearance (known as headspace) between the breech face and the face of the cartridge due to wear. The gun will recoil badly as a result.

A gas-operated semiautomatic is often the best choice for a starter gun, provided that the individual is capable of handling such a gun. Semiautos are always front-heavy, and this can result in what is known as forward inertia as the shooter tries to swing the gun.

The weight of a heavy gun can also result in a lightly built shooter's attempting to counterbalance the weight forward distribution by rocking onto the back foot. This results in poor muzzle control when the gun is moved onto the line of the target.

Felt recoil is always more with a fiber wad than with a plastic wad (plas-wad), even though the shot and propellant content may be the same. That is because it is the acceleration of the entire contents of the cartridge that affects the recoil, not just the shot charge. Fiber wads are heavier than plas-wads and recoil slightly more as a result. Also, plas-wads

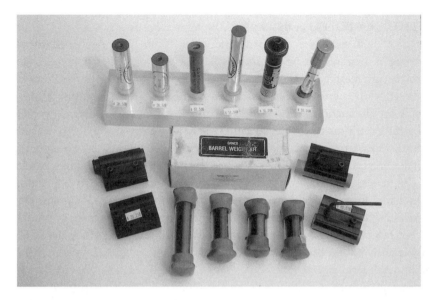

A tube filled with mercury, which is fitted inside the stock of the gun, can substantially reduce the amount of perceived recoil. Inertia slowly moves on the heavy liquid mercury inside the tube, slowing the gun movement rearward, during the first phase of recoil. Barrel weights of different size can be attatched underneath the barrel to reduce both recoil and muzzle flip. They can also be used to alter the handling dynamics of a shotgun.

have a compressible piston effect that cushions some of the initial acceleration, unlike the fiber wad, which does not compress as easily.

Try before you buy, if possible. I owned a gun shop for many years, and I was amazed that two guns, identical in every apparent respect, can recoil noticeably differently. This is due to small differences in balance because of the density of wood used for the stock and also variation in mechanical tolerances. When all else fails and there is no turning back from an investment that has already been made on a new gun, there are one or two tricks of the trade that can be used. The heavier the gun, the more resistant to movement it will be (inertia), and therefore it will have proportionally less recoil. Adhesive lead strip is readily available at hardware stores. Strips of lead can be applied to the wood on the fore-end between the wood and the barrel on an over-and-under. The butt pad can be removed to expose the bolt-hole in the end of the butt on most guns, and modeling clay can be added there with the addition of small pieces of lead to balance the gun. An increase of a few ounces can make a big difference to the amount of felt recoil.

THE COMPETITION GUN

Recoil reduction is a critical consideration with competition shooting where multiple shots are fired, and over the last decade or so, mainly due to the interest in sporting clays, there have been huge improvements in the search for efficient ways to make the shooting process more enjoyable for all. Manufacturers lengthen forcing cones, back-bore (overbore) barrels, and port muzzles to change the internal dynamics of the barrels in an effort to reduce recoil and muzzle flip. I personally have never liked ported barrels because the noise level to the shooter and bystanders is increased, but they do help defeat muzzle jump. Barrel weights and mercury tubes can also be fitted to reduce recoil and manipulate the handling dynamics of the gun. Many guns are now factory fitted with a recoil system and a fully adjustable comb. Failing this, there are now several hydraulic and mechanical precision-engineered pads that are fully adjustable and can also be fitted. The Gracoil, Rad, and G-squared are three examples. Of course, these modifications to the stock can be expensive, but if the gun is eventually sold, it will now be fully adjustable to the facial dimensions of the new owner, which is a good selling point. A recent development are the soft, space-age rubber recoil pads (called Gooey pads); they can have a dramatic effect on the amount of felt recoil with only modest expense involved.

Finally, remember that *all* new recruits are apprehensive about firing a shotgun for the first time, whether they admit it or not. There are more part-time "expert shooting instructors" in this industry than fleas on a hedgehog's back, and they will all volunteer advice on the best gun

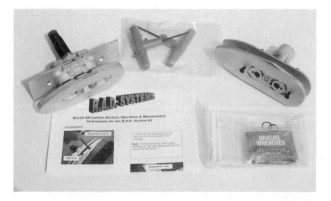

These Gracoil and Rad recoil reducers can be easily adjusted for length of pull, toe in, or toe out to suit the user's shoulder pocket.

In this picture, "Red" Meador of Meador Stockworks puts the finishing touches to a finished Gracoil pad on the stock of a competition gun.

for a new recruit. Shotguns are not cheap. It is best to politely decline their offer and do it right the first time. These people mean well, but bad advice is worse than no advice. Bad advice in the early stages of shotgunning can be a deterrent, and I have personally witnessed ladies refusing to *ever* fire a shotgun again due to a bad experience with recoil. Instead, seek the advice of a reputable gun dealer or, better still, the professional instructor who earns his living by teaching people to shoot.

Rubber recoil pads come in all shapes and sizes. Soft "space-age" rubber pads (in a dazzling array of complementary colors for the competition gun) are often used as an inexpensive way to reduce recoil.

CHAPTER 5

Eye Dominance: Diagnosis and Some Eye Problems

With shotgunning, your eyes and your shotgun must work as a team to achieve consistently successful results. Eyesight, the most complex of the sensory systems, must be utilized to its maximum potential if we are to achieve mechanical excellence. We may use our eyes to see, but our success with a shotgun depends on what we do with what we see.

The ocular stimuli the brain receives must be converted into a physical response to move the intermediary, the shotgun, accurately onto the line of the target. There should be a subtle blend of these neurological and physical ingredients, which we call hand-eye coordination. There are many other sports that depend on this basic hand-eye coordination for success. The baseball player or golfer simply keeps his eyes on the ball and unerringly hits it, in the same way that a carpenter drives a nail into a piece of lumber. No consideration is given as to which is the dominant eye to enable them to do this; they simply focus on the target and hand-eye coordination does the rest. So why then do we go to such great lengths to get an accurate diagnosis of eye dominance in shotgunning? Because we do not mount a shotgun centrally to our line of vision in the middle of our chest—we mount it to the side on one of our shoulders. Although the gun may feel that it handles better on one side than the other, if the eye above the rib isn't the one we use to see the correct target-barrel relationship as we trigger the shot, we may have problems.

EYE-OPENING ADVICE ON DOMINANCE

"I have to keep both eyes open when I shoot a shotgun, don't I?" inquired the new client.

Once again, this controversial topic bubbled to the surface. If I had $10 for every time I have been asked this question in the last twenty years, I would have bought myself a retirement home in Florida by now.

For many of us, the answer to the question is no, and I will explain why. There is no doubt that when using a shotgun, complete binocular vision throughout the act of shooting a moving target is an advantage, but only if everything is as it should be and the eye above the rib is the dominant eye. Stereopsis (depth perception) is better with two eyes. Closing one eye will also restrict the peripheral vision on that side. Peripheral vision is very sensitive to movement, an obvious advantage when we hunt in the field. But some shooters, for some reason, fall into the trap of thinking that they can ignore diagnosing eye dominance and shoot successfully with both eyes open regardless. They can't. So, in an effort to clarify the situation (and probably step right into the middle of a huge hornets' nest in the bargain!), let's take a look at the facts.

Fact 1. Our central nervous system, which we use to coordinate, regulate, and control our bodily actions in response to various stimuli, is complete by late childhood, around ten years of age.

Fact 2. Eye dominance is fixed at the time of this neurological maturity.

Fact 3. Contrary to popular belief, it is visual fixation, not eye dominance, that can switch due to tiredness or stress, but this is an involuntary action and part of the body's normal defense system. We cannot switch eyes voluntarily.

Fact 4. This is the most important one: contrary to some beliefs, we cannot train the sub-dominant eye to "switch over" and become the dominant eye. Depending on the degree of dominance, under certain circumstances we can try to ignore the dominant eye for certain monocular sighting tasks. But there is always an underlying neurological dominance, which will re-appear periodically.

If you shoot off of the right shoulder with strong left eye dominance and you have both eyes open during the act of shooting, you will experience "crossfiring" and shoot inconsistently as a result. It is easy to demonstrate this by shooting at the center of a pattern board. The main shot concentration will be approximately 18 to 24 inches on the left-hand side of the pattern board at 20 yards with both eyes open. (The diagram explains this.) This will have the effect of shooting behind a left-to-right crossing shot, and in front of a right-to-left. To continue shooting from the right shoulder with both eyes open if you have a left

Cross firing. The eye that is above the rib must be the one that the shooter uses to make the correct target/barrel relationship. If it isn't, the wrong eye will take over as the gun is brought to point of aim, and the barrels will be pointing in the wrong place as the shot is triggered. The right-shouldered, left-dominant-eyed shooter will shoot behind a left-to-right crossing target and in front of a right-to-left.

dominant eye will also complicate the process of applying lead. Exaggerated lead will need to be given on a left-to-right crossing shot and less lead on a right-to-left, in order to score a hit.

Some shooters attempt to ignore the dominant eye, proudly claiming that they have "trained" their cross-dominant eye to take over. They can't. All that happens is that they concentrate hard on the visual impression of the barrel, which corresponds to their shooting shoulder, in the hope that this will eventually reverse their dominance. By doing this, they are making a *conscious* effort to influence which eye sees the target in the correct relationship to the barrel, and by doing this they are compounding the problem of what is already a complex process, that of applying lead. The practice of attempting to do this has limited success, which is directly proportional to the degree of dominance. Eventually, however, they will be able to build up a huge and complex memory bank of sight pictures to enable them to hit some targets with some success, some of the time.

We can use the targets on a skeet field as an example. The laws of physics dictate that on a skeet field both station 4 targets (high house and low house) require approximately 4 feet of lead if shot with the sustained lead method. A cross-dominant shooter would need to give the high house target 6 feet lead and the low house 2 feet to score a hit. Quite a difference and very confusing for the shooter! Unfortunately, on certain target presentations, the dominance mismatch will manifest itself at some inopportune moment and bite the shooter in the proverbial butt! Once again, if you are left-eye dominant, you simply cannot voluntarily "train" your right eye to counteract this dominance and make the

Testing for dominance. Make a circle with the fingers of both hands, but keep the hands below the waist at this stage. Keeping both eyes open, focus on a small object in the distance, here I'm using the top of the flagpole at the Dallas Gun Club. With the hands extended, bring them up to look at the object through the circle that the fingers make, and then quickly bring the hands back towards the face. The eye that remains framed by the fingers is the master eye.

right eye become the dominant eye. Advice to the contrary is incorrect and misleading.

One of the first things I do with a new student is to diagnose eye dominance, and there are several ways to do this. Point at an object in the distance with both eyes open. Close first one eye then the other—the one that stays in line is the dominant eye. Or make a circle with the fingers of both hands, look through it and then alternately close each eye to see which one remains in line. There are many other ways. Unfortunately, although all these methods certainly tell us which eye is dominant, they don't tell us by how much. The confusion seems to arise when we try to assess the degree of dominance. Also, some of us will have what is known as "central vision," with neither eye dominant to a measurable extent.

Once I have diagnosed eye dominance in a new student, I prefer him to shoot one-eyed for the first few lessons. I do this because I believe that in the early days of learning to shoot, many beginners can benefit from closing the left eye (right shoulder, right master eye shooter) just as the gun comes onto the target, even though the test for

Left: Right master eye. *Right:* Left master eye.

eye dominance seems to suggest irrefutably that the right eye is the master eye. Doing this gives them a clearer sight picture than the normal recommendation (keeping both eyes open). For the first time in his life, the new student has a shotgun barrel central to his line of vision, and often he will see a "ghost" image of the barrels. This is, I believe, something called physiological diplopia, and it is the same reason why most of us see a ghost image of two fingers instead of one when we do an eye dominance test. Unfortunately, for a new shooter this can be confusing. Which image, the left one or the right one, does he use to determine the correct target/barrel relationship?

Closing the off eye (the one that is not above the rib) clarifies this. This is only a temporary measure. I am not suggesting for one moment that the right-shouldered, right-master-eyed shot should always close his left eye. As he becomes more experienced and knows what sight picture to look for, he will probably shoot better with both eyes open. For some people with central vision or slight match-match, the type of gun used, even the type of rib on the gun, can influence which eye takes over as the gun is brought to point of aim. This is in effect physiological diplopia in reverse. In some cases, if the rib or muzzle configuration is seen too clearly, it can lead to the shooter's eyes flitting back and forth between the barrels and the target, with disastrous consequences.

Many people insist that they never see their barrels during the act of shooting. How can they avoid seeing them? Our barrels are central to our line of vision as we intercept each target, but we should not be *looking* at them. It is impossible to direct the gun accurately onto the same line as the target unless we have some visual indication of where the barrels are as we do this. The answer is that we do rely on seeing the barrels but only subconsciously in our peripheral vision, because we should have our eyes locked onto the target to collect as much visual information as possible. The stimulus that the eye receives provides an ocular "link" to convert the information into muscular coordination, moving the gun onto the same line as the target.

Here's another interesting point. The importance of gun fit has always been stressed as one of the primary considerations for successful shotgunning. The main reason why we have a shotgun fitted is so that the aiming eye will be above the rib and the gun will shoot where we look. Therefore, what would be the point of going to this expense if there was a degree of cross-dominance involved and the wrong eye was taking over?

As an illustration of just how much the barrels can subconsciously influence our eyes, many years ago I had a client who had shot well all his life with a side-by-side, but every time he tried to shoot an over-and-under, he would shoot down the left side of the target. After much head scratching, an eye dominance test revealed that he was left eye dominant, but the dominance must have been slight, almost central vision. The dominant visual impression, as he brought his side-by-side up to point of aim, was the one of the wide, horizontal view of the barrels, which his right eye was receiving. However, when he did the same with the over-and-under, the situation was the reverse and the dominant visual impression was the one that his left eye would see of the barrels. Because they were now stacked vertically, his left eye would take over and he would shoot down the left side of the target every time.

There are some shooters who claim that a high-visibility, glowing bead on the rib gives them a better target/barrel relationship sight picture. There is no doubt in my mind that some people may benefit from one of these, but only if the cross-dominance is slight. These "glow-worm beads" work by enhancing the barrel/target relationship as it is seen in the *peripheral* vision, but once again, this is entirely dependent on the degree of dominance. In some cases where strong dominance mismatch exists, the shooter may be tempted even for a millisecond to switch his focus onto the bead instead of the target at the point of pulling the trigger. The gun will stop as a result. This attempt to enhance the barrels of shotguns in the peripheral vision isn't a new idea by any means. In low-light conditions, dawn and dusk, for example, seasoned wildfowlers on the Solway coast in Scotland would rub chalk or light-colored wax crayon down the rib of their shotgun to make it stand out more clearly. (This is explained in more detail in chapter 12.)

So, to recap, the shooter that is left eye dominant (or has almost central vision) and shoots from his right shoulder will hit some targets. But he will shoot *better* and more *consistently* if he makes absolutely sure that the eye above the rib is the one he is using to determine the correct sight picture. There is no substitute for making sure that the eye that is above the rib is the one that is relied on to give the brain the correct ocular information. We can do this in several ways.

The simple answer, if you have cross-dominance and it can be diagnosed early enough, is to learn to shoot from the same shoulder as the master eye, and there is no doubt in my mind that this is the best medicine and the shooter will be cured *for life*. With a youngster or someone who has never shot before, this should not be a problem, and it is as easy to accomplish as any new motor skill. This is good advice, since it is not as difficult as most people think to achieve and because it is impossible to change one's master eye. But anyone who has shot for a few years will usually object strongly to the suggestion to switch shoulders, for two reasons. First, he will have already developed some "muscle memory," and it will now feel strange to mount the gun on the opposite shoulder. Second, most people expect instant results, and when this does not happen, they quickly abandon this approach and go back to the shoulder that they are more comfortable with. I never push my clients with this, I can only advise. It depends on how determined the individual is to succeed.

When I first moved to the States, I had already been driving on the left side of the road in the United Kingdom for thirty years. Now I had no choice but to learn to drive on the right. After three or four days, I was driving competently, using a stick shift in my opposite hand. Driving on the roads in the United States was an exact "mirror image" of driving in the United Kingdom. But I was doing everything as spontaneously as though I had driven on the right for years. But as I said, I didn't have a choice; there was no "easy way out."

The second way is to block the cross-dominant eye with one of the weird and wonderful "cure-all" devices on the market. These can be different-size patches for sticking on shooting glasses or "obliterators," which fit on the sides of shotguns. There is nothing new in this. Over a century ago a device called the Monopeian sight was described by Greener in his 1892 book *The Gun*. Later, John Pesket of Cogswell and Harrison designed another similar device, known as the eye corrector or Obliterator. Modern versions of these are available today. Do they work? Sometimes, but they also have their drawbacks. They all interrupt the shooter's binocular vision in some way, which gives partial loss of peripheral and stereoscopic vision *on certain targets.* Lens dots are the same. The size of the dot is crucial. Dot too big, peripheral vision is sacrificed. Dot too small, the shooter will attempt to see around it. The position of the dot will change slightly if the shooting glasses slip for some reason. If the gun mount is less than perfect, the position of the dot relative to the barrels is questionable as the gun comes to point of aim. I think that these lens dot remedies are more acceptable for skeet and trap because the eye is perfectly aligned with the rib each time *before* calling for the target. For sporting clays and wing shooting, certain target presentations will cause problems.

The third way (this is the one I prefer; it was the cure for the guy in my example) is to close the off eye just before the shot is taken. It does not take much, just a quick blink as the correct forward allowance is established. By doing this, the shooter has retained his full peripheral vision, full stereoscopic vision (needed to judge speed and distance accurately), and full binocular vision, by keeping both his eyes open throughout the whole of the shooting process as he takes the shot, until the last millisecond. He now has a crystal-clear picture of his target/barrel relationship with no chance of cross-dominance kicking in. The only problem here is that some people cannot wink an eye, and the only alternative for these people is to use a *correctly positioned* lens dot.

Finally, although we have recognized for centuries the importance of diagnosing eye dominance in the United Kingdom, before writing this I took the precaution of making sure of my facts by consulting some of the most prominent ophthalmologists and strabismus (eye alignment) experts in the United States. The answers always came back the same. You simply *cannot* make your eyes change dominance. With shooting, the rules are not written in tablets of stone. No one can make a sweeping statement and insist that it is more beneficial for all people to shoot with both eyes open all of the time. We are all different; it depends entirely on the ocular nerve hook-up of the individual. There are some excellent world-class shots out there that close an eye.

So, for the people who have questionable eye dominance I would suggest this: experiment. Try shooting a variety of targets a variety of ways, eyes both open and one eye shut. One way may give you more consistent results than the other, and I suspect that many of you will be delighted if you try this. You may be quickly breaking more targets than you would have dared to imagine, and of course, that is what really matters, isn't it? And the next time someone tells you that you *must* shoot with both eyes open when you use a shotgun, smile politely and walk away. Then do what works for you.

SOME EYE PROBLEMS

Visual stimulus is the only "contact" we have with a moving target. Vision problems associated with successful shotgunning are more common than we think, and over the years that I have been a shooting coach, I have come across some extraordinary eye problems. Any eye problem directly influences the shooter's ability to hit moving targets consistently. Most of these problems are fairly straightforward for the experienced coach to diagnose, but some of them can be more complicated. I will give you three examples.

I once had the pleasure of instructing three pretty young ladies who were sisters. They were the daughters of a very accomplished shot, a titled gentleman, who loved his driven pheasant and grouse shooting. I will refer to him as "the Brigadier." Two of the sisters progressed rapidly and quickly became competent shots, but Margo, the third and youngest sister, just could not get the hang of it and struggled to connect with even simple targets. I decided that Margo should come back for lessons on her own, to eliminate the possibility of her being intimidated by the presence of her sisters, who were showing better progress.

With simple going-away targets, Margo could hit some, but never with any consistency, and easy incoming targets were just as bad. In desperation, I lined some clay targets up on the ground at a distance of about twenty yards and asked Margo to mount the gun and fire at them, and once again there was no consistency, even at stationary targets! What was the problem? Well, it took a bit of head scratching to figure it out, but Margo had developed a completely subconscious visual flinch and was closing *both* eyes just before she pulled the trigger. This flinch was not accompanied with the usual noticeable reflexive jerk, and it was hard to detect because I was always standing behind her.

The reason for the flinch? Margo, the youngest and most slightly built of the three sisters, admitted that several years previously, at the age of about twelve, a well-meaning uncle had tried to teach the girls to shoot with a light 20 gauge, which had kicked her badly, and she had developed a deep resentment of shotguns. I'm pleased to say that with a lot of patience and perseverance, Margo overcame the problem and can now bring down the long-tails with the best of them, much to the delight of the Brigadier.

The second example is a visual problem that was a result of physical damage. A friend of mine, Jock McKee, a police officer who was a reasonable shot, called me late one night in an obvious state of concern. Jock had three passions (four if you count pure malt whiskey)—Labrador retrievers, rugby, and driven pheasants. As a result of a nasty accident during a rugby game, another player's thumb had almost gouged Jack's right eye out during a scrum, the thumbnail cutting the cornea quite badly in the process. Thankfully, as later proved to be the case, the damage was not permanent, but Jock's main concern was that his right eye was badly damaged with just two weeks to go before the opening of pheasant season. What should he do?

Now Jock is a big guy, over 250 pounds, and his gun needed a good dose of cast. As luck would have it, quite by chance I had a nice side-by-side Charles Boswell boxlock that had sat in the gun rack of my shop for too long because it had a large amount of cast-on, i.e., cast left, usually correct for a left-handed shooter. I loaned the gun to Jock on the condition that every night he would practice his gun-mounting technique, the gun on his left shoulder, at least fifty times per night. Jock agreed. A week later, we went to my shooting ground to try a few shots off the high tower, and the results were encouraging. There was another week to go before pheasant season, and Jock went home with the promise that he would not let up on the gun-mounting practice. A week later, on the evening of opening day, I received an excited call from Jock. He had shot very well and was delighted with his performance. Several months later, when pheasant season was over, Jock walked into the shop. His right eye had healed, with only a barely noticeable scar across the pupil, and the vision was perfect.

"You'll be returning the gun then?" I inquired.

"Not if we can agree on a price" was the reply. "I found out that I have always been left eye dominant. I can shoot better than I would have imagined from my left shoulder."

Needless to say, we did agree on a price, and the deal was sealed with a suitable bottle of single malt. An appropriate ending to what seemed at first to be a disaster.

The third example is more complicated. Many years ago I was the chief instructor at a large shooting facility in the south of England, Clifford Farm Estates. One of my clients, an engineer with the Thames Water utility company, was struggling with left-to-right crossing shots. When I asked him to shoot a few high station 4 targets on the skeet field, he was well behind all of them. Low-house station 4 targets weren't a problem, and I could see a perfect target-barrel relationship as each target was systematically pulverized.

My initial diagnosis for his failure to connect with the left-to-right targets was the obvious one of a simple left-eye dominance problem, but this was not the case, as blocking off his left eye with a lens dot revealed. Also, it was not the physical fact that a right-handed shooter needs to see more lead on a right-to-left target, because a right-to-left gun swing is a push and the left-to-right movement a pull. Physically, a pull is an easier movement to make; this is why we put the cart behind the horse instead of in front of it. It wasn't reduced gun speed either, because he was shooting sustained lead, so I concluded that his visual impression of target-barrel relationship was wrong. Now, I have always been blessed with the ability to see the shot swarm on most shots, and this client was shooting a long way behind a twenty-yard crossing shot, by my calculations probably three to four feet. The conversation went something like this:

"OK, double your lead and try again." Another miss, still behind. The client was becoming increasingly frustrated.

"Double your lead again and try another shot." Another miss, still behind, but nearer.

By this time, I was becoming agitated. The day was overcast, and the shot swarm was a crystal-clear indication to me where the pellets were going. All the shots were still a long way behind. In desperation, I stood behind the client and moved the gun for him, giving him the signal to fire when the lead looked right to me, and the target was smashed. The client was wide-eyed with amazement. For some reason, his perception of lead on the left-to-right crossing shot was at least three times what he saw on a similar right-to-left target. When I questioned him about this, he insisted that he needed about a ten- to twelve-foot lead on a left-to-right no. 4 skeet target. It was the only way he could connect with them. I have seen this phenomenon several times with various clients over the last twenty years or so, but I have no idea what causes it.

I found out later that this guy was dyslexic. Was that the reason for his problem? I have no idea, but the moral of the story is this: only the man pulling the trigger knows what he sees, or *thinks* he sees. Mother Nature can get it wrong in isolated cases, and there was no doubt in my mind that this shooter had a defective neurological connection somewhere, which was giving either an extended delay time with his reaction to trigger the shot or a completely different perspective of the target-barrel relationship. This client had to make a deliberate effort to shoot almost three times as far in front of a left-to-right crossing target to hit it.

CHAPTER 6

Gun Fit

My ten-year-old daughter enjoys wildlife programs. Recently, we were both watching a documentary where a cheetah was stalking a Thomson's gazelle on the Serengeti. As the cat started its run, reaching speeds in excess of sixty-five miles per hour, its eyes were focused intently on its desperately fleeing target. Despite the extreme contortions of its accelerating body, the cat's shock-absorber system allowed its head to remain almost motionless and perfectly balanced, hardly moving, never bobbing about uncontrollably. Every movement of the gazelle was anticipated and the cat reacted accordingly. This is in effect what we are looking for in a perfectly fitted gun. The head must remain level, moving smoothly in the direction of the target as the mount is completed, allowing the user to visually lock onto the target to develop the line. Once this perfect fit is achieved, there is no mistaking it. The result is a shotgun that is tailored so perfectly to our personal physical requirements that it can be lifted smoothly into place, instinctively and comfortably, with a perfectly controlled mount, without conscious thought. With a perfect fit, the gun will shoot to point of aim, or in other words, the gun will shoot *exactly* to where its user looks.

The science of fitting sporting shotguns can be traced back in the United Kingdom as far as the 1830s. Earlier shotguns were so cumbersome in both barrel length and stock dimensions that before this, there was no need to fit them—shotguns were used to take (unsporting but necessary) pot shots at flocks of birds on the ground. However, flintlocks were in production by the eighteenth century that were fairly accurate and could be used successfully in the pursuit of flying game. These guns were similar in shape to the shotgun as we know it today. Proficient

74

shotgunning was a critical factor, in those days, in the social standing of the late Victorian and Edwardian sportsmen. Raised birds, which were released in the hundreds earlier in the century, were now released in the thousands. It is worth noting that between 1802 and 1853 Colonel Peter Hawker bagged only 575 pheasants, but Lord Ripon, renowned as one of the greatest game shots of all time, shot an incredible 111,190 between 1867 and 1895. Many previously remote areas of Britain were now readily accessible largely due to the spread of the railway system, and it became fashionable for the owners of the great sporting estates to invite the "crack" shots of the era (providing they were of suitable pedigree) to compete with each other for the largest bags. If Lord So-and-So's team of guns could "wipe the eye" of Lord Bees Knees' men by having the advantage of properly fitted shotguns and regular visits to the shooting school, so be it.

Over the years that I have been a shooting instructor, I have listened intently to more than enough conversations about gun fit to last me a lifetime. Self-professed experts delight in handing out free information on the subject to anyone with the time and inclination to lend an ear. But who really tries my patience is the fellow who thrusts a gun that is incompatible in every way into the hands of the new shooter with the advice of "Never mind the gun, lad; just point it in the right place."

Most experienced wingshooters, the ones who have been shooting for years, know all they need to know about gun fit, don't they? Of course! They mount the gun a few times, and if their gun-side eye is more or less aligned with the rib, the gun fits, right? Wrong. Most of the time, they are *consciously* aligning their eye. Would they do this in the field? What do you think? A hunter is moving through a mesquite-filled gully and the telltale whistle of startled mourning dove pinions reaches his ears. He isn't sure where the dove is coming from at this stage of the game, but suddenly, it shows itself and the hunter gets off a shot. Did he have time to double-check and make sure his eye was aligned with the rib? I don't think so.

Correct gun fit is crucial to successful shotgunning, especially in shooting situations with unpredictable targets, but just what exactly is gun fit? The explanation is simple. *Gun fitting* means exactly that—tailoring the dimensions of a gun stock so that it fits our personal physical requirements. The four basic variables of gun fit are length, drop, cast, and pitch. Alterations can be made to each of these to make the gun fit the user. The shotgun is the necessary intermediary between a shooter and the target. There is no rear sight on a shotgun—the shooter's eye must become the back sight. Therefore, it makes sense that any alterations we can make to allow this to take place as naturally as possible must provide an advantage.

However, before these elusive magical adjustments are made, the user must learn to mount and swing the gun correctly. A gun may be altered to fit its user as perfectly as the proverbial glove, but if his gun mount and swing are sloppy before the gun is fitted, he has wasted his money on the gun fit. On the other hand, we are all perfectly adaptable and resilient animals, and the human body is highly contortive. So if the gun does not fit, we can always wriggle our head about; this is just as good, isn't it? I am afraid not. We should be keeping our eyes on the target or, more exactly, the space in front of the target, where our shot needs to go, and not on the rib, or our fingernails, or the bead, or anything else. Providing we are of average build, we should be able, over a period of time, to accommodate any gun, but if we are wider or taller than Mr. Average, then we have problems.

This semiauto Beretta 391 has a standard, straight field stock with off the shelf dimensions of 1^1/$_2$ drop at "nose" of comb, 2^1/$_4$ drop at "heel," and a 14^1/$_4$-inch length of pull. This gun may shoot well for a five-foot ten-inch guy of average build, but the same gun will shoot high and left for a 250-pound, six-foot two-inch guy who needs a longer length of pull and a dose of cast, simply because he has broad shoulders and is looking down the side of the rib. He will also creep his head up on the stock, which in turn will elevate his eye above the rib.

Within reason, someone who needs a short length of pull can hold a standard gun with his front hand farther back on the fore-end, and someone who needs a longer length of pull can hold farther forward and compensate. A standard, straight field stock with off-the-shelf dimensions of 1½ inches at the comb, 2½ inches at the heel, and a 14-inch length of pull may shoot well for a 5-foot 10-inch fellow of average build. But the same gun will shoot high and left for a 6-foot 2-inch guy who needs a longer length of pull and a dose of cast, simply because he will "creep" his head up on the stock, which will elevate his eye too far above the rib or force him to mash the comb into his cheek too hard.

So, if a gun is not the right prescription for its user, he *may* learn to shoot it by wriggling his head about to align his eye in the right place. Perhaps he will even become a reasonable shot, but he will never reach his full potential until he is using a gun that is tailored to his personal physical requirements. A correctly fitted gun inspires confidence, and the shooter experiences subconscious, tactile assurance that his master eye is where he expects it to be, in correct alignment above the rib. With

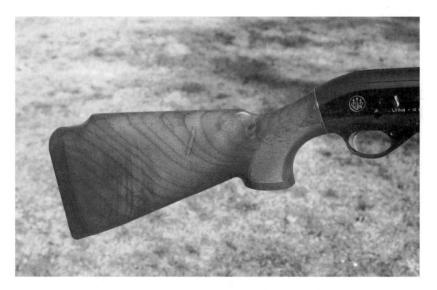

This is the same model of gun, but this time the stock is a high-combed, Monte Carlo–type stock. This stock was produced by Beretta to meet the demand for long-necked female shooters. The stock comes in two lengths, the RL (reduced length) and the SL (standard length), and the grip radius is smaller on both to accommodate smaller hands. Both types have a parallel comb. As a general rule, women typically have longer necks than men and can benefit from this type of stock.

sporting clays and in wingshooting situations, it has to be. A pheasant or dove that flushes from cover gives a hunter little time to evaluate his quarry's fleeing flight, and there is seldom time to consciously align the eye with the rib.

Many shooters, some of them with years of experience, have no more than a general idea of where their gun is pointing as they shoot it. Usually, the cause is erratic eye alignment due to bad gun fit or a sloppy mount. Some shooters will buy, sell, and trade guns in an effort to find the one that feels just right, but never take the time to have it fitted properly. In some cases, they proudly proclaim that for the first time in their shooting careers, they have found the perfect gun and it has so drastically improved their shooting ability that they are connecting with birds that had previously proved impossible. Usually, this is nothing more than new gun syndrome and is short-lived.

A new gun is often like a honeymoon or new girlfriend—exciting and exhilarating at first, then boring and mundane as the novelty wears off. When we buy a new gun, our mental focus is better and initially we hit more targets because of this and nothing more. Then, after a few months, the new gun becomes old hat, and we start missing again. It was always a standard joke in the gun trade that if you wanted to sell a gun to someone, let them try a couple of shots and then take it off them. Usually the ploy worked, and the guy who tried the gun would put his hand on his wallet, absolutely convinced that the gun was right for him.

How do I know this? Well, for many years I owned a gun shop. Unfortunately for me, this honeymoon syndrome worked both ways, and owning a gun shop can have its downside for a keen hunter and competition shooter. If I won a tournament or managed to pull down a cloud-scraping, stratospheric cock pheasant with a certain gun, it instantly became the best gun in the world and I had complete confidence in it. I would vow never to part with it, but once I had a bad day, I unceremoniously abandoned the gun in favor of the next one. Believe me, I speak from experience.

I have noticed that some Americans have a very laid-back attitude to gun fitting, and for a long time, it has been frowned upon as some sort of unnecessary, archaic poppycock, carried out for centuries by the Brits so that their English sidelocks (some of which cost an arm and a leg already) could command even higher prices. Over on this side of the pond, attention is usually given only to stock length, or only marginal consideration to comb height, cast, and pitch. Stock too long? Whack a lump off. Too short? Get a thicker recoil pad. Grandpappy never had a gun that was fitted and it was good enough for him, wasn't it?

Maybe so. For years, this "if it was good enough for grandpappy, it's good enough for me" attitude has prevailed in the United States. Unfortunately, this one-size-fits-all approach may have sufficed once upon a time, but times have changed, mainly because of the massive interest in sporting clays and double-guns. If you really want to shoot straight and transform those frustrating whiffs into confident hits, maybe it is time you cared about gun fit. A complacent attitude is a mistake if you want optimum results.

Although we routinely accept that other things that come into bodily contact need to "fit" our requirements, for some reason, in the eyes of some people, shotguns do not fall into this category. What do you do, for example, when your daughter or wife has been using your car? My guess is that you readjust the seat height and driving position, tweak the side mirrors, and adjust the seatbelt to restore your optimum driving position. What about clothing? Would you wear a pair of shoes or pants that didn't fit? If you expect maximum performance from your shotgun, isn't it worth having it fitted? Absolutely. Despite all the evidence of the benefits of a good fit, however, there are still some people who do not bother and, even worse, some people who will try to adapt to the gun instead. So let's spell it out: the *shooter* should be the starting point. The gun should be made to fit his requirements, not the other way around.

I have come across this ass-about-face attitude (as we say in Scotland) dozens of times in the last twenty years or so, usually, but not always, when the gun is a hand-me-down or an impulse buy. Some people will abandon logic and tolerate a gun that does not fit them for the strangest of reasons. Some years ago I had a call from a client who had been a regular customer for several years. This particular client, a really nice, jovial guy and a prominent dental surgeon, loved his pheasant shooting. At an auction sale of fishing tackle and firearms in Dumfries, as an early retirement present to himself (strange how lots of keen wingshooters often buy themselves guns as presents), he bought a nice Westley Richards sidelock. Like a dog with two tails, he gleefully opened the superb leather-bound case to display the contents. It was obvious that he was very pleased with himself.

"Bought this at auction last week, Pete," he beamed. "What do you think? Was £1,500 (about $3,000) too much to pay for it?" Though I did not say so, for me it was a bit steep, but as I said, this was a few years ago. I examined the gun, and it was a nice one. The well-figured French walnut glowed amber and black like the cape of a November cock pheasant, and there was some tasteful engraving. The action was as sweet as a nut, as tight as the day it was made, and the gun had obviously seen only light use.

"Soon be time for the old long-tails," he said cheerfully, "and I thought I'd better get my eye in before the start of the season."

So off we went to the high tower. Now, this client was normally a pretty fair gun, but he failed to connect even one of a half dozen or so shots.

Something was wrong, and the pride in the new gun began to fade as fast as late spring snow off a dry stone dyke. Targets sailed by untouched, and I could sense his disappointment.

"Okay," I said, desperately trying to make light conversation and salvage the situation, "let's try a few on the pattern board." From a distance of twenty yards, his first shot nearly missed the board completely. Bad gun mount, I thought.

"Try another one," I said. Sure enough, that time he did miss the board. The problem? The gun was cast left for a left-handed shooter. Immediately my genetically engineered cynicism kicked in. So that's why this gun was in the auction, and that's why it was a bargain price. I admit that I had not noticed the problem, and the client had obviously parted with his cash because the gun was so seductively pretty in appearance and he unfortunately did not know any better. So I pointed the problem out to him, suggested a good gunsmith who could bend the stock, and told him to come back when the work was complete. And that, I thought, was that. A year later, just before the start of pheasant season and when I had almost forgotten about him and the incident, the phone rang.

"Hello, Pete, Bob Bentley-Jones here. Any chance of my coming in for a brush-up lesson tomorrow?" We made all the usual peripheral pleasantries and agreed to a time at the shooting grounds next day.

Upon his arrival, I immediately recognized the Westley Richards and we made our way straight for the high tower. The first targets were pulverized perfectly.

"I see the shooting's improved, Bob. See what a difference a well-fitted gun makes?" I asked smugly.

"Oh no, it isn't that," he said. "I took it to the gunsmith, as you suggested, but he told me that he would need to bend the stock quite a lot to make it fit. He couldn't guarantee that it would work without

These prints on the pattern board are an indication of poor and inconsistent gun-mounting technique. For this reason, it is a complete waste of time to fit a shotgun (apart from length of pull) to a new shooter until he has acquired a few months of shotgun technique, learned to mount the gun properly, and also learned to stay "in the gun" as the shot is taken. One thing is certain: if the basic fundamentals of mount and swing are lacking, a perfectly fitted shotgun will not compensate for gun-mounting errors or miscalculations of lead.

damaging it. It's such a lovely piece of walnut that I didn't have the heart to risk it."

Suitably perplexed, I asked, "So just how are you hitting these targets?"

"Oh, it's easy," he said. "On the driven targets (incomers), the gun shoots a long way to the left, so I hold out to the right a couple of feet."

What about the crossing shots? I wondered but did not ask. The visual corrections and compensations for a gun that did not fit would drive me daft, but he was convinced that it worked for him, and it did, sometimes.

Some of the clients that come to see me say they are "inconsistent" and are convinced that the blame lies with their gun fit. While that is often the case, inconsistency can often be narrowed down to simple human indulgences like the one-too-many double-malt whiskeys the night before. Seemed like a good idea at the time, didn't it? The blonde barmaid who served the drinks was nice, too. Now the aftereffects of a late night and one too many makes your elegant, fast-handling Damascus-barreled sidelock feel like a sack of Irish potatoes as you attempt to swing and connect with the long-tails. With wingshooting, this sort of inconsistency can happen to anybody at some time and can be excusable, but inconsistency that is directly attributable to a badly fitted gun and a sloppy mount and swing is not. It always amazes me that some guys, obviously very serious about their shooting, will spend a small fortune on their guns, without ever having any of them fitted properly! They all *think* about it at some time or other, usually when they have had a particularly bad day, but like the visit to the dentist or doctor, they procrastinate in the hope that the problem will miraculously go away. Well, it won't. Consistency in shooting depends on two things: good basic technique and good gun fit. The road to consistency with a shotgun is a long and winding one, and the correctly fitted gun will help to straighten out some of the bends.

I have fitted guns to a lot of shooters over the last twenty-five years or so, and when someone calls to make an appointment for a gun fit, I always insist that they practice their gun-mounting technique every night for at least a week beforehand. Despite this, some people do not bother, and when they come in, it is very obvious to me that the gun and its user are unfamiliar with one another. It is a complete waste of time to fit a shotgun (apart from length of pull) to a new shooter until he has acquired a few months of good shotgun technique. One thing is certain: if the basic fundamentals of mount and swing are lacking, having a perfectly fitted shotgun will not compensate for gun-mounting errors or miscalculations of lead.

STOCK CONSTRUCTION
A shotgun stock is more complex than most people think. The three main parts of a stock are the grip, comb, and butt.

Grip
The grip, sometimes called the wrist, is the portion of the stock behind the trigger guard that is gripped by the rear hand. There are three main styles of grip: straight (or English), half pistol (sometimes called Prince of Wales), and full pistol. The grip can have a greater influence on the way the dominant hand raises the stock to the shoulder and on the amount of recoil that is transferred to the shoulder than most people realize. The full-pistol grip can be either straight-sided or with a palm-swell, which is exactly as the name suggests—a slightly convex side designed to fit neatly into the user's palm. Palm-swells are usually restricted to competition

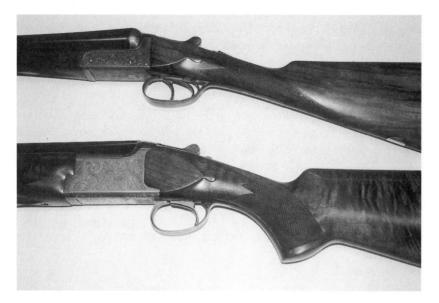

Types of grip. Pistol grips help to reduce felt recoil better than the English straight stock, simply because the hand will grip and control the gun better. English side-by-sides usually have two triggers, and the straight English stock was originally intended to allow the user to slide his hand backward or forward to reach these.

guns. Pistol grips help to reduce felt recoil better than the English straight stock, the simple reason being that the hand will grip and control the gun better, enabling the arm of the gripping hand to absorb more of the recoil. This added control also means that as the trigger is pulled with the forefinger, the thumb and the other three fingers retain a comfortable grip. This control is reduced with the English straight stock, which is more usual on a side-by-side double-gun, and the backhand can slip backward and forward. This was originally the intention of the design, because English double-guns always had two triggers, and guys with short fingers could move their hand backward and forward to compensate for this. However, some people will find that depending on the frequency of shots fired, the straight grip of the English gun causes discomfort due to the unnatural angle of the wrist as the gun recoils.

Comb

The comb is the top of the stock, the part that makes contact with the shooter's face. The front end of the comb is known as the nose, and the rear is known as the heel. The comb is traditionally thinner on an English stock than on a competition stock for two reasons: weight reduction and elegance.

Butt

This is the part of the stock that comes into contact with the shooter's shoulder. The top of the butt is called the heel, the middle is called the center, and the base of the butt is called the toe. For accurate pitch adjustment, it is essential to take each of these three measurements from the center of the trigger.

THE VARIABLES OF GUN FIT

The four variables of gun fit are length, drop, cast, and pitch.

Length

This refers to the length of pull, which is measured from the center of the trigger (front trigger, usually, on a double-gun) to the center of the butt plate (or pad.) The widely used method of holding the gun at the grip and seeing if the butt makes contact with the biceps is *not* a conclusive way to determine correct length of pull. The procedure is an old wives' tale that really works only sporadically. The stock should be as long as the user can comfortably mount and swing. Longer stocks point and control recoil better, but if they are too long, they will catch on the clothing and be slow to mount. A stock that is too short will result in bruising to the nose and face (with your thumb) as the gun recoils. Somewhere in between is what we are looking for.

Comb Height or Drop

If a straightedge is placed along the top of the barrels, the measurement from the bottom edge of it to the top of the comb is known as the drop, usually expressed as "drop at nose" and "drop at heel." However, the place where the face comes into contact is the drop measurement that really matters and should be marked when the stock is measured. There is a big variation, on a standard field stock, between the drop measurement at nose and at the heel. Most field stocks have a standard drop at nose of about $1\frac{1}{2}$ inches and a drop at heel of about $2\frac{1}{4}$ inches. This makes the angle of the comb in relation to where the cheek touches it quite steep. Where bruising to the top of the cheekbone is a problem, this steep slope is usually the culprit. Because of this relatively steep angle, a gun with a stock of these dimensions will cause the height of

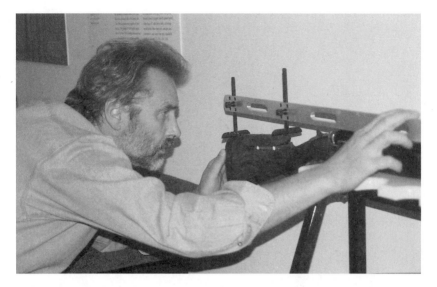

Drop-at-comb should be measured with a drop gauge. The most important measurement is drop-at-face, where the shooter's face actually touches the comb of the gun.

the eye above the rib to vary depending on not only facial structure but also length of pull needed. Although the gun may be perfectly acceptable to a shooter of average proportions, it will shoot low for someone who needs a short length of pull, and high for someone who needs a long length of pull.

Any alteration to comb height will influence the position of the shooter's eye above the rib. The gun will shoot high if the eye is too high and low if the eye is too low. If the shooter's eye is so low that it is hidden behind the breech, the wrong eye will take over as the gun is brought to point of aim. Many competition shooters favor a Monte Carlo–style stock with a comb that is parallel to the (top) rib. This means that regardless of the length of pull, the eye remains at the correct height. Most competition guns now have the luxury of an adjustable comb, and this makes a lot of sense—as our body and/or mount changes, our stock prescription changes with it. Weight loss or gain and flexibility change due to age or injury, and other factors can affect the way we bring the gun to point of aim, and therefore the drop we need.

Cast

Cast is the deviation between the centerline of the rib and the centerline of the stock, measured in inches at the butt, viewing the gun from

Left: Fitting for the female form. This rather well-endowed lady has an off-set butt plate to make allowance for the female form. The toe of the butt plate has been angled out so that the recoil is transferred equally onto the full surface area of the shoulder pocket. Without this, the toe would dig in and cause discomfort from the effects of recoil. The woman's gun also has an adjustable comb.
Right: As you can see from this picture, the butt of the gun fits snugly into the woman's shoulder pocket.

above. The reason for cast is to be sure that the eye is not to the left or right of the centerline of the rib. Cast is usually measured at the heel, but as with drop, what really matters is the amount of cast at the point where your face contacts the stock. Because of this, $\frac{3}{8}$ inch of cast may be perfect for you with a thin stock, but not nearly enough with a thick stock. Also, in the case of large-chested men (or buxom women), the amount of cast at the toe will be important. For these people, a stock without a pronounced toe-out will do two things—dig into the flesh of the shoulder pocket in the wrong area and cause the gun to be canted over at an angle as the gun recoils. The shot will be off to the side, if this happens, and there will be poor recovery for a second shot. A stock that is angled to the right is said to be cast-off (because it is "off" the face of a right-handed shooter), and one angled to the left is known as cast-on. To avoid confusion between right- and left-handed shooters (a gun that is cast-on to a lefty is cast-off to a righty), it would probably be better if we used the terms cast right and cast left, but cast-on and cast-off are fairly entrenched.

As a general rule, broad-shouldered people will need more cast than slightly built people. Any alteration to the cast of a gun will move the center of gravity, and depending on the gun type, the gun may then side-flip as a result. Finely built side-by-sides with a small grip radius were extremely susceptible to this and would noticeably pull to one side, especially when the choke barrel was fired. Years ago, eye dominance problems were sometimes rectified by means of a "crossover" stock, which greatly increased this side-flip effect. I had clients who shot with these guns when I lived in the United Kingdom, and believe me, I found them extremely difficult to shoot because of this side-flexing. I am sure that with regular use, the owner would subconsciously control this side-flip, depending on which way the gun was swinging at the time the trigger was pulled.

A gun should be brought smoothly to the face with the head erect, not canted over. This sideways cant of the head is often to make up for lack of needed cast, and it is often the reason why we experience bruising to the face upon recoil.

Pitch

Pitch determines how well the gun fits the contour of the shooter's shoulder. It is the angle of the butt of the gun relative to the axis of the bore. Most guns have some down pitch, and it is easy to measure this by placing the butt of the gun squarely on the floor next to a wall, then sliding the gun toward the wall until the receiver touches it. The measurement between the muzzles and the wall is the pitch measurement. Small pitch adjustments can dramatically influence the way recoil is transmitted to the shoulder. Too much down pitch and the butt will slide up during recoil, resulting in a whack under the cheekbone. Too little, and the gun will slide down, producing excessive muzzle flip and causing the gun to shoot high. Pitch and cast adjustments must complement each other. Just as with cast adjustment, a shooter with large pectoral muscles (or a well-endowed lady) will benefit from careful consideration to pitch adjustment. Failure to do this will mean that the butt plate is in contact with only a small area of the shoulder pocket, and when this happens, recoil is transferred to part of the pocket instead of the whole. If this main area of contact is the toe of the butt plate, there are painful consequences for the shooter. If the shooter's shoulders are fairly narrow but he has large pectoral muscles, a recoil pad that is fixed

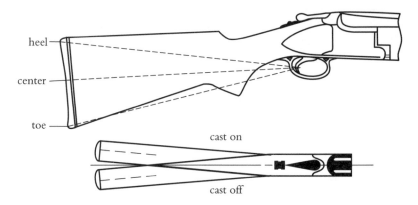

Length of pull should be measured in three places: heel, center, and toe. Failure to do this can result in an incorrect definition of the pitch of the gun. Small pitch adjustments can have a dramatic effect on the way recoil is transmitted to the shooter's face. A stock that is angled to the right is known as cast-off, and angled to the left is known as cast-on.

at an angle may be an advantage. This means that the heel of the pad would be in the shoulder pocket and the toe slightly farther out, toward the armpit. This is a much more comfortable solution for many people, especially women.

Something else we must consider as part of gun fit (but most shooters do not) is the fore-end of the gun. The front hand does the pointing, so it seems logical that if the shape of the fore-end can influence the way the gun assists this pointing attitude in the hands of its user, so much the better. Fore-ends come in many different styles, from the elegant "splinter" found on the traditional side-by-side to the "beaver tail," also usually found on a side-by-side. The splinter is found on all traditional English side-by-sides, and this type of fore-end is supposed to be held in conjunction with the barrels. The disadvantage is that in situations where multiple shots are fired, the barrels quickly become too hot to hold, a serious problem on a productive driven pheasant shoot. The answer is the leather hand guard, of course, but I have often seen some blistered fingers and heard some choice obscenities when, for some reason, this essential piece of equipment was left at home.

The only guns in the United Kingdom that I saw beaver tails on were the Winchester model 23 and the AYA no. 3. Over-and-unders routinely have a bulkier fore-end. The semibeaver tail and Schnabel, or

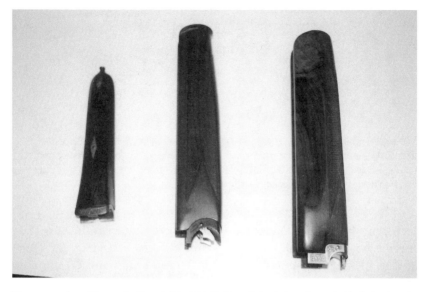

Three examples of fore-ends. From left to right: Splinter, Schnabel, and rounded half-checkered fore-ends.

Tulip, are found on many over-and-unders. The hunting or standard semibeaver tail is slightly slimmer, without the "beak" of the Schnabel. The semibeaver tail is found on many skeet and trap guns, and the full over-and-under beaver tail is, in my opinion, a real handful. I have only ever seen it on two guns, both of which were made for the American market.

PATTERN BOARD EVALUATION

Brits, in contrast to many Americans, are particularly picky about gun fitting. They use a method to determine their optimum driving position that has been used for decades by Purdey, Holland & Holland, and virtually all the best English gun makers. So just what is the best way to check gun fit? I believe that the most conclusive way to find out whether your gun fits is to shoot it! Since the main purpose of fitting a gun is to get it to shoot where you look, doesn't that make sense? You can peer down the barrel in front of the mirror as much as you like, but the final evaluation of the gun in the hands of its owner is an individual thing and can only be positively identified on a pattern board. This is a thick steel plate about four feet square, the center of which is about four

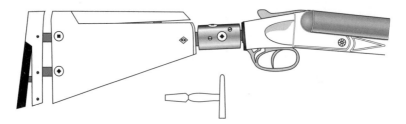

With side-by-side shotguns, the adjustable try gun was often used to determine the shooter's individual measurements. By using the square-ended key, the gun could be altered for cast, drop, or length of pull. The final evaluation of the gun's performance in the hands of its owner was then made at the pattern board.

feet from the ground. There is a central mark, which is the target. To use the board, stand about sixteen yards away and focus on the target area in the center. Mount and lower the gun twice, and on the third time, *as the gun hits the shoulder,* fire. Do not aim the gun like a rifle. An area should emerge, after five or six shots, showing where the bulk of the shot is concentrated.

For every inch that the pattern is off-target, the stock will need to be adjusted by $^{1}/_{16}$ inch. If, for example, the main shot concentration is four

Shots go high. Shooter's eye is elevated above the rib, usually an indication of excessive comb height or maybe incorrect pitch adjustment, with the gun rotating around the point of impact with the shoulder as the gun recoils.

Shots go low. Shooter's eye is below the sighting plane of the rib. If the shooter's eye is so low that the left eye is persuaded to take over, the result will be the same as a gun without enough cast. With a light, thin-barreled side-by-side, this may also be an indication of downward flexing of the barrels as the gun recoils.

inches high and four inches left, the stock needs to be given ¼ inch of cast right and ¼ inch additional comb height. The ideal shot distribution is usually about 60 percent above the centerline of the target and 40 percent below, unless a higher shooting gun is favored. A trap gun, for example, should pattern high because in the initial stages of flight the targets are always rising. A gun that is to be used for shooting flushing birds should also shoot high for the same reason, and in the United Kingdom, many English guns are designed to shoot high to give built-in lead to high incomers for the driven pheasant specialist. It is up to the individual, but regardless of his personal requirements, he should make it his business to find out *exactly* where his gun shoots, and he must do this on a pattern board. A few shots at the pattern board can reveal a multitude of sins to the trained eye, and if it is done right, pattern board evaluation will make a difference—in some cases, a *big* difference. Only after the gun is fitted, unless the shooter is extraordinarily lucky, will it shoot where he thinks he is pointing it and those frustrating whiffs be transformed into confident hits.

Occasionally, point-of-impact problems can be attributable to more than bad gun fit. I once took delivery of a 20-gauge shotgun that

Shots go left. Insufficient cast, shooter's eye looking down the left side of rib *or* left master eye (right-shouldered shooter).

impacted left of the target because the barrels were out of alignment when they left the factory. Guns fitted with screw-in chokes can have the same problem. Certain high-end competition guns come with adjustable spacers, or hangers, to permit quick and simple realignment of the barrels.

Shots go right. Too much cast, shooter's eye looking down the right side of the rib.

A WORD TO THE UNWARY

Good gun fit is dependent upon having a proper and consistent gun mount and upon getting a good fitter. Choose a professional with a proven track record. Word-of-mouth references are the best. The size of the advertisement in the glossy gun magazine may look impressive, but there is simply no substitute for experience. In the time I have been in the States, I have seen guns "fitted" by people who have been self-elevated to the level of "gun fitter." They could do this because they know that there are a lot of guys out there who are willing and, in many cases, more than able to part with a substantial quantity of cash in the effort to get a gun that shoots where they look. After a "fitting session," these gullible fellows emerge convinced that the fit will transform them overnight into a champion.

Just like a pair of shoes, the only person who knows if the gun is comfortable during use is the user. After paying for a fit, if there is a feeling of discomfort and bruising in normal use, provided the problem

"Into" the gun. Robert Paxton, thirty-two-time all-American and one of the best skeet shooters in the world, demonstrates how it all comes together. It doesn't matter what we are shooting, with the perfect fit the shooter will experience subconscious tactile assurance that tells him his eye is where he intends it to be, in perfect alignment with the rib of the gun. Only then will the gun shoot to where he looks.

is not a sloppy gun mount, take it back. My guns all fit me. We are perfectly matched; we work as a team. The measurements are complementary to my facial and bodily dimensions and my muscular capabilities. I
suffer absolutely no discomfort when I use these guns. I prefer to reserve
any painful experiences I must endure for my visits to the dentist!

HANDLING DYNAMICS

Finally, there is one other aspect to the gun–fit equation, apart from the
dimensions of the stock. There must also be a reactive relationship
between the user's physical capabilities and the balance of the gun. If the
interaction between the two is wrong, the shooter will become frustrated. We have all heard the axiom, "We aim a rifle, we point a shotgun." Absolutely, but rifle shooting is different—rifles are aimed, with
emphasis on a rock–steady, unerring hold as the shot is triggered. Shotguns are dynamic; they must be moved in exact empathy with the target
in order to intercept it. For the gun to respond to the user's natural
pointing ability, the shooter must be able to move his gun efficiently.
Poor-handling guns will cause the shooter to expend more energy than
necessary, and toward the end of a long day in the field, this will take its
toll. With the shotgun, balance is a key consideration for many, and conversations about the balance of guns are common. I read somewhere that
a prominent shooting man once described the handling dynamics of a
particular gun as being "like a pig on a shovel." I have no idea which
particular make or model he was referring to, but I am sure you get the
idea. But what exactly is balance in a shotgun? Most guns balance somewhere around the hinge pin, but the balance point is not the critical factor in the way that the gun handles. Two guns may weigh the same but
not require the same amount of muscle effort to mount. Both guns may
also balance at the hinge pin, but the handling dynamics will be completely different.

Perhaps the easiest way to begin to understand what handling
dynamics is about is to imagine a four-foot steel bar (similar to the bar
used in a set of barbells) with a three-pound weight on each end. There
is a point in the middle of the bar where it will balance perfectly. If the
weights are then slid into the center of the bar, until they are almost
touching, it will still balance in the center. In both cases, the weight is
the same, but the way the bar can be moved around will be noticeably
different. If the bar is gripped in the center with the weights at each end,
it will be difficult to start, but also difficult to stop, because of the inertia
of the weights. If the weights are then slid into the center, it will be

more willing to rotate with similar muscular effort, but it may rotate too freely. There will be a point where there is a happy medium and the weights can be positioned somewhere in between the ends and the center. The bar can then be moved freely, but not so freely that it feels unstable and too willing to change direction. The overall weight of the gun will influence the *directional* maneuverability of the gun, but the way in which this weight is distributed can influence the *rotational* qualities of the gun. Ideally, we should be looking for a gun that is not only responsive to the physical capabilities of the user but also controllable and steady. With a traditional side-by-side, for example, the weight will usually, but not always, taper off quickly in both directions from the hinge pin, and the gun will be fast handling as a result, because the bulk of the weight will be distributed between the shooter's hands as he moves the gun. I say "not always" because I have handled a lot of long-barreled side-by-sides with thin walls, and others with thick walls, and the dynamics surprised me. It is not that simple.

Usually, with an over-and-under, the weight will be distributed more evenly over the full length of the gun than with a side-by-side weighing the same amount, and the gun will be less responsive and steadier as a result. Both guns may react differently and vary from shooter to shooter, depending on the shooters' individual reflexes and physical strength. A powerfully built person will sometimes overpower a light-handling side-by-side, and a lightly built fellow may feel the effects of forward inertia on a heavy over-and-under. A muzzle-heavy gun will be slow and steady to swing and point; a butt-heavy gun will feel "whippy" and "wave-about-y." Once we have done enough shooting, weight and balance become secondary, and it is the overall feel of a shotgun that matters to us most—in other words, the handling dynamics. Unfortunately, there are no shortcuts. The path that we tread in an attempt to find a shotgun that suits our physical capabilities is never clearly marked, and with new shooters this "what feels right" factor is difficult to identify until they have acquired several years of shooting experience. Eventually, the dynamic qualities and tactile attributes of a particular gun will integrate, and it will feel just right to the user—and that is all that matters. A client once said to me, referring to his exquisite Westley Richards sidelock in the middle of a pheasant drive, "I just have to look in the right place and it responds as smoothly as a BMW gearbox." Although I'm not lucky enough to own a BMW, I am sure he was right. Later that day, I swear I caught him talking to that gun more affectionately than he would have to a lover.

CHAPTER 7

Stance, Mount, and Swing

Have you been to the U.S. Open? Before you get excited, I mean the U.S. Open golf tournament. Ever watch Tiger Woods make an incredible drive or sink an impossible-looking putt? I have. It seems amazing that he can eye the ball, eye the cup, eye the ball again, and then sink a twenty-five-foot putt, doesn't it? Ever stop to think what goes through his mind before he hits the ball? Well, I don't know Tiger Woods, but I do know some good golfers, and they told me this: with every shot, they make a calculation of the angle they need to hit the ball on, the speed they need to hit the ball at, and the terrain the ball must cross. To make it all come together, they need to hit that golf ball in *exactly* the right spot. A tiny fraction of an inch to either side and they have blown it. All golf professionals, when teaching new students, stress that there are several peripheral issues, all of which require detailed consideration in the early stages of participation in the sport. These are correct stance, compatibility of the golf club to the personal physical requirements of the individual, and smoothness of swing.

The foundation for successful shotgunning involves the same three considerations, substituting the gun for the club, of course. Many years ago, I watched John Bidwell win the world FITASC championship, the top sporting clays competition, for the third time. There was naturalness in his shooting, and he seemed to stroke the targets out of the sky with a confident flourish. Anyone who has seen John shoot will know what I mean. When he called for the target, he was ready. I don't mean *nearly* ready. I mean absolutely, 100 percent mentally prepared and focused, eyes looking for the target in the right place, body poised to make his move to intercept it. Everything was spontaneous and unhurried. His eyes locked onto the target at the same time his gun was moving smoothly into his shoulder pocket to complete the mount. The computations of speed, distance, and angle were complete by the time the ocular stimuli from his brain gave him the signal to trigger the shot. Don't forget we're talking FITASC here, mandatory low gun. Just like the miss-hit on the golf ball, if the mount had terminated in anything less than perfection, the shot would have been unsuccessful.

So just what do a world-class golfer and a world-class shooter have in common? They have similar objectives. Both are using basic hand-and-eye coordination to hit a target with an inanimate object. Instead of a shotgun, the ball is the golfer's equivalent of the shooter's shot-string, and he uses his club as an intermediary to propel the ball to his target. Physical mechanics still need to be perfect to enable him to do this with any success, and both the golfer and the shooter need economy of motion, grace, and elegance from the first preliminary move to the final follow-through. If there is one main reason why people miss targets with a shotgun (apart from the obvious one of miscalculation of forward allowance), what do you think it might be? The inability to move the gun efficiently to develop the line of the target. Unfortunately, many experienced shooters consider proper gun-mounting technique, correct stance, and a smooth swing to be "the basics" that apply only to beginners. Not so. I have witnessed many experienced wingshooters demonstrating such alarming gyrations with a shotgun that they would put a Turkish belly dancer to shame. When the pressure is on and they are in the hot seat, with plenty of birds about, they fall apart even worse.

So let's not fool ourselves—if you cannot move the gun *smoothly* onto the line of the target after making an accurate computation of the lead requirement, you have missed. As the eyes lock onto the target to analyze the variables and compute where the gun must be pointed relative to the target at the moment of ignition in order to hit it, the hands, legs, and body should be working in unison to move the gun *precisely* to that destination. For far too many shooters, this destination is "somewhere in the vicinity" of the target, which is not the same thing at all.

There are only four ways we can miss a moving target: above, below, in front, or behind. This means that if we learn to move the gun correctly on the same line as the horizontally moving target, we have eliminated two of the variables—we cannot miss above or below it. This gives us a much better chance of hitting it, and provided that we have made good visual contact to read the line, our natural hand-eye coordination should do the rest. Our ability to do this is directly influenced by one thing—gun fit, gun mount, and smoothness of swing. Now hold on, aren't those *three* things? Not really. Most shooters, when asked what they would like to achieve, come up with the same answer: consistency. With successful shotgunning, our ability to move the gun accurately, developing the line of the target, is of paramount importance and is totally dependent on these three peripheral issues. Combined, they are the Holy Grail of shotgunning. But any one of these key elements is useless without the other two. To achieve success in shotgunning, all three must be brought together to work simultaneously. I am therefore reluctant to separate them. Now, I am not a gambling man, but I am prepared to bet an ale in a pub that some readers have already decided to skip this bit and turn the pages to read about things that are "more important," such as forward allowance, evaluating range, or shot-string.

"Oh no! Not the old gun-mount stuff *again*," I hear you say. "I've been shooting a shotgun for years, and *my* mechanics are as smooth as silk."

Maybe they are. Maybe you have such elegance and exactitude when you shoot that you would put Rudolf Nureyev and the dancers from the Royal Ballet to shame, but let me tell you this: I have had hundreds of clients over the last twenty-five years who had shot for years and who genuinely believed that their ability to move the gun was flawless and beyond reproach. I estimate that *at least 80 percent* of them could have used some improvement. And I believe that a much greater proportion of moving targets are missed "off the line" than we realize (i.e., we mistakenly believe we failed to get the lead right), because of our reluctance to practice the basic fundamental of developing a smoothly engineered mount and swing. Did I say our *reluctance* to practice? Absolutely. Most shotgunners do not even consider it to be necessary. This ability to move the gun accurately on the line of the target is even more important than a correct computation of how much forward allowance is needed. Even experienced shooters often overlook this basic step. Most birds, especially after they have been shot at, are not obliging enough to come back and give you a second chance. For some reason, people who practice religiously in other activities that require hand-eye coordination often fall short in the shooting arena. The golfer practices his footwork and swing (can you imagine what your golf game would be like if you didn't?) and the tennis player practices his serve, but many shotgunners never bother to work on fundamentals. Instead, they expect it all to happen miraculously. Wingshooters as a class are more guilty of this than competitive shooters. They put their guns away at the end of dove season, bring them out again a year later, and expect to shoot well. I've got news for you, regardless of what some guys would lead you to believe: it does not work. Everyone needs to practice. Now I know there are always exceptions to the rule, and some people, the so-called "naturals" of the shooting world, do not seem to need to bother with practice. Some people get there quicker than others because they have more natural talent, and every once in a while along comes a phenomenon who is incredibly talented and makes things look too easy. But for every person like that, there are a thousand who get there because of hard work and determination. They have the will to succeed. A good gun mount and swing are the combination of several peripheral factors, and achieving them is one of the most important prerequisites to consistent shotgunning.

"The gunners who are most productive in the field all seem to have this flawless mount and swing and stroke the birds from the sky with confidence." Most of us would not have a problem with that statement, would we? "They also have a gun that fits them perfectly, don't they?" Yes, absolutely. "The expert shot does not bag more birds by accident." Correct.

Where are we going with this? Well, despite the three statements above, I see lots of folks who have been shooting for years that have not, despite all the informative articles and videos available, grasped the importance of a good mount and swing. They have a genuine desire to shoot better, but they think there is an easy way. There isn't; you only get out of this game what you put in. Nothing more, nothing less. There is a ton of information and instructional data on the subjects of proper stance, foot position, posture, and mounting procedure, but some shooters do not get it.

Stop and think for a minute what it costs you to shoot. First of all, there are the expensive guns. They look so impressive in the elaborate, walnut, glass-fronted gun cabinet, don't they? Don't forget why you bought them in the first place. Unfortunately, all this is meaningless if the fundamentals of mount and swing are not good, and make no mistake, the wheels come off very quickly when the chips are down. A smooth, coordinated movement, with the gun in exact empathy with the target, is sine qua non of successful shotgunning. It can pay the biggest dividend of all when we shoot in the field. The best thing is that it will not cost you a dime to make sure you get yours right.

For the shotgunner, the gun is the necessary intermediary, the connection with the target. Although a gun may fit its user perfectly, if that user's mount and swing are sloppy, he has wasted his money on gun fit. Alternatively, perfect technique cannot overcome the handicap of a badly fitted gun. There needs to be a subtle blend of the mount and swing, which will complement the perfectly fitted gun. Shooting a shotgun well requires development of our natural pointing ability; the shotgun should become an unconscious extension of our arms. It always amazes me, when I teach a new shooter, how complicated they often try to make this. Ask them to point at a simple crossing target with their index finger, and they can do it with ease. Give them a stick and ask them to do it again, still no problems. Then put a shotgun in their hands, and more often than not, the natural coordination skills go out the window and the gun starts waving about all over the place. Sometimes this can be caused by a gun that does not match the physical attributes of the user. A heavy gun and a lightly built student, for example, will be mismatched to the point where smooth, coordinated movement will be impossible. A poorly balanced gun will have the same effect.

What do I mean by this? A gun that has a lack of weight forward will feel whippy, and the barrels will tend to come up before the butt

The typical, weight-backward stance of the new shooter. This young lady is attempting to counterbalance the weight of the gun by adopting this stance. As a result, all her weight is distributed over her back foot. As the gun recoils the situation will be aggravated, and recovery (for a second shot) will be poor.

In the initial stages of learning to shoot, patience and perseverance are essential for any new shooter. The correct stance must be adjusted carefully *before each shot is taken.*

comes into the shoulder pocket. The opposite is true of the badly balanced, barrel-heavy gun. This often happens when an inch of length is removed from a stock because it is too long for the user. Over the years, I have seen many such situations where this occurs—for example, the lightly built lady or youth who struggles with a heavy, thirty-two-inch-barreled, hand-me-down shotgun. Well-meaning people tell them that a longer-barreled, heavier gun will swing better and reduce the possibility of committing the cardinal sin—stopping the gun. Well, a heavy gun will indeed do that, because of the effect of momentum, but they will also be harder to start. Others may tell them that a heavier gun reduces the effects of recoil. I couldn't agree more, but let's be realistic here—some of my students bring guns that are hopelessly unsuitable for them. A gun that is too heavy often results in a weight-backward stance that is wrong. A shooter will experience, by attempting to mount and swing a gun that is too heavy, something that is known as forward inertia (resistance to movement) as an attempt is made to move the gun smoothly

The same youngster two weeks later. Note the much-improved forward stance after two weeks of gun-mounting "homework." This 75-pound eleven year old was easily and consistently breaking most targets on a skeet field after her third shooting lesson.

from a stationary position. Also, heavy guns in the hands of those who are incapable of handling them will result in fatigue that will eventually result in mismounting, which will in turn result in recoil being transferred to the wrong place. This is a sequence of events that must be avoided, especially with beginners. Choosing a gun that will match the physical capabilities of its user is important.

Watch a good shot in action. Everything is spontaneous and unhurried. His eyes will be locked onto the target, and at the same time, his gun will be moving unerringly into his cheek and shoulder pocket to complete the mount. The computations of speed, distance, and angle will be complete by the time the ocular stimuli from his brain give him the signal to trigger the shot. This culmination of events should ensure that the shooter will not "track" the target unnecessarily and he will "stay in the gun" instead of lifting his head. "Wood to wood," as we say. Tracking and head lifting are two of the most common shooting flaws. There is no place for them in the proper mount and swing.

GUN UP OR DOWN?

So, if a good mount is so critical, why don't we always premount the gun—like serious trap and skeet shooters do—to reduce the possibility of a mismount? Don't forget that in these situations we are dealing with more predictable targets, and in most wingshooting situations, this is impossible due to the unpredictability of the birds. It is simply impractical to walk about with a mounted gun because until we see the birds flush, we have no idea where they are coming from or going to. Also, with sporting clays, the nature of the beast dictates that many target presentations may have unpredictable trajectories.

With many situations on many sporting clays targets, a low gun will give better target visibility. Visual contact with the target is better if the gun is out of the shoulder, and this also encourages us to shoot more rhythmically. The shot can then be triggered within the dynamics of the swing, as the gun comes into the face and shoulder, without the distraction of the rib/barrels. But just how far out of the shoulder? It depends entirely on the target presentation (more on this in a minute).

The only exception to this is the new shooter. The new shooter has enough to think about in the early stages of learning, and because of this, I *always* have new students shoot for the first two hours or so with a mounted gun. This makes sure that the gun is in the correct position in the shoulder pocket. Do it the other way and the youngster will seldom get the gun in the same place twice as he triggers the shot, which will cause two undesired results—a lot of misses and bruising to the top of the arm. Now I know there are some people who will be critical of this (the "you don't walk about with the gun in your shoulder when you hunt" guys), but don't forget that although a youngster can point easily with his finger at a moving object, that ability is severely handicapped when the weight of the gun is added. The youngster will need to reprogram his young muscles to control and point the gun accurately. Then as gun-mounting procedure improves and young muscles strengthen, he can try shooting with a low gun.

So just what are the ingredients for a good, smooth, unhurried mount and swing? A perfect mount starts with perfect foot position. Get your feet wrong and it will be impossible to shoot rhythmically, swing smoothly, and, most important of all, remain balanced and in control. Good balance and body weight distribution are all-important. The weight should be slightly over the leading leg, or "nose over toes," as I tell my students. Why? Because the shooter's feet must provide a stable

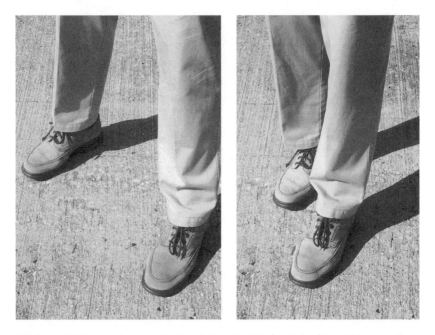

Left: In competition shooting, a good stance is important, the foundation from which a smooth swing will develop. This stance is often seen, but the feet are too far apart. This will restrict smooth movement in the direction of the target. I feel that the shooters who adopt this stance succeed in spite of it, not because of it.
Right: Here, the feet are too close together. In certain situations, feet as close together as this will be a problem; balance and stability will be difficult to maintain as the swing develops.

platform so that the gun can be moved with perfect control, and this slightly weight-forward stance will help to soak up the recoil of the first shot so that there is quick recovery for the second.

With competition shooting, sporting clays, for example, the target "address" position is with the leading foot (left foot for the right-shouldered shooter) toward the *approximate* kill zone. If you can imagine that straight ahead, where the shot will be taken, is at twelve o'clock, then the front foot should be at one o'clock, and the rear foot at three o'clock. The heels should be approximately nine to ten inches apart. The stance should be *relaxed*. What do I mean by relaxed? Well, next time you are standing in a bar having a beer with friends, stop and look down. My guess is that your feet will be approximately nine to ten inches apart at the heels and your legs reasonably straight.

So why do so many of us adopt a different stance, with legs wide and knees bent, as soon as we get a gun in our hands? I have no idea.

This nice, relaxed stance is about right. If we imagine that a line straight in front of us is 12 o'clock, the front foot will be (for a right-handed shooter) at approximately 1 o'clock, the rear foot about 3 o'clock. The heels will be approximately nine or ten inches apart. This will give stability with good freedom of swing. The weight should be over the leading leg, or "nose over toes."

Tension in any muscle that we intend to use is unadvisable; the muscle must first relax before it can move efficiently. The muzzles of the gun should be under the flight line of the target. When calling for the target, the body should lean forward *very slightly* to shift the weight forward over the front foot. Not too much, because with nearly all the weight over the leading leg, the heel of the back leg will lift off the ground. This is what I call ballet dancing and should be avoided. This is an unstable, badly balanced stance that will impede the smoothness of the swing in the latter stage, which will in turn result in poor muzzle control.

The gun hold point is dependent upon the shooting method preferred (swing-through, sustained lead, etc.). The head should remain erect and move slowly in the direction of the target throughout the whole process, and the gun should be lifted to the face and shoulder by using both hands in unison. The back hand should *never* move the butt to the shoulder first and allow the barrels to pivot around the front hand. Initially, the front hand should push the gun forward and start to guide the gun onto the target line. At the same time, the rear hand lifts the gun *smoothly* to the cheek and into the shoulder pocket. The trigger hand should pull the gun firmly into the shoulder pocket, and as the

Left: Address position: the toe of the leading leg should be pointing toward the intended break zone. The gun should be under the flight line of the target. The upper torso should be rotated back toward the trap so that the eyes make good visual contact with the target as soon as possible. At this point, the thighs and upper torso should be under slight tension and "wound up," i.e., rotated toward the visual pick-up point of the target.
Right: The mount should be a progressive movement, an integrated combination of legs, body, and arms. As visual contact with the target is made, the body and legs start to unwind and the upper torso should rotate smoothly in the direction of the target. There should be no point where the mount ends and the swing begins. The gun should be lifted smoothly into the face and shoulder with the *equal movement of both hands,* not with the back hand first.

butt of the gun arrives there, the muzzles of the gun are brought onto the line of the target. The front hand will absorb some of the recoil as the shot is taken. Doing this will reduce the recovery time between shots.

The swing, as the gun mount is developing, should move the gun onto the line of the target smoothly. The power driving the gun should come from the ankles up, using the legs, thighs, hips, and upper torso, a perfectly smooth, fluid flow of physical movement using all the muscles. The perfect mount and swing are a subtle blend of arms and body movement; there is no point where the mount ends and the swing begins. The movements are fluid and rhythmical, not erratic and jerky. By doing this, you will get maximum efficiency with minimum effort, without tiring one set of muscles, usually the arms. Ideally, the mount is completed; i.e., the gun comes into the shoulder at the same time that the brain gives the order to trigger the shot. This culmination of events should ensure that the shooter will not track the target unnecessarily and he will "stay in the gun" instead of committing the cardinal sin—lifting his head. This bit is important; many shooters develop this slight lift of the head as the mount is completed, especially on incoming and driven shots. Don't do it. Keep your head down or, as we instructors say, "wood to wood."

Many inexperienced shooters use a two-part gun movement: they mount first and then try to move the gun accurately onto the trajectory by using upper body movement. This is a mistake. The human torso pivots easily on a horizontal plane. If you put the gun in the shoulder early, at the end of the swing the muzzles will be prescribing an arc known as "dropping off-line." Also, there is a good chance that the gun will be laying *across* the closed shoulder pocket instead if in it. This is why a hurried mount often results in a recoil into the top of the arm instead of the shoulder. The hurried mount, where the gun is slammed

The mount is completed, and the shot is taken. At this point the body is unwound completely. The shooter should be into the gun at this stage. The head should be locked down onto the stock ("wood to wood," as we say), and the butt of the gun will be exactly where it should be, firmly embedded in the shoulder pocket. This culmination of events should ensure that the shooter will not track the target unnecessarily, and he will stay in the gun as he triggers the shot, instead of lifting his head.

into the shoulder with such force that it almost comes out again (what I call a bouncy mount), should also be avoided. It is unnecessary and only adds to the effects of recoil. The upper torso and head, as the hands and arms are producing this controlled lift, will be turning in the same direction, so the eye that is above the rib will remain in the correct position. Push through, but don't rush through, or your face will not be where you expect it to be as the mount is completed.

The position of the butt of the gun relative to the shoulder pocket will depend on the target presentation. What if the target is a trap-type target or a narrow-angle quartering shot requiring minimal gun movement? On the sporting clays course, these targets are more vulnerable to the gun when they are nearest to us, so logically it is better to shoot them early. To do this, the gun should be dropped just out of the shoulder, and by doing this, there will be a reduction in movement as the gun is raised, which will result in a much quicker mount when there is less time available. This is known as economy of movement, and it is the hallmark of all great shooters. Also, if the gun is held too low, the butt will usually be raised first, allowing the muzzles to pivot around the axis of the front hand. This is known as chopping down on the target, and poor muzzle control will be the result.

Now what about the complete opposite? On long, slow incomers or long crossing shots off a high tower, a common mistake is to mount the gun too early and track the target all the way in. The longer you have the gun in your shoulder with this target presentation, the more time there is for something to go wrong, and this should be avoided. The same is true of birds in incoming wingshooting situations. How many times have you seen a dove or a duck coming toward you from a distance, mounted the gun, tracked the bird all the way in, and missed? Lots of times, I bet. Following a bird with a mounted gun will result in the shooter becoming mesmerized by the gun. Instead, stay relaxed and do not mount until you are ready to take the shot; keep the muzzles moving with the bird but the butt of the gun out of the shoulder. This will allow good visual contact with the target, instead of attempting to see around the barrels, as you would have to do with a premounted gun. By allowing the bird to come to you, there will be plenty of time to compute the necessary variables, and the mount and swing will be more fluid as a result. As a general rule, the distance the gun is away from the shoulder pocket is directly proportional to the amount of movement required.

What about the stance for the wingshooter who has no idea where his birds are coming from? How can he align his feet correctly? The answer is that he can't, but most bird hunters are too hurried in their movements and shoot as though they are rooted to the spot. There is more time than you think with most shots. The muzzles should start to move in empathy with the bird as soon as it is flushed, and the feet should be set up for the shot by turning in the same direction. This is known as "stepping to the bird." With practice, this is easy to achieve. To allow a more fluid swing in the direction of the target, the right heel should be raised for a bird going from right to left, the left heel for a bird that is going from left to right. This will ensure that the shoulders remain level throughout the shot.

Now what about flushing birds over dogs? The way the gun is carried when walking up birds can have a dramatic influence on the outcome of the shot. In these circumstances, many hunters will bring the

When walking behind the dogs, it is perfectly acceptable to carry the gun close to the body like this. By doing this, the center of gravity of the gun is closer to the body and the apparent weight of the gun will be less than if the gun was held out at an angle. However, if this position of the gun is maintained as the birds flush, precious seconds will be lost. As the shooter tries to get on his bird and the butt of the gun comes up into his shoulder, there is only one thing that can happen—muzzles of his gun will dip down. Unfortunately for the hunter (but luckily for the quail) this is exactly the opposite of what the flushing birds will be doing.

gun from well below their waistline in an attempt to complete the mount, even when they know that the sudden appearance of the birds is likely. The long trip with the gun from this position is unnecessary and encourages rushing, often resulting in a mismount as the gun comes into the shoulder. Also, many quail hunters, as they follow the dogs, will carry the gun at an angle across the front of their chest. By doing this, the weight of the gun is close to the body and is obviously less tiring than holding the gun out at a slight angle. This is the best way, especially if long distances are to be covered. But what happens when the dogs go on-point? If a covey rise *is* anticipated, think about this for a moment. Birds that flush from ground level will obviously be rising targets, and if the gun is still in this position (across the body) as the birds flush, the butt of the gun will be coming up into the shoulder pocket and the muzzles will be going down as the gun is mounted. This will be exactly the opposite of what the flushing birds are doing. Do it this way: If the dogs are on a point, hold the gun out in front at an angle of roughly 45 degrees to the ground (which will be well above the dogs) and look ahead just over the muzzles of the gun. With this gun-hold position, the mount will be more fluid as the birds flush and there will be less wasted residual movement. There is another point worth mentioning here. With any birds that are flushed over dogs—grouse, quail, or pheasants, for example—it would seem logical to watch the ground in front of the dogs when they are on-point. Most hunters do this to give themselves maximum time to see the birds the moment they flush, and therefore a better chance for a successful shot, but there is a better way. Most times as the birds flush, it will be difficult to bring them into hard focus early for two reasons. The first is that they will blend in with their background; the second is that it takes the human eyes approximately one-fifth of a second to focus. Instead, avoid maintaining a hard focus in the area where the covey rise is expected; look ahead, above the ground at about head height, with your eyes relaxed and in soft, or wide, focus. Flushing birds always rise into this horizontal plane, and as they do, they will be easier to distinguish from their surroundings with this approach. The rapid movement of their wing beats will be picked up quickly by the peripheral vision. Peripheral vision is more sensitive to movement than central or hard-focus vision. By doing this, the eyes will lock onto the bird, and if the mount and swing are good, this will occur at roughly the same time the gun comes into the face and shoulder and the shot is taken. This is a technique used for walking up red grouse that I learned

When the dogs are on a point and a covey rise is expected, avoid maintaining a hard focus in the area where the dogs are, and instead, look ahead, above the ground at about head height, with eyes relaxed and in soft, or wide, focus. Flushing birds always rise into the horizontal plane, and as they do so they will be easier to distinguish from their surroundings. The rapid movement of their wing beats will be picked up quickly by the peripheral vision. If a covey rise is anticipated, this gun-hold position will ensure a much smoother, quicker move onto the bird. As the birds flush, there will be no wasted, superfluous movement with the barrels moving momentarily in the wrong direction. On some birds (especially bobwhite quail), there is often no time to waste.

from one of the keepers on the Duke of Buccleuch's estate in southwest Scotland. I can assure you that it works very well.

PRACTICE AND EXERCISE

Expert shots, both in the field and in competition, have a stylish smoothness that makes it all look easy, but to achieve this, they must practice, practice, practice. A few energetic, erratic slashes with the gun the day before dove season is not the answer, if we are to achieve anything that is close to perfection. Good gun management skills are crucial if we are to develop the line of the bird properly. A good place to start perfecting your mount is in your living room or bedroom. Stand at one end of the room and mount and swing the gun by using *a combination of body and arm movement,* not just arm movement, on an imaginary target moving along the line where the ceiling and wall meet. Do this again and again, from left to right and then from right to left. Then change position slightly and repeat. These exercises can be practiced on any suitable line and will greatly improve coordination and make the mount consistent.

These exercises are necessary to make the mount spontaneous. What exactly is spontaneity? The best description I can give is rapid muscular coordination of a series of movements until they can be repeated *without* conscious thought. Any new motor skill or repetitive task must be practiced slowly at first, like the steps of a dance routine or a karate move, until it becomes spontaneous. Think back to your childhood days. Remember learning to ride a bike? Steering was easy. Pedaling was, too. How about balance? Not quite so easy, but you got there in the end. Each separate task was repeated, coordinated, and entered into the equation until you could ride without conscious thought.

The workers on a production line putting components into computers have this same subconscious spontaneity. They carry out their repetitive tasks with ease, but put a newcomer in the line and it is a different story. The newcomer's efforts will be clumsy and deliberate until he acquires muscle memory and can repeat the tasks without thinking.

Many years ago, when I owned a fishing tackle and gun shop in Scotland, I sold trout and salmon flies. Two of my fly tiers were ex–Hardy Brothers employees. Hardy's of Alnwick in Northumberland was then probably the most famous fishing tackle manufacturer in the world and still is. These fly tiers, with fingers so incredibly nimble, could display amazing manual dexterity. Their blurred fingers would produce identical trout and salmon flies subconsciously, and they would carry on a normal conversation as they did this. The amazing thing was that if I asked them to slow down so I could see more clearly how they performed a particular intricate step in the process, winding a hackle on, for example, they could not do it. By attempting to become more deliberate, the spontaneity of the movements was reduced.

With practice, the mount and swing will become a spontaneous, subconscious action, as natural as blinking an eye. It should be achieved without conscious thought, and with sporting clays and bird hunting, this is important. The shooter, by doing this, will allow his conscious mind to concentrate on the more important task of analyzing all the important variables. The perfect mount and swing should be silky smooth with no wasted, superfluous movement. Don't forget, on some targets there may be no time to waste.

CHAPTER 8

Application of Lead and Various Shooting Methods

A woman called me last week to ask advice on what instructional shooting video she should buy. Before giving her an answer, I asked her if she had ever tried to lose weight. The surprised woman admitted that some years ago she did indeed try after the birth of one of her children. How had she gone about it? Just as I suspected, she bought one of those exercise videos that, along with a rigorous diet program, is guaranteed to melt away the excess pounds. And of course, if you follow the instructions, it works . . . sometimes. Okay, so what have weight-watcher videos got to do with shooting?

Some time ago, Sunrise Productions released George Digweed's instructional shooting video, describing a swing-through technique. Months later, Dan Carlisle launched his video, also produced by Sunrise Productions, outlining his pull-away technique. Before this, there was former world champion John Bidwell's *Move, Mount, Shoot* using a sustained lead variation, and Roger Silcox with the CPSA "method," which is basically pull-away. Long before any of them, in the 1920s, the legendary London gun maker Robert Churchill taught his Edwardian students his theory of allowance by eye method.

There are many others that offer anyone thirsty for knowledge and prepared to part with their cash a surefire way of smoking targets, claiming that theirs is the method that really works. Over the years, the battle over the merits of swing-through versus pull-away or maintained lead has raged. With the baffling array of how-to shooting videos on the market at this time, who is right and which method is the best to use for sporting clays are a puzzle. There is no doubt in my mind that the thinking shooter needs all of them, and a sound knowledge of how each method works has to be an advantage, so let's take a closer look at the window of opportunity for each one.

There are six ways that we can attempt to successfully place a cloud of pellets into the anticipated flight path of a moving target, but usually only four of these are mentioned. I will start with the one needing the least gun movement and finish with the method requiring the most.

1. *Ambush or spot shooting.* This is where the gun is stationary and the trigger is pulled when the target appears to be the correct distance behind the muzzles to give successful interception. Sometimes a clever course designer will present this type of target and there is no time for any shooting method other than this one. An example of this would be a narrow window shot, like when a rabbit target appears briefly from behind a straw bale and vanishes behind another one, or when a bird appears through a small gap in the trees. For some reason, these target presentations are more popular in the United Kingdom than in the States.

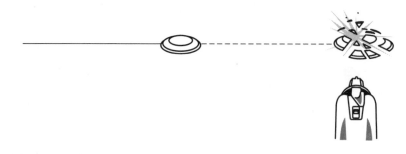

Ambush or spot shooting.

2. *Maintained lead.* Here the gun is mounted in front of the target and moved with it until the correct sight picture is seen. There should be no residual gun movement as this happens, and the gun and target speeds will be synchronized. This sight picture is maintained briefly until the shot is taken. There can be a problem with this method of slowing or stopping the gun, especially on long crossing shots requiring a lot of lead. It is useful for fast quartering shots.

3. *Decreasing maintained lead.* This method is a slight variation on maintained lead where the gun is inserted *on* the correct lead and the trigger pulled as the mount is completed. The gun insertion point

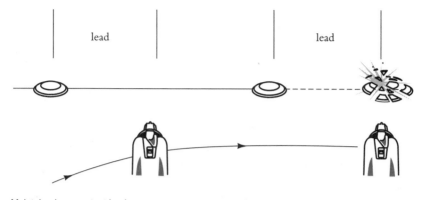

Maintained or constant lead.

should be about halfway between where the target is seen clearly (not as a blur). To use this method correctly, there will be too much lead in the initial stages of the mount because the target will be traveling much faster than the gun, but as the gun is moved onto the target line, this excess lead will "bleed off." A point will be reached where the speed of the target and the speed of the gun synchronize, and if the gun-hold point is correct, and the correct sight picture is seen, the trigger should be pulled immediately, usually as the gun hits the shoulder. This method is basically the same as John Bidwell's *Move, Mount, Shoot* method. It is probably the most favored method for FITASC, where a low gun is mandatory. Once again, there is a chance that on long crossers the gun can be slowed down or stopped as it hits the shoulder to complete the mount. This method can be useful for simultaneous pairs when it is necessary to "buy" extra time for the second target.

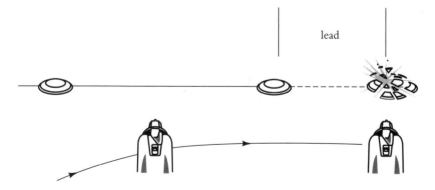

Reducing maintained lead.

4. *Pull away.* This is also known as the CPSA method, popularized by Roger Silcox. The technique involves mounting on or slightly ahead of the target and accelerating the gun away from it until the correct sight picture is seen. Because pull-away is a two-part gun movement, it is less useful for close targets requiring small amounts of lead, but it is excellent for long fast crossers or targets that are not noticeably slowing down or dropping, for example, edge-on teal, chandelles, battues, and long crossers off the high tower that are dropping under power. The main advantage is that on long and fast crossers, a controlled acceleration is produced, which eliminates the tendency to stop the gun.

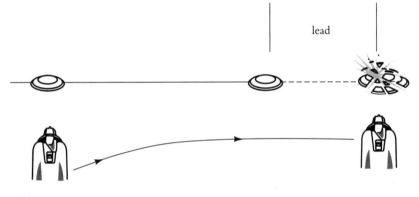

Pull away.

5. *Controlled swing-through.* This is where the gun comes from behind the target and is accelerated through it on the same line but in a smooth and methodical manner. The trigger is pulled as the correct sight picture is seen. This method is useful for driven targets, springing teal, or anything that has a predictable trajectory. The inevitable muzzle momentum produced with the swing-through method means that the gun may be difficult to control. More gun movement equals less control. Also, on a long, fast crosser, it is difficult to repeat the gun speed if using a swing-through technique. Many people who shoot swing-through confuse it with Churchill, but with this method, the lead is consciously applied, unlike pure Churchill.

6. *Churchill swing-through.* This method is sometimes called the English or instinctive shooting method. Robert Churchill was a famous London gun maker and firearms expert who inherited his uncle's gun-making business in 1911. He suggested that swinging through a bird and

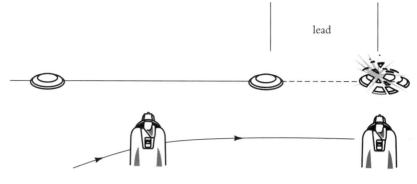

Controlled swing-through.

deliberately seeing lead was a waste of time, and that with proper gun-mounting technique (or drills, as he called them), the proper forward allowance could be made subconsciously. This was his theory of allowance by eye, and it can be used with some success at slow- to medium-paced, reasonably close clay targets and also live birds. On fast crossing targets or extended ranges, it will favor the guy with the slow reactions. The method works because initially the gun barrels are held behind the target until the speed is evaluated, and then accelerated through it on the same line. The amount of acceleration needed on extended ranges is often excessive, which gives poor muzzle control. Pure Churchill is extremely inconsistent unless the gun speed is the same each time, and it is perhaps more useful for live bird shooting because of this. A point worth mentioning here is that the enterprising Robert Churchill often recommended that the success of the method depended on the purchase of one of his very fast handling twenty-five-inch-barreled guns.

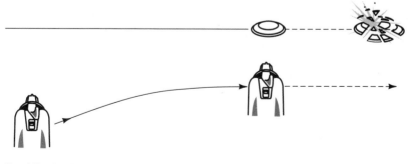

Churchill swing-through.

One thing is certain, in order to hit any moving target, we must shoot in front of it. If we apply basic physics, the velocity of a standard 12-gauge shell is somewhere around twelve hundred feet per second, which is eight hundred miles per hour. If the target we are shooting at is traveling at forty miles per hour, this is a ratio of 20:1. In other words, for every yard the target flies at forty miles per hour, the shot load travels twenty yards in the same time interval. (Neither the speed of the shot nor the speed of the target is constant, but their rates of change are similar enough that we can ignore that aspect for these purposes.) The shot charge will take approximately $\frac{1}{20}$ of a second to travel twenty yards, but almost twice as long to travel thirty yards, and nearly three times as long to travel forty yards, due to the deceleration of the shot.

A target that is traveling at forty miles per hour will travel three feet, six feet, and nine feet in those same time intervals, but there are other things that we must consider. The main one is gun speed, that is, how fast we are swinging the gun as we fire. Some people believe that it is possible to influence the length of the shot-string by the speed of the swing, the jet-of-water-from-a-hose effect. This is an erroneous mental picture. The shot column may be only an inch long as it leaves the gun. The difference in the time interval between the front of the shot column exiting the barrel and the back may be less than 0.00005 of a second, during which time the gun barrels would have hardly moved. After the shot leaves the barrels, it starts to spread longitudinally and laterally; this is known as shot-string. Shot-string does give a slight advantage in that the shooter may be too far in front of the target and still hit the front edge with the back end of the shot-string. But one millionth of an inch behind, and he's missed.

The second factor we must consider is something called shooter reaction time. Human reflexes vary enormously from person to person, day to day, hour to hour, and even shot to shot. The guy that starts the day with lightning reflexes and strong physical capabilities may be feeling the strain on his mental and physical reserves after tramping around a tough sporting clays course for three hours.

The last thing we must consider is time up the barrel. This is a complex equation involving lock time of the gun, i.e., the fraction of time it takes for the trigger-pull to disengage the sear and allow the hammer to fall, the time it takes for the primer to ignite the propellant, and the ignition time of the propellant to build up enough pressure to push the shot charge out of the barrels. The combined shooter reaction time and up-the-barrel time is probably only about one-twentieth of a second. It does not sound like much, but if you think about it, in a twentieth of a second a fifty-mile-per-hour target will travel three to four feet. Stop the gun as you pull the trigger, and all the lead will evaporate. A miss behind is the inevitable result. This combination of neurological, physical, mechanical, and ballistic events influences our shooting consistency. So which methods of shooting do they least affect?

Two of the six methods listed above produce much more consistent results than the other four, and the effects of gun speed, shooter reaction time, and time up the barrel are reduced. These are maintained lead and decreasing maintained lead. In both these methods, the target is used as a moving reference point, and the lead requirement is more precise as a result. But isn't this the way it used to be done? Back in 1660, King Charles II and his noblemen used shotguns for hunting flying birds. In the days of the flintlock, ignition times were variable due to the doubtful recipe of the powder, primitive lock mechanisms, dampness, etc. These early sportsmen had absolutely no choice but to keep the gun pointing the correct distance ahead of the target until the shot charge had left the barrels, and no doubt they shot with some success.

The method they used was a version of maintained lead, and it is the oldest method for intercepting a moving target with a cloud of pellets. If this is done properly, the gun and target speeds should be synchronized at the point of pulling the trigger; therefore, there is no excessive gun speed. During the short interval that this synchronization occurs, the trigger is pulled as the sight picture is maintained (with the flintlock on a thirty-yard target, this may have been half a second or more), so the shooter's reaction time and time up the barrel are inconsequential.

Three of the other methods can be adversely affected by shooter reaction time and gun speed: pull-away, controlled swing-through, and Churchill swing-through. This is because it is possible for the same shooter to vary his reaction time subconsciously on two identical shots, and if he does this, how will it affect his consistency? Let's look at the effect of this on a forty-mile-per-hour target crossing at twenty yards from the shooter and shot by the swing-through method.

Let's say the shooter's speed of swing is fifty miles per hour faster than the speed of the target. Fifty miles per hour is seventy-three feet per second. As the shooter accelerates his gun onto the line of the target, the picture looks right and the shooter's ocular stimuli give his brain the order to fire. His reaction time for this shot was about 0.05 of a second. Since $0.05 \times 73 = 3$ feet 8 inches of lead, which is about right, the shooter breaks the target. He then shoots the same target again, but this time his reactions are slightly faster as he pulls the trigger, with a reaction time of 0.03 of a second. Since 0.03 × 73 = 2 feet 2 inches of lead, he would miss behind. When using a swing-through technique, 0.02 of a second is all it takes to make a difference between a hit and a miss!

Now let us consider the effects of variable gun speed. With any method that relies on gun speed to produce the correct amount of forward allowance, it is almost impossible to repeat the exact speed of swing accurately on every shot without some sort of reference for the speed of the gun. Perception of lead varies as gun speed varies. Perceived lead is the amount of lead that the shooter thinks is necessary, and it is directly proportional to his gun speed.

Take a target that is traveling at forty miles per hour and is crossing approximately thirty yards away (which we have already calculated requires six feet of actual lead). If the gun is moving at twice the speed of the target, the shooter's perception of the lead required may be about three feet instead of six feet. If the gun is moving at three times the speed of the target, the shooter may feel that he is shooting straight at it. With a gun speed that is even faster than this, it is possible that negative lead will be seen in order to hit the target.

We have already calculated that for a swing-through shooter to hit a forty-mile-per-hour target crossing at twenty yards, he needs a gun speed of about fifty miles per hour and a reaction time of about 0.05 of a second. (Note that when I describe a gun speed as being X miles per hour, I do not mean the muzzle is actually moving at X miles per hour; I mean that it is swinging at the speed that would keep it pointing directly at a target traveling X miles per hour.) Suppose this time the shooter accelerates past the target at about twenty miles per hour faster than the target speed, i.e., thirty feet per second faster than the target. His reaction time is the same: 0.05 of a second. Since 0.05 × 30 = 1 foot 6 inches, a miss behind is the result. Of course, when wingshooting, gun speed and shooter reaction time are less important, because with live quarry the bird is never flying at the same speed each time. That is why Churchill and controlled swing-through are often successful—the sudden appearance of the quarry triggers a spontaneous reaction, and the resulting fast gun speed and follow-through do the rest.

But competition shooting is different, and we need to be able to make repetitive shots to compete. Both gun speed and personal reaction time can vary from day to day due to stress, tiredness, etc., so logically it would make sense for the competition shooter, wherever possible, to use a method that is unaffected by these. With spot shooting, there is no gun speed involved, but the success of the shot is still affected by shooter reaction time and time up the barrel.

So if more consistent results can be obtained by using sustained lead, why don't we stick with it for everything? In many circumstances we can, and it is without a doubt the most effective way to produce perfect scores at skeet. But we are not shooting skeet. The extreme variety of target presentations, and the variable angles and trajectories and specialty targets we encounter on a challenging sporting clays course dictate that we use a variety of methods if we are to be successful. For example, what happens when the second target of a following pair gets the jump on us and we have to chase it? Then the gun must come from behind to restore the correct sight picture, and we must use a swing-through technique to do this. And what about a long, fast crossing target or a long target that is still under power? I mostly use pull-away here, because with swing-through, it would be difficult to keep the gun on-line when it is so far in front of the target, but the pull-away must be controlled, just slightly faster than the target's speed, not sudden and erratic.

What about driven targets and springing teal? Controlled swing-through or sustained lead is often best for these. There is no single shooting method out there that will give you a way to handle all the target presentations, but I always teach a new student by using sustained lead. Why? Because by doing this, his brain will establish how much forward allowance is needed without having the problems of excessive gun speed and shooter reaction times to influence the sight picture. Of course, when shooting in the field, we cannot always use a swing-through method, because on occasion our gun will be coming from behind the bird as we see it. Then we must apply a controlled swing-through shot. The shooter will be looking for the correct sight picture based on the information he has already stored in his memory bank, and the shot may be carried slightly farther in front of the bird due to the faster gun speed that results. The worst-case scenario when this happens is that the bird is hit in the head, which is quite a good problem to have, really.

So just like the woman at the start of this chapter, there are many ways to lose weight, just as there are a variety of ways to apply the correct forward allowance to a moving target. Of course they all work— sometimes. But there is no doubt in my mind that the guy who has developed a mental awareness of the amount he needs will be the most successful shot, regardless of the method he uses. Lead, like beauty, is in the eye of the beholder.

CHAPTER 9

The Modern Shotshell

One of the hallmarks of society is the tendency to take everyday things for granted. Take the humble shotshell, for example. As we go hunting or amble around the sporting clays course, we never really give it much thought. Stick a couple in the gun, pull the trigger, the gun goes bang (twice), and the targets break. Simple. Today's shotshells are widely available, conveniently packaged for the discerning shooter, still relatively inexpensive, and superbly reliable. Nowadays, misfires are almost unheard of.

It wasn't always like this. Although the past six hundred years or so have seen the shotgun evolve from the cumbersome, archaic muzzle-loader of the sixteenth century to the intricate and refined instrument of recreation it has become in the twenty-first century, the quest to find a way to propel the shot charge up the barrel efficiently was often an elaborate, painstaking, and sometimes extremely dangerous procedure. In terms of ballistics, a cylinder-bored shotgun of the mid-1800s loaded with an ounce of shot and black powder propellant gave a range and penetration similar to those of a cylinder-bored modern shotgun. The main difference is the ease with which we can now achieve this. So let's look at the evolution of the modern shotshell and what makes it tick.

As soon as the visual information that the brain receives triggers the order to fire, finger pressure on the trigger releases the sear of the lock mechanism and the hammer strikes the firing pin. The firing pin then hits the center of the primer, which in turn ignites the main propellant, and the charge of pellets is on its way to intercept the target (if we're lucky). The primer plays a critical role in the successful ignition of a cartridge. Necessity is the mother of invention, and to understand how the

A dazzling array of choices. The application of modern technology has greatly improved the shotgun shell over the last few years so that there is a shell out there that will fit the bill for any shooting situation.

primer works and how it evolved, we have to rewind about 250 years, to the era of the flintlock.

The priming powder, with the flintlock, was held in a receptacle or "pan" at the side of the touchhole, and the main charge was situated next to this, inside the barrel. Unfortunately for enthusiastic shotgunners in those days, inclement weather had a detrimental effect on this priming powder. If it was windy, it would blow away. If it was raining, the priming powder became damp and would not ignite. Even if it did ignite, there was always the danger of a blow-back, and the hunter could lose his eyebrows, or worse. It was frustrating, to say the least, and certainly not for the fainthearted, but there was no choice if you wanted to shoot. The hunter who had hungry mouths to feed often faced many problems because of the early firearms.

As if this were not bad enough, things could get even worse. On the battlefield, for example, a pyrotechnical hiccup just as a bloodthirsty hoard of battle-ax-wielding adversaries appeared on top of the next hill would spell disaster. Tough times indeed! A satisfactory solution to the situation was needed, and in 1807, the Reverend Alexander Forsyth, a minister from Belhelvie in Aberdeenshire, Scotland, began experimenting with a substance called fulminate of mercury.

Fulminates were not a new invention. They were first researched as far back as the late 1600s by French chemist Peter Bolduc. The difference between a fulminate and ordinary explosive powder was that although striking ordinary black powder between two metal surfaces could ignite it, the explosion produced by doing this was not as violent as if it had been ignited by a burning match or spark. Fulminates, on the other hand, were much more unstable and could be easily ignited by a sudden blow. The resultant explosion was of a much more violent nature.

Another Frenchman, Henri Bayen, chief army physician to Louis XV, discovered mercury fulminate in 1774. Although Bayen experimented with its explosive properties, he did not apply this effect to firearms in any way, and the honor of inventing the percussion system was awarded to Reverend Forsyth in a patent dated April 11, 1807. The applications of Forsyth's invention were numerous, and over the years it was improved, but the most successful application was the invention of the copper cap. As the name suggests, this was a small, cup-shaped primer with a small amount of fulminate inside that fit over the "nipple" of the flintlock. This fulminate was ignited by the fall of the hammer, and in turn it ignited the secondary charge in the barrel.

The main problem with these early primers was the corrosive residues that remained on the bores and attacked the steel of the barrels after the gun had been fired. All the guns in those days were, of course, muzzleloaders, and without almost constant maintenance, the breech of the gun soon became badly corroded and unusable. Cleaning the bores in those days was a major task that involved unscrewing them from the breech block and pouring boiling water down them to neutralize any corrosive residues that remained. Fortunately for us, modern priming powders are not corrosive. They use a substance called lead styphnate.

For many years, gun makers strived to produce a weapon that could be loaded and cleaned more efficiently than the muzzleloader but failed to find a way to successfully lock the barrels. However, in 1812, Paris gun maker Samuel Johannes Pauly, from Geneva, Switzerland, produced and patented one of the first breechloaders. Inextricably caught up in the development of the breechloader was the need for gun makers to develop a self-contained cartridge to go with it. In 1829, Clement Pottet of Paris took out a patent on a self-contained cartridge, and it was further developed by French gun maker Houllier in about 1850. This was known as the pin-fire cartridge. The cartridge case was paper molded to a brass base, with a brass pin that projected through the side, which in turn made contact with an internal percussion cap. The hammer, as the shot was triggered, would strike this external pin and the cartridge would explode. There were serious drawbacks, and this particular cartridge had a few nasty disadvantages. Loading was difficult; the firing pin needed to be aligned in exactly the right place for the hammer to strike it successfully. The pin could also corrode easily and either break off or become stuck, but the worst was yet to come. Because the firing pin was prominently sticking out of the side, and because these cartridges were loaded with black powder instead of the safe powders that we use today, a sharp knock could cause them to explode. Walking up pheasants in those days with a pocketful of unexploded bombs was scary stuff. George Daw of London eventually solved this problem, and in 1861, he perfected a cartridge that consisted of a paper case and a brass base containing the primer at the bottom. This cartridge closely resembled our modern cartridge.

So if this is how a primer and priming powder function, what about the main propellant? Usually anything that burns requires a supply of oxygen to support combustion. Gasoline, for example, needs to vaporize and mix with air before it will successfully ignite. Propellant powders, on the other hand, need to be able to ignite and burn rapidly within the airtight confines of a shotgun or rifle chamber, and in order to do this, they produce their own oxygen.

The black powder that was used as a propellant before the modern nitro powders was made from a mixture of saltpeter (potassium nitrate), sulfur, and charcoal. Modern gunpowder is known as nitrocellulose. Treating different substances with nitric acid forms nitro compounds, and the most common of these is gun cotton, which, as its name suggests, is produced by soaking cotton or cellulose in nitric acid. Although we consider this to be a modern compound, an alchemist named Christian Schonbein was the first to manufacture gun cotton, in about 1846.

When ignited outside the confines of a cartridge case, gun cotton does not explode (don't try this at home), but burns fairly slowly. Any product that produces its own oxygen to aid and support combustion begins with the word *nitro*. All nitro powders are made more violent in their explosive capabilities by confinement, and in the confines of the cartridge case, pressure builds up rapidly and the mixture produces huge

Components of the modern shotshell.

amounts of hot, expanding gas that quickly accelerates the shot column from standstill to twelve hundred feet per second in less than one-thousandth of a second. Modern powders can be regulated to control this pressure by the addition of amounts of nitroglycerin. These powders are called double-based powders. Regulation of the rate of burn is necessary to control the pressure involved relative to the shot load. A fast-burning powder may be required to accelerate ⁷/₈ ounce of shot from standstill to twelve hundred feet per second, but a slower-burning propellant may be used to accelerate a heavier goose-hunting load of 1¹/₂ ounces so that the breech pressures remain reasonable. A comparison would be the difference in the amount of effort required to throw a tennis ball or a bowling ball.

Although both powders produce gas as they burn, nitro-based powder has a huge advantage over the old black powders. The first advantage is the clean burning properties. Black powder produces approximately 65 percent residue and 35 percent gas, whereas the nitro compounds are the opposite—35 percent residue and 65 percent gas. Because of this, the second advantage is the volume of powder needed. About half the volume of nitro powder is required to produce the same volume of gas.

So there we have it, the evolution of the shotshell. On a hunting trip or sporting clays course, in the unlikely event that you get a misfire, keep the gun pointed in a safe direction for twenty or thirty seconds, and then open the gun at arm's length, because these misfires can go off after a delay. Outside the confinement of the chamber, the shell will explode with reduced force, but the primer may still be ejected from its pocket with great force. You certainly don't want to be examining it when it goes! Modern primers are usually superbly reliable, but if you happen to get a dud, don't be too hard on the manufacturer. Remember, it was not always this easy. Besides, it is an extremely rare dud that was not caused either by the firing pin or striker not hitting the primer hard enough for one reason or another, or by the shell getting wet internally.

So now you have a dilemma. Modern technology has greatly improved the shotgun shell over the last few years. There is a shell out there that will fill the bill for any shooting situation. You, the shooter, have to decide among the dazzling choice of shotgun shells available today which is the best one for you to use for maximum penetration and pattern density on your particular choice of target. All the manufacturers, with the aid of aggressive marketing and attractive packaging, will try to tempt you to buy theirs. Of course, you can always buy a reloading press and roll your own magic formulation of ingredients.

The confidence factor always plays a big part in shotgunning. When someone becomes proficient with a shotgun and either runs a station at a sporting clays tournament or makes several successful shots while winghunting, there is always one question that observers ask more than any other: "What shells are you using?"

Some guys, in an effort to boost their confidence, painstakingly pattern, chronograph, and test their shells, and in certain situations, there are benefits. Usually these benefits are what I call individual perceived benefits, and as an example of this, two guys are walking around the sporting clays course or the quail lease, or sitting in the duck blind. Bill knows that his 20 gauge loaded with $3/4$ ounce of $7\frac{1}{2}$ shells is the perfect medicine for the doves out to thirty yards, just as John knows that his 20 gauge loaded with 1 ounce of 8 shells is the right answer. Ask these guys to trade shells, and instantly doubt begins to creep in. If either misses a bird, the miss will usually be incorrectly blamed on the shells.

And that psychology works in reverse. You are out on the river for a quiet afternoon's trout fishing. You already have three nice fish in the bag, using your favorite trout fly. You move downstream, and as you go around the corner to the next pool, you notice that another guy is fishing there.

"Any luck?" you ask.

"Yes, got a couple of nice ones." He opens his sack, and sure enough, two nice rainbows. You then show him your fish.

"Caught them on one of these. Never fails," says the other guy. He gives you one of his favorite, infallible flies. As soon as he vanishes downstream to try his luck, you tie the fly on the end of your line, don't you? It is exactly the same with shooting. Anyone who has a good day with a particular shell, either in a wingshooting situation or at a clay pigeon tournament, is unlikely to change his particular brand of shells until they let him down badly. We all do it. We stick faithfully to our chosen brand, sometimes for the flimsiest of reasons, and it isn't always a bad thing. Believing in one particular brand of shell, correctly or incorrectly, always inspires some degree of confidence and, as a result, often produces better performance.

Okay, so there are lots of circumstances where "specialist" shells may be more appropriate, but most of the time, the failure to connect is the fault of the person at the other end of the gun. Do I ever pattern a shotgun? Very rarely, except as a way to check gun fit to see where the gun shoots. Why? In certain circumstances, trap shooting, for example, a nice tight pattern on the board may inspire confidence. For pass shooting high geese with a forty-mile-per-hour tailwind? I doubt if we could convincingly blame the miss on a hole in the pattern. Usually the blame rests squarely on the shoulders of the person pulling the trigger; in other words, the miss or hit is dependent upon the shooter's proficiency. Just plain old pilot error causes our misses. So now we come to the crunch. Just like in the trout fly scenario, when someone asks what shells you use, the answer should usually be, "The ones I have confidence in." It seems to work for me.

CHAPTER 10

Internal Dynamics, Chokes, Barrels, and Forcing Cones

Nowadays, it is a pretty safe bet that anyone who decides to buy a gun for the purpose of competitive target shooting, especially on sporting clays, will choose one with a set of interchangeable choke tubes. Sometimes, though, this can be a problem. Choke choice on the sporting clays course causes more frustration and indecision, and is a more frequently debated topic than perhaps any other. Manufacturers, quick off the mark and eager to exploit the growing market, have jumped on the bandwagon with a huge choice and combination of interchangeable chokes, all of which are guaranteed to improve (and confuse) the dedicated competitive shooter, not to mention the poor bird hunter. Is all this really as necessary or as worthwhile as they would have us believe?

The actual origin of choke is not firmly established. One invention, patented on April 10, 1866, by American gunsmith Henry Roper, was probably the first-ever screw-on choke, but this was detachable, not an integral part of the tube. Even earlier, another American, Jeremiah Smith of Southfield, Rhode Island, reputedly discovered the merits of choke boring in about 1827, but I suspect that this claim is apocryphal, as I can find no concrete evidence to support it.

Although a system of choke boring was used by William Rochester Pape, a celebrated gun maker from Newcastle-upon-Tyne in the north of England, as early as the 1860s, the proof as to which individual should be credited with the initial idea has apparently been lost in the mists of time. But perhaps I can help to unfold some of the mystery.

William Rochester Pape, son of James and Dorothy, was born in 1831 in Amble. His father had a fishing tackle and gun shop in Collingwood Street, Newcastle, and in 1857, William set up in business as a

Chokes for competition guns come in a variety of shapes and sizes, which in some cases only serve to confuse and confound the shotgunner.

gunsmith and gun barrel maker at 44 Westgate Street, Newcastle. Now, as luck would have it, my gun shop in the Scottish borders was only sixty miles from Newcastle, and many of my customers, who came to either shoot or fish for sea trout and salmon in the Langholm area, lived either in or around the Newcastle area. One of them I was lucky enough

Manufacturers, quick off the mark and eager to exploit the growing market, have jumped on the proverbial bandwagon with an alarming choice and combination of interchangeable chokes, all of which are guaranteed to improve (and confuse) the dedicated competition shooter and often also the avid bird hunter.

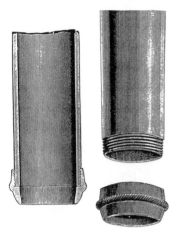

This invention, which was patented on April 10, 1866, by American gunsmith Henry Roper, was probably the first-ever screw-on choke, but this was detachable and not an integral part of the tube.

to become acquainted with was Stewart Pape, a deer keeper for the Duke of Buccleuch in Langholm.

Through the course of conversation, I found out that Stewart was distantly related to William Rochester Pape. More importantly, Stewart's father, who owned a gun and tackle shop and game dealer's business in Appleby, Cumbria, had in his possession copies of some of the original patents that were issued to his great-uncle William Rochester Pape. One of the patents, dated May 29, 1866, clearly stated that the "muzzle end of the barrel was tapered inwards." Was this in fact hard evidence that the original spark of genius to which we can credit the origins of choke boring began with William Rochester Pape? I would like to believe so. There have been many claims over the years as to who the original discoverer was, including Fred Kimble, an Illinois duck hunter; W. W. Greener; and others. Unfortunately for Pape, he never renewed the original patent, and it lapsed in 1873. Many other gun makers were quick to seize the opportunity to "jump into the breech," and there is no doubt that others exploited the invention to its maximum during the same period.

Until the advent of choke boring, all barrels were bored as straight cylinders, and ranges were short as a result. The only way to extend the range was to use bigger (or larger quantities of) shot. Many gun makers were quick to seize the opportunity and exploit the new invention. One of these was W. W. Greener, who saw the potential and wrote a book on the subject, *Choke Bore Guns*, published in 1876. Suitably inspired by Pape, Greener perfected a way to bore barrels so that there was a constriction at the end.

The effect of this was dramatic, so much so that Greener guaranteed that at forty yards, his guns would give a tighter pattern than any other, which was a claim previously unheard of. Extensive and exhaustive tests of Greener guns were made at the London Gun Trials of 1876, where his fully choked 20-gauge guns could easily beat the 12 gauges in both pattern and penetration. These tests were convincing enough for many, but some of Greener's competitors suggested that the constriction at the end of the barrels would wear out in a short time, reducing the choke effect. In response to these cynics, *The Field* conducted wear-and-tear trials in 1875. These trials involved firing two hundred shots per day until each gun had fired twenty-five hundred rounds. Once again, the Greener guns triumphed in both pattern and penetration, proving conclusively that the performance of the choked barrels was far in advance of anything yet attempted with the shotgun. As if this were not enough, further trials were carried out on July 21, 1876, this time using live pigeons at the Notting Hill Gun Club. There were nine guns on each team, five birds each at thirty yards, and the prize was a silver cup, presented by Mr. J. Purdey. The Greener-choked guns reigned supreme and won the day.

Choke in a shotgun barrel is exactly as the name suggests: the degree of constriction at the end of the barrel that influences and regulates the pattern of the shot as it passes through the muzzles. An open choke gives a

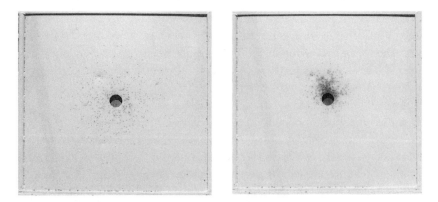

Left: Improved cylinder pattern at a distance of twenty yards.
Right: Full choke pattern at the same distance. Most birds are not as far as we would like to believe. At close range overchoking is a distinct disadvantage, both from an accuracy point and to avoid smashing the birds up so they are useless for the table.

The Cutts Compensator works by allowing the shot to expand rapidly as it exits the first part of the barrel, then compressing it again to produce the choking effect. Side slots are cut in the side of the tube. The end is slightly flared to allow the pattern to spread as rapidly as possible as it finally exits the barrel. This combination of internal dynamics opens up the center of the pattern, which gives an elongated shot string. Skeet is one of the few situations where this can be an advantage.

wide pattern; a tight choke gives a tight pattern. The actual choke area itself consists of three distinct measurements: the standard internal diameter of the barrel (nominal boring); the taper or lead in to the choke proper; and the actual choke area itself, the walls of which are parallel. The actual length of this choke area can be anything from ⅜ inch to about 3 inches. Each manufacturer has its own specifications, and dimensions vary considerably. To add to the confusion, there are many types of choke, e.g., conical, retro, Tula, Russian, recessed, and "jug."

So why exactly is choke so important? As soon as the shot charge leaves the barrel of a gun, it begins to spread longitudinally and laterally. It is the cumulative effect of multiple strikes from the pellets of the shot charge that breaks the target or cleanly kills the bird. At a given distance, the effectiveness (density) of this pattern is reduced to such an extent that the pattern becomes ineffective. But if we can increase the density of this swarm of pellets, we can also increase the range of effectiveness. That is what choke does—it gives us control over the pattern density at various ranges. Increasing the amount of choke (constriction) will increase the range at which the shot pattern will be effective. Decreasing the amount of choke (constriction) will give us a larger, more effective pattern at close range.

The skeet gun, with its very open chokes, is optimally effective at twenty to twenty-five yards, the range at which skeet targets are shot. The three-inch magnum duck gun, which is usually full choke, is effective at extended ranges, up to fifty yards. Horses for courses, as we say.

For centuries, the size of the bore of a shotgun has been denoted by the number of lead balls to the pound that would fit down the barrel.

For example, with the 16 bore (gauge), sixteen balls of lead exactly the diameter of the bore would weigh exactly one pound. With the 12 gauge, twelve balls the diameter of the bore would weigh one pound, and so forth. Nominal standard bore diameters (in inches) are as follows:

28 gauge	0.550
20 gauge	0.615
16 gauge	0.670
12 gauge	0.729
10 gauge	0.775

The .410 is classed as a *caliber,* but if measured in gauge, would be 67 gauge. Many years ago, some shotguns were designed to fire solid lead balls rather than shot. These guns were used by the aristocracy of the period for big game hunting in Africa and India.

A barrel without any choke constriction in it is referred to as a true cylinder, or as being choked cylinder. The degree of constriction is stated in measurements of hundredths-of-an-inch increments from the cylinder to the maximum, which is usually full choke, about 40×0.001 (0.040) of an inch in 12 gauge and about 0.024 in 20 gauge.

To determine the amount of constriction a given choke produces, first measure the inside diameter of the barrel behind the choke area. This is known as bore diameter. Then measure the choke at its tightest point. The difference between these measurements is the amount of choke (constriction) in the barrel. If that difference is 0.020 (or within a thousandth or two of 0.020) in a 12 gauge, then that barrel-choke combination is said to be modified choke. But the same amount of constriction in a 20 gauge is said to be improved modified.

For 12 gauges, the nominal choke constrictions are usually expressed in increments of 0.005 inch from the diameter of the bore (0.005 = skeet, 0.010 = improved cylinder, 0.015 = light modified, 0.020 = modified, etc.). As the gauge is reduced, the degree of constriction becomes proportionately smaller. For the 20 gauge, for example, the constrictions are in 0.004-inch increments (0.004 = skeet, 0.008 = improved cylinder, 0.012 = light modified, 0.016 = modified, etc.).

Contrary to somewhat popular belief, it is the open choke that gives longer shot-strings, not the tighter choke. Also, the shape of the shot charge in flight and the resulting pattern are not influenced as much by the degree of choke as they are by the amount of lead in or taper from the bore diameter to the tightest part of the choke section. As a rule of thumb, short taper will produce a wider pattern, and long taper will produce a tighter pattern. Modern gun manufacturers each have their own preference and recommendations as to the ideal choke tube length and lead-in (taper) dimensions. This is why chokes of the same internal diameter in the same gun can produce very different patterns on a pattern board.

Internal barrel dimensions can also influence pattern and spread. A back-bored (i.e., slightly overbored) barrel and a standard barrel, when each is shot using the same choke tube, will give different results at the same range. Since it is the amount of constriction that matters, that same choke tube provides a greater constriction in the back-bored barrel than it does in the standard barrel. The back-bored barrel can also produce a reduction in perceived recoil, simply because the length of time the recoil is occurring is proportionately increased. The shooter will feel a long push rather than a short, sharp jab.

Regardless of bore diameters, constriction measurements, lead-in tapers, etc., what really matters with a given choke is how it patterns on paper or board. Expected percentages of pellets put into a thirty-inch circle at a range of forty yards are usually as follows:

True cylinder	35%–40%
Improved cylinder	45%–50%
Modified	55%–60%
Full choke	70% +

In ballistic terms, at a range of forty yards a full choke *should* deliver about twice the number of pellets into the thirty-inch circle as a cylinder barrel, somewhere around 65 to 75 percent. In a 12 gauge, full choke is usually accomplished with about 0.040 constriction. More constriction than 0.040 is not necessarily better because the amount of deformation the pellets are subjected to is increased with tighter constrictions, and deformed pellets fly erratically.

The deformation occurs when the shot charge, merrily cruising the length of the bore with elbow room to spare, suddenly slams into the much narrower choke. This crushes the clump of pellets together laterally, distorting some of them. It also causes the shot charge to suddenly slow down, which has the effect of crushing and distorting the pellets at the rear of the shot charge so that they are aerodynamically inferior to the

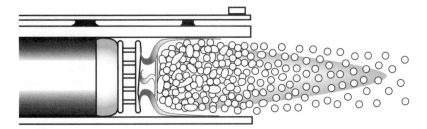

Due to the massive acceleration forces as the shell is detonated, the rear pellets will become more distorted and compressed, the front ones progressively less so, before the shot charge leaves the barrel. As the choke area is reached, some of the pellets will be deflected inwards, giving even greater distortion. This degree of distortion is dependent on several factors: degree of choke, size and hardness of pellets, and type of wad are the main ones.

front pellets. Under about 0.040 constriction, adding more constriction usually results in a tighter pattern, but beyond that, the increase in pellet deformation outweighs the benefits. This is known as a blown pattern.

Also, as the size of shot is increased, the deformity that will occur as it passes through the constriction of the choke will increase. Therefore, while 0.040 might produce the tightest possible pattern in a barrel with small shot, less constriction might produce the tightest possible pattern with large shot. The chapter on shot-string describes this in greater detail.

Too high a velocity can have the same adverse effect, reducing the pattern density and increasing the length of the shot-string. This is exactly what happens with the Russian or "jug" choke. This choke was reputedly developed by the Russians for their skeet team and was a huge success. The area of the barrel behind the choke area is opened out so that it allows the shot column to expand as it passes up the barrel. The shot charge must then compress rapidly as it passes through the choke area, which causes a massive deformation of the pellets, opening up the center of the pattern, resulting in rapid spread and a long shot-string. Skeet is one of the few situations where this is a big advantage, because of the short ranges involved. In most other situations, this is not recommended. Although a visible piece may be broken off a skeet target at close range, in most cases with successful shotgunning, we are trying to make sure that the shot charge reaches the target more cohesively.

Basically, there are only two ways to eliminate this problem. The first is to try to reduce pellet deformation as much as possible before the shot exits the barrels, and the second is to keep the mass of pellets as uniform as possible for as long as possible to reduce the length of the shot-string. Uniform pattern density and a reduction in the length of shot-string would obviously be maximized if the transition from the chamber to the end of the barrel were as smooth as possible. This is done with a combination of lengthened forcing cones and back-boring. The forcing cone is, as the name suggests, the area in front of the chamber that tapers into the barrel proper. By giving this area a more gradual taper, shot deformation is reduced, as is felt recoil. Back-boring is boring out, by up to about 0.015 inch larger than nominal bore size, of the bore between the chamber and the choke area. Once again, pellet deformation and the effect of recoil are substantially reduced.

Besides this combination of back-boring, lengthened forcing cones, and gradual choke taper to ensure an as smooth as possible transition for the pellets, what else can we do? Several things. Manufacturers have applied modern science to the problem, and ammunition has dramatically improved over the last decade or so. The addition of antimony to make the shot harder, and copper and nickel coatings to protect the shot, help to reduce deformation of the pellets. This in turn increases pattern density because there is a reduction in the number of "flyers." Trap loads usually have the highest antimony content of all. Antimony is expensive in comparison to lead, so the price of ammunition for trapshooting is higher, in proportion with the antimony content. European trap loads for international trap can have as much as 6 percent antimony. Quality skeet loads usually have about 4 percent, and most good hunting loads about 2 percent.

Modern plas-wad plastic shot cups are designed to do two things. First, they reduce shot distortion inside the barrel by cushioning the massive pressure as the propellant is ignited, and second, they protect the pellets from abrasion as they travel up the barrel. Biodegradable fiber wads are often used in hunting loads. By using a slower, more progressively burning powder, it is possible to gradually accelerate the shot charge from rest to the required velocity without subjecting the pellets to the rapid acceleration that a faster-burning powder would produce. The problem here is that to do this effectively, more powder is required, which raises cost.

Today many field guns are still equipped with fixed chokes; that is to say, they do not have the interchangeable or screw-in choke tubes that most competition guns have. Some people inherit guns or buy them used and never bother to check how much choke is in the barrels. Their shooting, and in some cases the things they shoot at, can suffer as a result, and this is far more common than most people realize. I have on many occasions given lessons to clients who shot a gun in the field that was choked far too tightly for normal use. One client came to me with a 12-gauge Winchester model 101 that he used regularly on dove-hunting trips to west Texas. When we measured the bores, I found the gun was a trap model choked full and extra full. This must have made for some frustrating dove hunting! Most of his birds were attempted at ranges of twenty yards or thereabouts, so of course most of them were missed. But the ones that were hit just about disintegrated!

So just how do we tell how much choke is in the barrels, short of having a barrel smith measure them? Usually, there will be a visible difference between one barrel and the other on a double-barreled gun, and looking at the end of the muzzles, you will easily see this. The wall of the barrel will be thinner on the tube with less choke and thicker on the one with more choke.

Most fixed-choke guns also have some indication as to the choke size stamped on the flats of the barrels. Sometimes these are asterisk-shaped marks. With these, **** indicates 0.010-inch constriction; ***, 0.020 inch; **, 0.030 inch; and *, 0.040 inch or full choke. But beware, many guns have been tampered with; i.e., a previous owner may have had a gunsmith open up either or both chokes, and the marks on the flats are no longer correct. Years ago, all the major gun makers in the United Kingdom would regulate the point of impact and pattern of their shotgun barrels to suit their clients' requirements by means of draw-boring with a lapping machine. The lapping tool consisted of a lead cylinder fitted on a central shaft that was fitted loosely down the barrel of the gun. This lead cylinder was coated with thin oil and emery powder, and as it rotated, it was moved back and forth inside the barrel to polish the bores and also carefully remove areas of the bore at the end of the muzzles. The expert barrel maker could reach a point of perfection where there was an optimum ballistic performance for certain choke and brand of cartridge at a certain distance. This was a painstaking process that involved many hours spent at the pattern board, because once the lapping process had removed the metal, it could not be put back. Wealthy clients would have faith in a particular brand of cartridge, and they would insist that their guns be regulated to this specific brand. In some cases, the guns involved were worth many thousands of pounds

The bore gauge is a precision instrument that can be used to find the precise amount of constriction at the end of the barrels and also any changes in the diameter of the barrels at any point in a set of barrels up to thirty inches long.

(or dollars) because of the labor expended on them. These skilled craftsmen had a lot of tricks of the trade up their sleeves, including the one of eccentric choking, where sensitive areas were removed by this lapping process, possibly changing the point of impact of the gun slightly.

The only way to truly tell how much choke is in a barrel is to use an internal-bore gauge, which any good barrel smith will have. This is a precision instrument that can be used to find out precisely the amount of constriction at the end of the barrels, and also any changes in the diameter of the barrels at any point in a set of barrels up to thirty inches long. In the past, I have surprised many quail hunters using 28 gauges with improved cylinder in both barrels—upon measuring, it was revealed that in fact there was a huge amount of choke present. Not particularly good for the ego or the quail at close range.

This is an excusable situation and a commonly made mistake, but we can also reduce our efficiency with a shotgun and miss more birds than we should because we *purposely* overchoke. As an example of this, it would always amuse me when visiting "guns" would come into my gun shop in Scotland to purchase ammunition for driven grouse or pheasant on the Westerhall and Buccleuch estates. Pheasant and grouse shooting had existed in the Langholm area for over a hundred years. In fact, the record grouse bag was an astonishing thirteen hundred brace on the duke of Buccleuch's moor in 1911. All the guns in those days would have been 12-gauge English sidelocks or boxlocks with a chamber length of $2\frac{1}{2}$ inches, designed for 1-ounce loads of no. 6 shot and probably choked $\frac{1}{4}$ and $\frac{1}{2}$ (about improved cylinder and modified). Remarkable bags were taken in those days with this combination.

Unfortunately, due to the insatiable appetite of the modern driven pheasant specialist, there is demand for more and more quality high birds, and with this demand comes the requirement for quality cartridges. Perhaps modern belief is that pheasants are a lot tougher and fly faster than they used to. Some of the visiting guns would bring with them their modern, bespoke Spanish and Italian guns chambered for 2¾-inch shells, and some of these guns would be choked full and full, presumably at the request of the owners when they ordered them. Despite the fact that cartridge manufacturers were producing quality specialist ammunition for driven pheasants, I had many requests for high-velocity, high-brass trap loads of 1¼ ounces, which were available only in 7½ shot size. The downside (for the pheasants, mainly) was that with very high birds, the 7½ shot size just did not retain enough energy to properly penetrate, certainly not as much as the no. 6 shot.

These gentlemen were probably insisting upon trap loads because of the reknowned quality of trap shot, but a much better bet would have been a standard factory duck load with an increase in 5 or even 4 shot size. The other problem with these trap loads was the punishment the shooter received. Push these shells through the gun they were intended for—an eight-pound trap gun—and 1¼-ounce loads are not a problem, but at extended ranges, this combination would defeat the purpose and produce a huge amount of felt recoil in these light 6½-pound side-by-side game guns. Most of these guys soon tired of being pounded mercilessly and switched to the softer, recommended standard loads. I doubt whether any of them could detect a reduction of birds bagged because of it.

So just what is the ideal combination of choke in a double-barreled 12-gauge gun that is to be used for a multitude of wingshooting purposes? At modest to long ranges, choke constriction over 0.030 will probably put fewer birds in the bag, not more. The tighter the pattern, the more precise we have to be at a given range. Unless the person at the other end of the gun is confident and competent enough, overchoking can be considered a negative move on the sporting clays course and a definite disadvantage at short-range birds in the field, not to mention the cause of the birds being blown to pieces. We nearly always overestimate range, and most of the time birds are not quite so far away as we would like to believe. My own personal preference is true cylinder in the first barrel, half choke (modified in the United States, i.e., about 0.020 inch) in the other. This choke combination (with the appropriate shot size) will cover most of the situations the shooter will come across with duck, pheasant, grouse, partridge, dove, woodcock, and pigeon shooting up to forty yards.

THE HARD-HITTING GUN

All the pheasant shoots on the large estates in Scotland depended on a good supply of "beaters"—the chaps who line up at the edge of the woods and tap their way with hazel sticks through the undergrowth to flush the birds. There would be twenty ot thirty beaters in a line on each drive, and the idea would be to keep the birds moving in front of this line at a steady pace until they reach a flushing point where they were forced out of the thick cover and over the waiting guns. Ideally, the birds (there could be as many as several thousand) should be released over the guns a few at a time, not all at once.

The estate keepers hold a keepers' day at the end of the season, where the beaters are invited to shoot for free. Beaters are usually all local fellows, and all are self-professed experts on such interesting topics as fishing, ferreting, fighting, the consumption of alcoholic beverages, and pretty ladies. Will was no exception. He was a gardener, mole catcher, and great salmon and sea trout fisherman, and his exploits as a good shot were legendary.

Each season, Will would appoint himself leader of the beaters and turn up at all the keepers' shoots in the Langholm area, invited or not. Unfortunately, Will had a liver and white spaniel (Foxy) with nothing but cotton wool between his ears, and a reputation for insubordination, that would accompany him on the shoots. At the end of each drive, strict orders from the keeper about leashing Foxy would go unheeded, and Will would let the dog have a bit of fun and scatter the birds. Warnings from the keepers about the unruliness of the dog made no difference—Will would bring him anyway—but there was a healthy respect on both sides. Will would boost morale on the cold wet days (there were lots of those), keep the new lads in check, and make sure the beaters' line was in order. In return, the keepers would tolerate the absence of discipline in Foxy, and it all seemed to work well.

Will was a good shot, and on keepers' days, he would delight in showing off. Woodcock that would slip like shadows from under the clumps of bracken would never be noticed by anyone except Will. They would curl back over the line like big brown moths and boom! Another woodcock would be in the bag. Late-season, wily cock pheasants, sitting tight as limpets on an estuary rock as the line approached, would suffer the same fate. As they launched themselves skyward at the last minute, Will would nail them, with remarkable accuracy, as they curled over the edge of the spruce plantations and into apparent safety. Will could certainly shoot, make no mistake.

Now, the lunch breaks on the pheasant shoots were always a time for jovial banter and indiscretions. Inclement weather, hangovers, and unruly dogs would all be forgotten. Always, the subject of who was the best shot would come up, and we would poke fun at the shooting skill of the guns we had seen throughout the season. Will would always be the one who would cast the most aspersions, some bordering on slander.

"D'you see that big guy with the red face? The purple head [anyone with high facial color that was made more intense by cold weather was called a purple head by Will] couldn'a hit the side of a barn if he was shut inside it!" Loud chuckles all round. "And what aboot that skinny guy with the specs? My auld lady could shoot better than him!" More laughter. "Aye, lads, good job I wasn't on one of the pegs with *my* goon! I'd have showed 'em."

"Mind if I look at your gun, Will?" I asked one day. Will handed it to me. It was an AYA no. 3 boxlock nonejector that had seen better days.

"Now *that* goon, laddie, can *hit!*" Will said as he winked at me.

The gun was old, and the flats on the barrels were marked full and full. Will had bought it new when he was a youth for £12 (about $20), and he was now over sixty. Over the years, he has used it for everything from goose hunting on the Solway Firth to fox drives and rabbit hunts. I pushed the top lever open and immediately noticed a sloppiness in the action. On closer examination of the gun, as I peered down the barrels, I was horrified. Both were badly pitted, and they had suffered several dents in the past that had been unprofessionally removed. I tried hard not to imagine how the pellets must have been distorted with their passage through the barrels; the internal dynamics were so appalling. There was no doubt in my mind that the gun was unsafe, and yet Will used it regularly and rarely missed. Despite my later pointing out these defects to him in private, Will, with his genetically engineered Scottish cynicism, no doubt thinking that I intended to persuade him to buy a new gun, dismissed my claims as paranoia. Now, I never had the chance to fire the gun, and if I had, it probably would have been at a distance with the aid of a long piece of string, but I often tried to imagine what sort of pattern it gave. My guess is that the pattern would be both long and wide, a sort of extralong retrochoke effect produced by the poor state of the barrels. This detrimental deformation effect on the pellets is known as bore scrub, and I have seen many guns with barrels so pitted that there is a huge pattern-opening effect as the shot transits. Was this the secret of Will's gun and its hard-hitting capabilities? I have no idea. Will has long since passed over to the happy hunting grounds, and his reputation as an expert shot will always be intact, so we will never know. Come to think of it, though, I never saw Will shoot or attempt to shoot at anything that was more than about twenty yards away, and at those modest distances, I swear I never saw him miss. Perhaps he knew something about the gun that we didn't.

CHAPTER 11

Proof of Guns

PROOF MARKS

Like many shooting men, I have always been a willing victim of the seductive charms of the old Damascus-barreled hammer gun. The first 12 gauge I owned was a double-barreled Charles Boswell with paper-thin barrels of dubious safety margins. There is no doubt that shooting such a masterpiece of elegance and grace from antiquity has a charm and satisfaction of its own, and I offer no apology for this affection with shotguns from a bygone era. However, there is a certain amount of risk associated with using these old guns. Due mainly to the resurgence of interest in English guns, I am often asked about proof marks, and there is no doubt that anyone who is considering buying an English gun should have some prior knowledge of these marks. Proof marks are an extremely complicated subject, and *anyone who decides to invest in an old gun would be well-advised to seek expert counsel before doing so, and certainly before shooting it.* It is always tempting to buy old guns because of the prestige involved in owning a piece of shooting history. But old guns are exactly that, and care should be taken to ensure that the proof marks on them are currently valid. The information given here is merely intended to provide a historical perspective and introduction to the subject. It is not intended in any way as a guide to, much less a guarantee of, safety.

The exact date when it became compulsory to proof firearms in England is unclear. Many gun makers supported compulsory proofing as a way to dissuade or prevent the manufacture of firearms by unauthorized persons, both to protect their livelihood and to protect the general public from injury by the unscrupulous manufacture of unsafe firearms. For years many barrel makers privately proofed their own barrels, and in

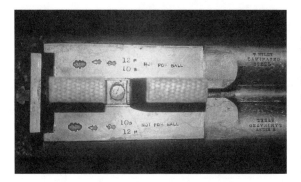

Proof marks were stamped on gun barrels to protect the user from injury due to defective barrels or work-manship. These marks cover caliber or bore size of the weapon, type and quantity of propellant, choking of the barrels, and suitability of the weapon for shot or solid ball.

London, a charter that was granted to the Guild of Gunmakers in 1672 included the power to search premises within a ten-mile radius of London to expose and proof any barrel that had not been made by a reputable manufacturer. To enforce the charter, a proof house was established in London. A similar proof house was later set up in Birmingham in 1813, but it was easy for bogus barrel manufacturers to evade using it. Eventually an act of Parliament was passed in 1868 making it illegal to either make or sell any gun barrel that had not been proved at the Birmingham or London proof houses.

The rules governing proof are lengthy and complex, covering black, cordite, and nitro powders; shotguns; handguns; rifles; and military arms. Since this is a book on sporting shotguns in general, we will deal only with the proof requirements for them. The rules of proof stipulated that for shotguns, there were three kinds of proof: provisional, definitive, and supplementary.

Provisional Proof

Provisional proof is the first proof a barrel is subjected to (and which, according to the complex rules, requires two proofs). It is applied only to new barrels, primarily as a means of showing early signs of weakness and defect in barrels. If this first test is satisfactory, the gun can then be finished and the barrels fitted to the action. If not, it prevents the manufacturer from wasting time finishing and fitting barrels that are defective in some way.

Definitive Proof

Definitive proof is the second test applied to barrels that the rules of proof stipulate need a second proof. This applies to all barrels either "in the white" (unfinished) or finished and fitted to the action.

Supplementary Proof

Supplementary is an additional proof that must be applied after definitive proof. It is for any shotgun that is to be subjected to unusually heavy loads. I'm afraid all this was as complicated as it sounds!

REPROOF

After the original proofing, any gun that is subjected to alteration in any way needs to be reproofed. "Alteration in any way" covers a broad spectrum. Some of the main reasons include:

1. Any enlargement of the original bore, lengthening of the chamber to accept heavier shells, fitting of screw-in chokes, or any repairs to the barrels that would require a heat buildup, welding, or brazing

2. Any repair to cracks, dents, bulges, or pitting

3. Any gun that was to be used for a purpose other than that for which it had originally been intended, for example, conversion from black to nitro powder.

SUBMITTING A GUN FOR PROOF

Anyone can submit a gun for proof in the United Kingdom. However, it is more usual to have this done through a registered firearms dealer, because most old guns require some work before they are presented for

1989 Rules of Proof

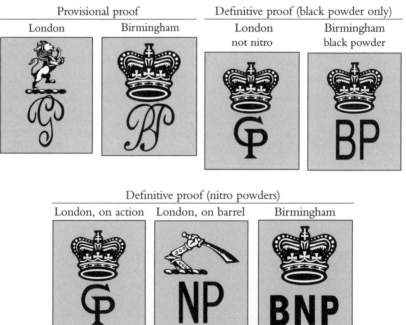

Ammunition inspection		Special definitive proof	
London	Birmingham	London	Birmingham

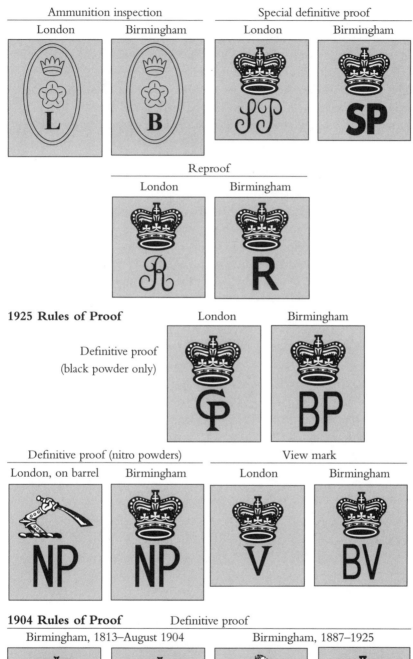

Reproof	
London	Birmingham

1925 Rules of Proof

Definitive proof
(black powder only)

London	Birmingham

Definitive proof (nitro powders)		View mark	
London, on barrel	Birmingham	London	Birmingham

1904 Rules of Proof Definitive proof

Birmingham, 1813–August 1904	Birmingham, 1887–1925

submission. Badly pitted barrels, for example, will need to be measured with a wall gauge to determine the degree of pitting. Actions should be in good working order, and the gun should be "tight on the face." The proof house will usually require that the stock be removed before proof. The proof marks are stamped on each barrel, within about three inches from the breech. The provisional proof mark is stamped on the convex surface of the barrel, and the definitive mark is stamped on the flats.

GAUGE SIZE

The gauge of the gun is also stamped on the barrels at the time of definitive proof. With barrels from 4 to 10 gauge, the size is divided into three separate parts; for example, a 10 gauge would be 10 (which would be the smallest bore) at 0.775, 10/1 would be 0.784, and 10/2 would be 0.793. In gauges from 11 to 17, this is divided into two separate parts; for example, 12 would be 0.729 and 12/1 would be 0.740. A table of bore sizes is shown below. Any barrel that has some degree of choke is also indicated with a letter *C* in a box.

DETAILS OF BARREL ENLARGEMENT SIZES

Bore size	1925 Rules Marking size	1954 Rules Diameter in inches	1986–1989 Metric size in millimeters
12	$^{12}/_1$	.740	18.9 down to 18.2
	12	.729	
	$^{13}/_1$	.719	
	13	.710	
16	$^{16}/_1$	.669	17.3 down to 16.8
	16	.662	
	$^{17}/_1$	.655	
	17	.649	
	18	.637	
20	19	.626	16.2 down to 15.6
	20	.615	
	21	.605	
	22	.596	

CHAPTER 12

The Pathway to Pointability?

I could see immediately what the problem was. The young client, like a lot of youngsters who make the natural progression from the BB gun and stationary targets to scattergun and moving ones, was focusing on his barrels and front bead as he moved the gun in front of the target. Of course the gun stopped every time he did this. We all know that a glance back at the barrels or the bead, however fleeting, is a mistake, certainly not conducive to good shotgunning.

"Don't look at the bead or the barrel, Andrew, look at the space in front of the target where you want the shot to go."

"Bang!" Missed bird.

"Don't look back at the bead or the barrels, Andrew, look at . . ."

"What's it there for then?" interrupted the falsetto voice.

I often wonder just how many times I have been asked that question over the last twenty years or so. So why is it there? Or why, for that matter, does not only the bead but also the type of rib on the gun have an influence on the way we can point it? This is confusing not only for the beginner, but also for many experienced shooters, so let's take a look at shotgun ribs, foresights, and sighting planes.

Shotguns *must* be pointed accurately. The rib guides the shooter's eye to the space in front of the target as he triggers the shot. There are many people who swear that they never see their rib, which I have never fully understood. None of us can deny that there is some degree of peripheral positioning of the barrels as the shot is triggered (although it may be subconscious), and for the majority of us, accurate muzzle perception is important. There must be some degree of visual correlation of the target and muzzle, and this is dependent on several factors—background

Although we should never look at the barrels or bead as we trigger a shot, there is no doubt that the rib influences the acquisition of the muzzle in relation to the shooter's eye as the gun is brought to point of aim. The sole purpose of the rib of the gun is to act as a guide for the eyes in the peripheral vision. Here the difference can clearly be seen with the sighting planes against the contrasting backgrounds of sky (top) and vegetation (bottom) with three guns, the over-and-under, side-by side, and the semiautomatic. In bright sunlight, the side-by-side barrels are almost invisible.

and target visibility against that background are the main ones. We somehow need to position the gun in front of the target, but this must be achieved by what I call peripheral positioning, and nothing else. I always tell my clients that they should *always* be able to see their rib, without actually looking for it. This explanation seems to work in most cases.

Just how much the barrels influence our subconscious aiming has always been a hotly debated subject. Many years ago, English shooting writer Gough Thomas Garwood, who for many years was the editor of *The Shooting Times,* carried out pointability experiments by using a spotlight projector in a shotgun barrel that was aimed in complete darkness at another beam of light randomly projected onto a wall. When I owned my gun shop in Scotland, I carried out similar experiments with the aid of a slim-bodied flashlight that was slipped down into the barrel of a 12-gauge gun and then connected to a snap cap. As the trigger was pulled, the light would come on. In the back room of my gun shop, in complete darkness, a shooting friend would point a similar light at a place on an expanse of wall, and then flick on the switch of another similar light to project a beam of light. I would then quickly try to point at this with my illuminating gun. The results of the experiments in both cases seemed to indicate that although some of the targets were hit by natural coordination in complete darkness, the number of "hits" increased substantially when the same experiment was carried out in daylight conditions. In other words, there is always some degree of sub-conscious aiming involved. Once the hunter or competitive shooter gets into the gun, recognizes the correct target-barrel relationship, and triggers the shot, the rib more or less ceases to be an aiming aid as such. Its only remaining job (in the case of a competition gun) is to diffuse the heat haze that is emitted from the barrels.

Early ribs were put on shotguns to hold them together; it was simply a feasible construction process, and there was no early intention to use them as a sighting aid. Unfortunately, the long-barreled double-guns of two hundred years ago shot low to the mark, a problem that plagued the gun makers of the era. The first person to come up with an idea to correct this low-shooting problem was Joseph Manton (1795–1835), who took out a patent for his elevating rib in 1806. Manton was always thinking up something new, and he was probably the most inventive London gun maker of the early nineteenth century. Joseph, along with brother John, was instrumental in perfecting the double-barrel sporting gun.

The idea for the low-shooting problem was a simple one—the rib was raised where it was attached to the barrels at the chamber end and tapered off toward the muzzle. This forced the user to look over this elevated portion, pitching the gun upward slightly, which in turn had the effect of bringing the muzzles of the gun to where the shooter's eye was looking. The shooter could now better keep birds in view since the barrels did not block his view.

The top ribs of shotguns obviously follow the curves of the barrels, and since barrels are thicker at the chamber end than at the muzzle end, all ribs taper slightly from the breech to the muzzle. Ribs can be Churchill, flat, concave, ventilated, or raised.

The flat, concave, and Churchill ribs are found on side-by-sides. They can be either swamped or straight. A swamped rib means that the rib follows the contours of the barrel tubes, and if you were to place a straightedge along the top, it would touch at the muzzles and breech, but not in the middle. The straight rib is exactly as it sounds—the top is level from the breech to the muzzle. Most live-pigeon guns and hunting

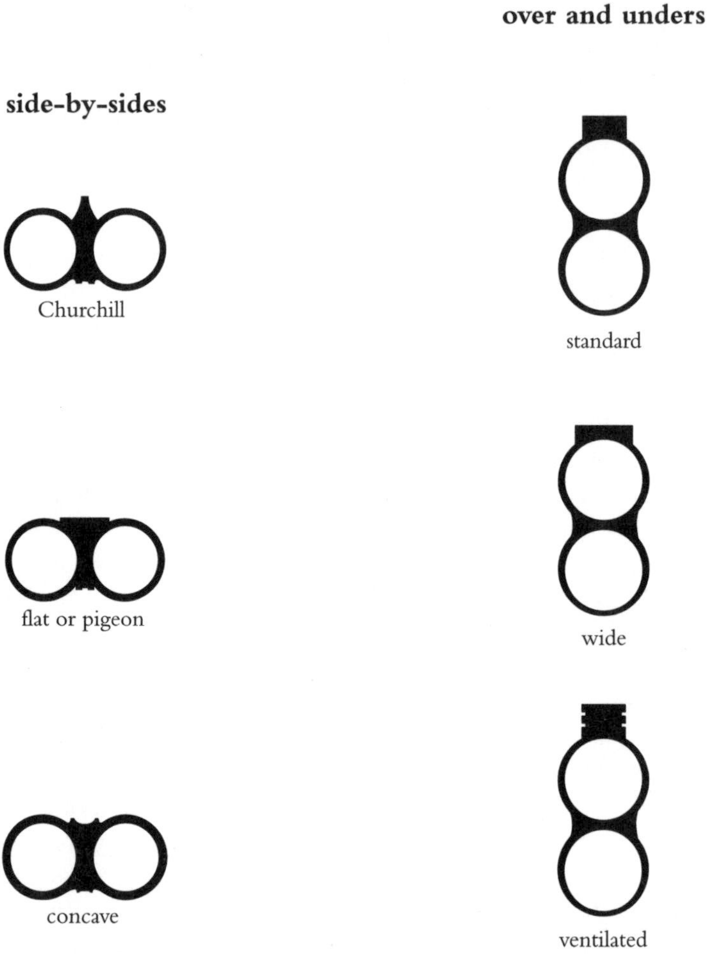

over and unders

side-by-sides

Churchill

standard

flat or pigeon

wide

concave

ventilated

Types of rib. Concave ribs on side-by-sides can be either straight, (where if a straightedge was placed on the top of the rib it would touch at all points from the breech to the muzzles) or swamped (where the straightedge would touch only at the muzzles and breech and be lower or "sagged" in between). The ventilated rib is usually found on trap guns. The mirage effect as the heat waves rise from the barrels can obstruct a clear view of the target. The fins on the ventilated rib help to disperse the heat quicker so that heat waves are reduced.

guns of the eighteenth century had these flat, straight ribs with an antiglare, file-cut surface.

The distinctive high, narrow, flat, file-cut rib, which is often seen on side-by-sides, is called the Churchill rib. Churchill's earlier guns, made in the 1920s, did not have this rib. They were instead the normal swamped ribs of standard width. Normal side-by-sides, with longer barrel length, were susceptible to muzzle flip due to down-flexing, but the shorter barrels of the Churchill XXVs did not have this characteristic. Because of this reduction in down-flip, the XXV was a higher shooting gun. Churchill designed his rib so that it was higher at the muzzle end, and by doing this, the eye was in turn raised above the breech. This gave the user the overall illusion that the barrels were longer. Of course the gun did shoot substantially higher as a result of this raised rib—an advantage on driven birds and rising targets, but a problem on crossing shots. Churchill called the rib the Churchill Narrow Raised Quick Sighting Rib. The thing that confuses me (and many others before me), though, is that although he described the rib as such, he also insisted in that during the act of shooting, the rib should never be seen.

The raised and ventilated ribs are usually found on over-and-unders and semiautomatic guns. The surface of all ribs should be antiglare. A smooth, swamped rib without a machine or file-cut surface is almost impossible to see in bright light. The opposite is true in fading light. Years ago, many Olympic trap shooters would paint the sides of their ribs white or yellow to enhance rib awareness. Many of the old-timer duck hunters I have met on the coastal flats of the Solway Firth in Scotland would rub chalk or a lightly colored wax crayon on the rib of their duck gun. Did it work? Absolutely—enough to make me do the same to mine. Of course, this is exactly the reason why some people can benefit from the fiber-optic Glo-Dots that are popular at the moment. Some people dismiss them as unnecessary and refuse to try them, insisting that they will cause bead fixation. Unfortunately, sometimes people form an opinion on something by listening to others instead of trying something new and forming their own opinion. There is no doubt in my mind that in *some* cases, these sights can be beneficial to *some shooters.*

Several years ago, when these fiber optics first came on the shooting scene, I too dismissed them as a gimmick, until I found myself in the embarrassing situation of wanting to answer a client's question untruthfully, because I had never actually tried one. My argument was the same as others'—that enhancing the barrel is one thing, but enhancing it to the extent that it was sure to detract from our true purpose was a mistake, and that in order to shoot a moving target, we should be looking at the space in front of it as the shot is triggered. So I reluctantly tried one, and you know what? They work. I was pleasantly surprised at how unobtrusive the effect was, while at the same time there was a noticeable, discernable improvement in distinguishing the correct sight picture. Many top-class shooters have bowed to this new technology, and I know

Although many hunters will insist that they do not see their barrels, we always need to see a specific target/barrel relationship by subconscious peripheral positioning as we trigger the shot, if we are to be successful. Here in the low-light conditions of thick undergrowth, the position of the barrels is unclear.

In the same situation, this time with a fiber-optic Glo-Dot on the end of the gun, the position of the barrels is made clearer.

several world-class shooters who swear by it on the sporting clays course, just as others find them a distraction and cannot use them because there is a diversion of focus away from the target. They really do enhance target-barrel awareness, especially for the shooter who really has no idea where his barrels are as he triggers the shot. This is a fundamental problem for many shooters, and in competition situations especially, these beads can solve the basic problem of establishing the correct target-barrel awareness. In competition, if you have no idea where your barrel is when you miss the target, you obviously have no idea where it is when you hit it, either.

There are many other situations where this light sight technology may make perfect sense, for example, heavily wooded hunting situations and dark backgrounds of vegetation of any sort. Surely I'm not suggesting that in deep woods and dense brush, in pursuit of woodcock or ruffed grouse, we should stick a Glo-Dot on the end of our beloved 28-gauge side-by-side? Well, that is exactly what I am suggesting, and I know plenty of people who do just that.

Do I use one? No, I don't, but then I have always had a crystal-clear indication of where my barrels are and do not need to. As I say in chapter 5, on eye dominance, only the guy who triggers the shot knows what he sees or thinks he sees. So if this idea sounds a bit distasteful to you and you just cannot face the sacrilegious act of sticking a high-tech blemish on the end of your gun, perhaps you could do what the old-time duck hunters do and use a wax crayon instead. But think of this: shotgunning has always followed a path of natural progression, whether we like it or not, and I'm willing to bet that in a few more years, in thick vegetation or low-light scenarios, this light sight modern technology will be widely accepted without question. I'm also willing to bet that many hunters will take more birds as a result. That's got to be a good enough reason for some of us to try it.

CHAPTER 13

That Shot-String Thing

Have you ever seen the Tour de France cycle race on the sports channel, where hundreds of perspiring guys pit their physical capabilities against the grueling, undulating terrain of southern France? Sometimes the top guys seem reluctant to blaze a trail for the others and prefer to lag behind the front-runners. What they are doing is using the effects of slipstreaming, also known as drafting, by letting the guys at the front do most of the hard work. Many years ago, a cyclist set a new world record by riding at speeds in excess of one hundred miles per hour. He did it by utilizing the full advantages of this phenomenon by riding in the slip-stream of a large truck. In nature, geese fly in V formation for exactly the same reason: the strongest birds in the skein take the lead, while the younger and weaker birds fly behind with less air resistance to fight.

Many years ago, I spent many happy hours hunting ducks and geese on the Solway Firth in Scotland. During a lull in the activity (somewhere in between fumbling with the top of a Thermos flask with frozen fingers and nudging the dog to make sure it hadn't succumbed to the freezing temperatures), I would absentmindedly watch the huge flocks of Barnacle and Pink-foot geese flying in to the feeding grounds in the early morning. I have often seen the lead gander, buffeted mercilessly by a strong offshore headwind, drop back and change places with the next in command as he tires. So what have Scottish geese and French guys on bikes got to do with shooting? Something known as shot-string effect.

We have seven hundred members at the Dallas Gun Club, so arguments and discussions on the merits of shot patterns and shot-string regularly bubble to the surface. To most of the members, shot-string is one of the topics of conversation that distinguishes the guys who know what

In nature, geese fly in V formation, the strongest birds in the skein taking the lead while the younger and weaker birds fly behind with less air resistance to fight. This is known as slip-streaming or drafting. Exactly the same thing happens with the pellets of a shot column.

they are talking about from the ones who like to sound as though they know what they are talking about. Shooting, and its associated experts (self-professed or otherwise), has always been like that. Most shotgunners know (or think they know) what shot-string is, along with what the effects of shot-string are on successful shotgunning. However, for most of us, it is a huge gray area, and it would not do us any harm to find out more about it.

We have ten skeet fields at the club, and directly in front of these, we have a large lake. On calm days, when there is minimal wind and the surface is like a mirror, this lake has a practical use, and I like to use it to demonstrate to my students the effect of shot-string. I must stress that there is absolutely no scientific relevance here; it is merely a visual demonstration. As soon as a cloud of pellets leaves the muzzle of a shotgun, the shot begins to spread both laterally and longitudinally and develops into a rough sausage-shaped cloud, which is usually more dense at the front than at the back. The greater the distance from the muzzle, the greater the length of the shot-string. The effect of this "stringing" can clearly be seen if a shot is fired into a smooth expanse of water, and from this demonstration, it is obvious that the charge of shot is three-dimensional.

Taking into account that at twenty yards a pattern from a cylinder barrel will be about thirty inches wide, and that obviously (depending on the angle to the surface of the water) there will be some difference between the arrival of the first and last pellets to hit the surface, there is a visually *progressive* difference—the pellets seem to "run out" along the surface. Wayward pellets and "flyers" can clearly be seen as the pattern hits the surface of the water. It is rumored that Lieutenant Colonel Sir Peter Hawker, "the father of game shooting," often used the fast-flowing river test (which would obviously give a better visual demonstration than my expanse of still water), using a river that ran past his ancestral home, for similar demonstrations almost two hundred years ago. It was mentioned in his book, *Instructions to Young Sportsmen in All That Relates to Guns and Shooting,* written in 1814. However, apart from this visual demonstration, there is also an audible one. When shooting from a distance at a steel pattern plate with different loads, there is an obvious *audible* difference between the impact of the first pellets arriving at their target and that of the last pellets. So what causes this, and how can it affect our performance? Perhaps more importantly, is it beneficial to our shooting in any way and in what respect?

Many shotgunners genuinely believe that there is a huge advantage to a long shot-string, and I have been involved more than once in (sometimes heated) discussions concerning the advantages and disadvantages of degrees of choke and the resultant long shot-strings. We all know, for example, that a tight choke gives the advantage of a longer shot-string, doesn't it?

Afraid not. What barrel constriction *will* give is better pattern density, not a longer shot-string. We also know that the first pellets to leave the muzzle of the shotgun will be the first to reach the target, right? Wrong again. Finally, we all know that it is possible to influence the length of the shot-string by the speed of the swing, the sort of jet-of-water-from-a-hose effect, don't we? One of the members was quite insistent that on an overcast day, he could see a "bend" in the shot-string, which was a result of him using a fast gun swing. He is not alone. Many people genuinely believe this. Well, can they? Does the stringing effect of the shot start to occur *inside* the barrel? Once again, simply not true. This effect is an erroneous mental picture and is easily explained. The shot column may be only an inch long as it leaves the gun. The difference in the time interval between the front of the shot column exiting the barrel and the back may be only less than 0.00005 of a second, during which time the gun barrels would have hardly moved, so there is no advantage regardless of how fast the gun is moved.

Extensive tests on the efficiency of gunpowder, the effects of choke, and also patterns, penetration, and shot-stringing were carried out at the public gun trials in London as far back as 1859. These gun trials were carried out at intervals in 1866, 1875, and 1879. Similar trials were carried out in America—the New York trials of 1873 and the Chicago trials of 1874 and 1879. Many of the tests at the London Gun Trials of 1879 were carried out by Mr. R. S. W. Griffiths, who was the ballistics expert for the Shultz Powder Company. Until Griffiths's experiments, the physical properties and effects of the shot-string were a mystery.

Griffiths realized that although shooting a charge of shot at a pattern plate would give a reasonable indication as to the density and effectiveness of the pattern at a specific distance, what it failed to do was give any indication of which of the pellets arrived first and which arrived last. The simple pattern board would not show the overall effect of shot-stringing. Two pellets on the pattern board may be only an inch or so apart, but in reality, as they traveled through the air, they may have been six feet apart or more. Griffiths carried out experiments that involved shooting at a stationary paper target, behind which there was a rotating circular target that was twelve feet in diameter. This target revolved at a specified number of revolutions per minute, and by shooting at this combination of static and revolving targets and then by comparing the two, Griffiths could measure with reasonable accuracy which pellets struck the target first and which struck last. The results of his tests were published in *The Field* magazine and later in *Land and Water.*

Another ballistics experimentalist and early shotgun writer, Major Sir Gerald Burrard, conducted his own tests in 1923 by shooting at a pattern plate mounted on the side of his Model T Ford. Even in those days, long before the advantage we have today with modern technology and photographic evidence, the results of the experiments revealed that the shot-string was considerably longer from the cylinder barrel than from a choke barrel. This is surprising to most people.

Finally, one person who has probably done more experimentation in this field than any other is Bob Brister. Bob is a member of the shooting club that I managed in Houston many years ago. The exploits of Bob and his brave wife, Sandy, who towed a moving pattern board on a trailer behind a station wagon at forty miles per hour while Bob shot it, are somewhat legendary. So just what causes this stringing effect, and is it beneficial in any way?

As soon as the charge of powder in a shotshell explodes, the sudden rapid acceleration from rest exerts a massive pressure on the rear pellets. These rear pellets in turn exert pressure on the next layer, and so on. The front layer of pellets is the least deformed in this process, and the rear layer is the most deformed. The small column of shot then pushes up the barrel until it hits the choke area, where more pellets become deformed as the shot charge is accelerated through the constriction because the outside pellets are deflected inward. Anything that is squeezed from a large diameter to a smaller one is subjected to some degree of acceleration. This is known as the Venturi effect.

When the main mass of pellets is forced through some degree of choke, it causes the center of the shot column to be slightly smaller than the diameter of the bore, and it will hold together better after exiting the barrel. The more choke, the greater the cohesion of the pellets over a longer distance. However, the rear portion of the charge begins to disperse more rapidly, for two reasons. These rear pellets have slightly less velocity, and they are more deformed and therefore aerodynamically inferior to the front pellets, which should be more spherical and therefore less affected by air resistance.

The pellets passing through the cylinder barrel are not deflected inward in the choke area, and the small cylinder of pellets emerges from the barrel more or less intact. As soon as these pellets meet air resistance, a drag effect begins to separate the pellets, and because there is no slightly faster central portion to the column of shot, unlike with the choke barrel, this happens quicker with the cylinder barrel. Air resistance does not act on the pellets equally, but acts more on the deformed pellets and less on the perfect ones. The leading pellets protect the trailing pellets from the effects of this air resistance, and these trailing pellets move along behind the leaders. This is why the slipstream effect occurs, but in order to understand this, you need to have a good imagination.

Try to imagine a perpetually peeling banana. The front part of the banana represents the forward portion of the shot column, and the skin of the banana represents the outer layer of pellets. These pellets, which are in various stages of air resistance, which is directly proportional to the aerodynamic properties and remaining energy of each pellet, "peel off" in stages. The energy of the leading pellets is dissipated as the pellets hit the air resistance, but the pellets *behind* these leaders are shielded by them, which has the effect of allowing them to retain more of their original energy. The second layer of pellets will push aside the first layer and overtake them. They may actually collide with the front pellets as

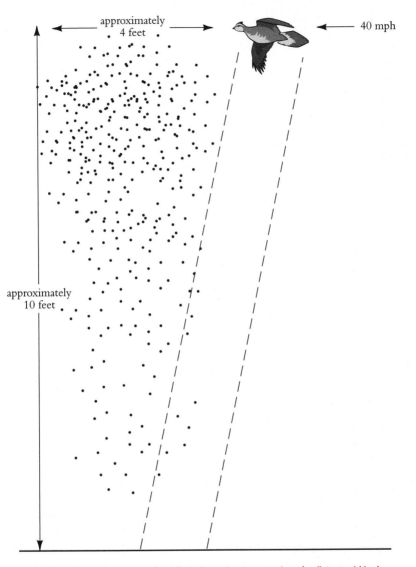

approximately
4 feet

40 mph

approximately
10 feet

Because of the slipstreaming or drafting effect, the main concentration of pellets would be in the front portion of the shot-string. The tail end of the string would contain proportionately fewer pellets and each of these pellets would retain less energy, so a dove flying at approximately forty miles per hour would probably not be hit and killed cleanly.

they do this, and by doing so, they create an even wider pattern and longer shot-string. All this passing and catching up continues until either the pellets strike their target or all their energy is exhausted and they fall to the ground.

The result of all this pushing and shoving, in ballistic terms, is that the bulk of the shot will be concentrated in the front end of the string. It also means that the energy retained by these pellets will be directly proportional to their position in the string; in other words, the greatest concentration of pellets and energy retained by each individual pellet will be in the forward portion of the shot-string. Is this significant in normal shotgunning activities? In bird-hunting situations in the field, with shots at extended ranges, a long shot-string is a distinct disadvantage, and any bird that flies into the tail end of a weak shot-string would probably be merely wounded.

So what conclusions can we draw? Pattern density, especially on crossing targets, is more important than you think, especially in wing-shooting. A long shot-string is produced at the expense of pattern density. Quality shot will produce a more efficient pattern with less stringing, which will in turn ensure cleaner kills. A shot at a stationary pattern board, with softer, inferior shot (although first impressions may be impressive), is always inconclusive. Economy shells may be perfectly adequate on the skeet field or the quail lease, but at extended ranges, these same shells will be inappropriate and should be avoided. What about on the sporting clays course? Because of the complex and varied target presentations, I believe that 99 percent of the targets we miss are missed due to our inability to put the muzzles in the right place as the shot is triggered—in other words, plain old pilot error. I think it would be difficult to prove *conclusively* that shot-string is a *definite* advantage on most of the targets, and the old perception that shot-string is an advantage just isn't true on anything except fairly close targets—twenty yards or so. As I explained in the section on choke, skeet is one of the few situations where shot-string may give a *slight* advantage. A few lucky pellets, on occasion, will retain enough energy to chip the front edge off a full, 90-degree crossing target (as these pellets lag behind the main pattern) on an otherwise lost target. With trap disciplines, straightaway shots, and narrow-angle targets, it is a different story, and this advantage is substantially reduced. For most of our shooting, the length of the shot-string is inconsequential. In the few cases where shot-string does matter, a short one is better than a long one.

CHAPTER 14

Pattern versus Penetration

In my youth, hunting books were my passion. The adventures of the big game hunters in Africa and India were a constant source of amusement for me, and I would read about their exploits over and over again. My favorite was *The Man-Eating Leopard of Rudraprayag,* a true story. The leopard claimed seventy-two victims before the author of the book, Jim Corbett, was able to kill it. The contests between man and beast in those earlier days were more equal than they are today, and a one hundred-yard shot at big game with a black powder rifle was considered a long one.

I owned a collection of these fascinating old books, and in one of them, *Shooting: Its Practice and Purpose,* written by Victorian gun maker J. D. Dougall and published in 1875, experiments that involved shooting conical lead bullets into soft clay showed that (contrary to popular belief in those days) as the velocity increased, penetration was proportionally reduced, down to certain limits. Why was this? The simple answer is that the deformation of the bullet during the early stages of penetration drastically reduces further penetration. From about 1890, the introduction of smokeless powders, the use of jacketed bullets, and other advances in ballistic technology dramatically increased both range and penetrative power of the rifle.

Unfortunately, the same was not true of the humble shotgun; the cylinder-bored shotgun of the mid-1800s loaded with an ounce of shot and black powder propellant gave a range and penetration similar to those of a cylinder-bored modern shotgun with modern loads. Some people still believe that because a small-diameter rifle bullet penetrates better than a large one (because of the deformation-resistant outer jacket), this is also true of the shotgun pellet. Unfortunately, this is not

163

the case, due to several factors. All shot round projectiles have inefficient ballistic properties when compared with a bullet from a high-powered rifle, for example. When these round projectiles are incorporated in a cloud of pellets fired from a shotgun, they shed energy rapidly and string out as they slow down. The greater the distance they fly, the more energy they lose and the more their efficiency is impaired. The ballistic properties of the humble shotgun pellet are pretty inefficient at extended range, as we shall see.

Over the past few centuries, more has been written on the subject of shot penetration and effective pattern than probably any other shooting-related topic, with the possible exception of forward allowance. As the golden age of game shooting reached its zenith in the United Kindgom, *The Field* published a series of articles written by Sir Ralph Payne-Gallwey. In an earlier chapter, I describe later how this great Victorian experimentalist dangled dead pheasants from a kite to determine the degree of penetration of the birds in both vertical and horizontal situations. This was to determine the effect of gravity on the pellets at perpendicular targets. He concluded that there was quite a difference between the extent of penetration on the vertical shots and that on the horizontal shots.

Sir Ralph's inquiring mind did not stop there. In another experiment, he designed an open-ended copper tube that he called a rack. He made saw cuts across this tube and in them placed cards approximately one-fortieth of an inch thick. By numbering each saw and counting the number of cards the pellets had passed through, Sir Ralph could measure the degree of penetration for specific distances and shot sizes. A similar device, called the card rack penetration register, is mentioned in *The Gun and Its Development,* by W. W. Greener. This device used straw board, an early form of cardboard, for the tests and was used at the Chicago Gun Trial of 1879. During this trial, the penetration of the straw boards was compared to the actual penetration of live pigeons and ducks that were placed in cages next to the device. The results were carefully tabulated in true laboratory fashion and contained such gory details as "Bird struck in body but not disabled from flying" and "Leg broken, one pellet in breast, bird could still fly." No doubt, the animal rights activists would have had a field day!

In those days (just as there are today), there were many spurious claims as to the range and penetrative powers of the shotgun. One such story appeared in *The Country Gentleman* magazine in 1903. In it, a gentleman shooter claimed that with a load of forty-two grains of Shultz powder and $1\frac{1}{4}$ ounce of no. 5 hard shot, using his twenty-five-inch-barreled 12 gauge manufactured by W. W. Greener, he cleanly killed two cock pheasants at seventy-five and eighty yards. Ah, if I could only get hold of a gun like that today! Another interesting story claimed that a 24-bore gun, made for a lady and weighing three pounds, shot and killed a fallow deer at a range of twenty-five yards with $\frac{7}{8}$ ounce of no. 7 shot. Very impressive! Presumably, in those days it was considered more sporting to reserve 12 gauges for charging bull elephants!

When I was about thirteen or fourteen, I was already a seasoned shotgunner. I had lots of guns, much to the dismay of my long-suffering mother, who could never understand why I did not play with train sets or have a stamp collection like other kids. Unfortunately for her, my hobbies included guns, fishing tackle, and explosives. Anything else that was not suitably dangerous did not hold my attention for long. Among my "armory" at that time were several air weapons in both .177 and .22 calibers. I could never understand why at the range of about twenty yards, the smaller-caliber .177 could easily pierce a bean can, but the .22 couldn't. The theory of kinetic energy just did not enter my head, and for a long time, I believed that smaller pellets always penetrated better than the larger ones.

But I had an inquisitive and experimental mind, and after reading about Sir Ralph's experiments in his *High Pheasants in Theory and Practice,* I decided to conduct my own shot-penetration tests. My experiments were not as elaborate as his, but there was a certain similarity. I lived in the north of England in those days, and one of the attractions of the area where my friends and I hunted was a high railway viaduct that spanned the Mersey River. We called it the seventeen arches. This viaduct was an impressive engineering feat, a monument of the industrial north, and locomotives carrying coal for the smelting furnaces of the iron and steel industry would trundle daily along the railway track that it carried.

However, the viaduct had an additional attraction. Clouds of pigeons would nest on the brick ledges, and my friends and I would spend hours shooting them in the evening as they flew in to roost. We were all pretty fair shots, but we could never fully understand why a long crossing shot at a pigeon would sometimes be successful, while one at a similar distance but overhead would result in a mere puff of feathers, with the bird flying merrily away. Was the penetration impaired by the effect of gravity, as Sir Ralph had concluded? We had lots of time on our hands during the summer holidays, and we decided to find out. Instead of the rack with the pieces of card, I used telephone directories, which were opened in the middle and hung loosely over a wire coat hanger for the horizontal shots. I would shoot at these directories at varying ranges and with different shot sizes. It was then easy to count how many pages the shot had penetrated. For the perpendicular shots, the directories were dangled over the side of the viaduct at a measured height of 120 feet in a landing net that we used on our fishing trips. This entailed some degree of risk, and the net had to be positioned when there was no danger of a locomotive coming.

It was immediately apparent that the penetration efficiency was directly proportional to the size of the shot and the distance to the target, and the difference in the degree of penetration was remarkable. Now it was not very scientific, I admit, but as a demonstration, it certainly worked. I can honestly say that I did not find a measurable difference between the horizontal and perpendicular shots, unlike Sir Ralph. My results were probably better than his because of the advance in technology in powders and the superior cartridge production processes we have today.

However, apart from the ballistic aspect of these experiments, I did agree with Sir Ralph on something else. All the shots, both horizontal and perpendicular, that I took at the directories were taken by carefully aiming the shotgun (a Charles Boswell Damascus-barreled hammer gun) like a rifle. On the horizontal shots, the muzzle of the gun is flipped up slightly during recoil. This is because the center of gravity of side-by-side shotguns is well below the barrels, and as the gun pushes backwards (providing the pitch measurement is correct) the resistance as the butt of the gun comes into contact with the shooter's shoulder will produce rotation around this center of gravity.

With the more perpendicular, overhead shot, the butt of the gun is positioned completely differently on the shoulder, and as the heel of the stock hits the unyielding bone of the top of the shoulder, it will slide up (or back), which will in turn push the muzzles down. This effect, combined with the vertical flexing of the gun if it is a thin-walled side-by-side, will mean the gun will shoot even lower. This is the likely reason that Lord Ripon, possibly the greatest driven bird shot who ever lived, gave the advice to "Aim high, keep the gun moving, and never check."

Another popular misconception pertains to velocity. Increased velocity gives increased penetration, doesn't it? Not always. In order for a shotgun pellet to penetrate anything efficiently, it needs to keep its shape as long as possible. If the deformity takes place after the pellet has reached its target, for example, if in the early stages of penetration, the pellet hits something that causes it to deform, such as a pinion feather or breastbone, any further penetration is substantially diminished. So if deformity of the individual pellets makes them aerodynamically inferior and opens the pattern considerably, is this a problem? That depends on the range of the target. At very close targets, quail and rabbits in thick cover at ten to fifteen yards, for example, open patterns of small shot work fine. On my first-ever quail-hunting trip in the States, one guy advised that I use size 6 shot because "you can shoot through the bushes with them and still get the quail." Needless to say, I made a mental note never to go quail hunting with that guy!

For competition shooters, here is something else to consider with high-velocity shells. How many times have you heard, especially on the sporting clays course, shooters say that they use faster shells because the increase in velocity will allow them to give the target less perceived lead? Many times, I'll bet. Unfortunately, this isn't the case. With a 7½ shot size shell and a muzzle velocity of 1,350 feet per second, the leading pellets in the shot column would reach a 40-yard target with an *approximate* remaining velocity of 680 feet per second. A shell with a muzzle velocity of 1,200 feet per second would reach the same target with an *approximate* remaining velocity of 629 feet per second. The faster shell would reach the target in approximately 0.127 of a second; the slower shell would reach it in about 0.139 of a second. The difference in the lead requirement (on a 40-yard full 90-degree crossing shot) between a 1,200-feet-per-second shell and a 1,350-feet-per-second shell would be a very humble 7 or 8 inches or, in other words, the distance that the target flies in 0.012 of a second. This very slight advantage is reduced proportionately as the angle decreases. On a narrow-angle shot, the advantage of the lead requirement with a faster shell may be an inch or less. The perceived recoil, however, would be considerably more and, in my opinion, certainly not worth the trade-off. The size of shot at extended range is also something to consider. A 7½ pellet with a muzzle velocity of 1,200 feet/second would take approximately 0.139 of a second to travel 40 yards; the smaller no. 9 shot would bleed off energy faster and take 0.146 of a second. Because of this, a larger shot size will be more effective at extended ranges for both live targets and clay pigeons.

What should be kept in mind here is that in some cases, pellets are badly deformed *before* they reach the target, for several reasons, and effective penetration is once again impaired. Deformed shots are aerodynamically inferior to spherical shots and lose velocity, thus striking power, quicker.

Why does this deformation happen? Softness of the shot used, for one thing. The explosive pressure on the shot charge before it makes it out of the barrel can have a dramatic effect on the eventual efficiency of the shot distribution and the penetrative power of the individual pellets. The plastic shot cup in the modern cartridge plays a major role in reducing deformity still further and identical shells—one with a plas-wad and the other with a biodegradable wad—will often pattern completely differently, despite having equal shot and propellant contents.

Eventually, the penetrative power of the pellets is reduced to such an extent that the pellets retain little of their original striking energy. Another point worth mentioning is that the faster round projectiles accelerate from rest, the faster they decelerate. This is directly proportional to the diameter of the pellet. As an example of this, a no. 9 pellet from a standard 1,200 feet/second shell would be traveling at only 625 feet/second at 40 yards, a loss of almost 50 percent of the initial velocity. A no. 4 pellet starting at 1,200 feet/second would still be traveling at 770 feet per second at the 40-yard range, a loss of only about 36 percent.

So now we have a problem. To be a successful shotgunner, we must find a balance between a load that will retain enough energy in the pellets and one that will retain enough pattern density to execute a clean kill on live game or chip a visible piece off a clay target. Unlike big game hunting, where a single projectile is used, when we shoot at a moving target, we are attempting to intercept it with a cloud of sufficient pellets. Ideally, the shot pattern should arrive at its destination as cohesively as possible, because a clean kill on a target will be dependent upon multiple pellet strikes to ensure success. But these multiple hits must be with pellets that are of sufficient size so that enough energy is retained to penetrate through to the vital organs. As the size of the bird increases, the pellet size must increase in proportion. The pellet size must be large enough to develop enough momentum, so as to retain sufficient energy to penetrate those extra layers of feathers, muscle, fat, and bone. Now I am sure that everyone out there has a share of stories involving evidence to the contrary. For example, we are on a quail hunt and a rooster pheasant explodes from cover like a thanksgiving firework. Up comes the 28 gauge loaded with no. 9 pellets and boom!—down comes the rooster as dead as a doornail. Does this mean that in the future we should use ¾ ounce of no. 9 pellets for our pheasant hunts? I hope not. All a lucky shot like this proves is that within certain limitations, the impact of a large number of pellets can inflict enough damage and dispatch a bird that is far bigger than the bird for which the shot charge was intended. The key words here are *lucky shot* and *large number of pellets.* Usually these shots are flukes, carried out at a distance that is well within the reserves of the penetrative power of even small pellets, and examination of the pheasant would probably reveal that at least one or two had penetrated a vital area.

There must be a balance. This is important. There is no excuse for using the wrong size shot. If the shot size is too large, a clean kill will depend on luck. Too small, and even the best shooters will fail to kill *cleanly consistently* because of the lack of penetrative power. If one of these criteria—sufficient size and quantity of shot—is not met, or even worse, if both are not met, wounded birds will be the result. There is no point in using a cartridge with shot size 8, which would be perfectly acceptable for dove hunting at thirty- to thirty-five-yard ranges, for duck hunting at forty yards plus. There simply would not be enough energy to penetrate through the thick feathers of the bird, the flesh of the bird, and one of the vital organs with enough force to kill. Both these criteria, with live quarry or clay targets, need to be met to ensure a clean kill, and one or two pellets are normally insufficient.

I know that some hunters out there, when cleaning birds for the table, have found that there is an obvious absence of pellet damage, almost as if the birds died of shock. Sometimes birds are brought down with a single pellet in a vital organ, but 99.9 percent of the time this is pure luck and usually results from a pellet that finds a direct route to the brain from underneath, in the throat area, or through the eye socket. By the same rule, as a clay target is launched from the throwing arm of a machine, it is spinning like a Frisbee. One or two pellets may shatter it early in its flight path due to the effects of centrifugal force, but as the clay target slows down and stops spinning, this is unlikely. Also, because of the ingredients of clay targets (pitch and chalk), cold targets shatter easier than hot targets. Here in Texas, in fact, I have picked up targets that have had several pellet holes in them but did not shatter due to the more elastic qualities of the targets. Farther north, trapshooters sometimes switch to size $7\frac{1}{2}$ to break the frozen targets better. There is no doubt that where clay targets are concerned, multiple strikes are necessary to ensure a clean break. As a rule, we can use small shot (no. 9 for example) for close sporting clays and skeet targets, and larger shot (no. $7\frac{1}{2}$, for example), for distant (trap) targets, and do just fine in any temperature.

My first introduction to deformed shot and how it could affect pattern density came many years ago, when, as a youth, I would spend many happy hours on my uncle's farm near Stoke-on-Trent in the north of England. It was considered a big farm in those days, but most of the land and spinneys where I shot wood pigeons as an adolescent have been long since bulldozed and swallowed up in the name of progress. Some of the outlying fields were rough pastureland, gorse bushes, and tussock grass, ideal habitat for that most unfortunate of the English herbivores, the lowly rabbit.

During the summer break, I would spend all my waking hours in pursuit of them, accompanied by my cousin William, two years my junior; two terrier dogs of dubious pedigree; and an old Damascus-barreled Charles Hellis side-by-side that had seen better days. The dogs would hustle the rabbits up, and we would shoot them—sometimes. Anyone who has shot bolting rabbits in thick cover will know what I mean. They don't just bolt; they are jet-propelled, turbo rabbits, as we called them. The shells we used in those days were Czechoslovakian and of doubtful consistency. One shot would leave you wondering whether the charge had even bothered to find its way out of the barrels at all, and the next would leave you with spots before your eyes and an aching head. How those old, paper-thin Damascus barrels must have stretched at times!

Our success rate was not good, and the dogs were losing faith, but one of the farmhands came up with a simple solution. Taking the shot out of each of the shells in turn, he poured the contents onto the black-smith's anvil in the barn and tapped it with a hammer to flatten it slightly. This flattened shot was then placed in the cartridge. The effect on the spread of the pellets was incredible, and the mortality rate of the rabbits rose sharply. Apparently, this procedure was usual among farm workers for increasing the average kill of both rabbits and partridges at close range. It certainly worked, but one thing was apparent, although we hit more rabbits, we certainly didn't kill them as cleanly because the penetration of the shot and the density of the patterns were reduced. I did not know it then, but for years the French and Italians, in an effort to achieve rapid pattern distribution, have been using disc- or cubed-shaped shot, called plomb disco or disparente, to produce more open patterns. Unfortunately, this is achieved at the expense of pattern density.

Years later, when I owned a gun shop in Scotland, I came across another application of the obvious advantages of deformed shot. I had a customer, Archie "Blackie" Nairn, who was a professional rabbit catcher. Rabbits were considered a major pest by the farmers, both as competitors with the sheep for grazing rights and because of their destruction of food crops. Blackie provided a valuable service within the farming community of the Langholm area, and in the spring, he was always busy and much sought after for his ability to rid areas of rabbits.

He used a team of ferrets, purse nets, and a Border terrier called Sid. Any unfortunate rabbit that ran the gauntlet of the ferrets, made it past the purse nets draped over the rabbit burrows, and then managed to avoid Sid, was unceremoniously shot as he bolted, usually at very close range. Blackie always reloaded his own shells, and he bought the powder and shot from me. He would always insist on the old "drop shot," never buying the then-modern chilled (hard) shot. Chilled shot is made with the addition of a percentage of antimony (1 to 6 percent), which makes it harder. Drop shot was pure lead, and sometimes this old shot was difficult to come by, but Blackie simply would not reload with the harder stuff.

Now, Blackie was a man of few words; he would never use a sentence if a single word would do. When he came into the shop one day to collect his powder and shot, I asked him why he preferred the soft shot to the hard. With a puzzled expression, raising his eyebrows as he pulled his wallet (and the odd ferret dropping) from the inside pocket of his old tweed jacket, he replied, "More spread, lad." So that was it. I found out later that Blackie always used a fast-burning propellant, which would rapidly accelerate the shot load from rest as the gun was fired. I dread to think just how much powder he used, but because he made his living killing rabbits, the actual formula for his success was a closely guarded secret. More by luck than a sound knowledge of ballistics, Blackie had stumbled upon a winning combination. The soft shot (which would deform quicker) and fast powder give a much bigger pattern at close range, which worked very well for him.

CHAPTER 15

The Logic of Lead

THOSE EARLY DAYS

"Don't shoot *at* him, laddie! Put t'shot where 'e's *going,* not where 'e's *bin!*" Of course! Why didn't I think of that? Andy McCloud, a gamekeeper on Lord Edgerton's estate, once growled that rather abrupt order at me as I made a hurried, uncoordinated poke at a flushing pheasant. Andy was a giant of a man with a ruddy, whiskered face and an accent as thick as a slice of Granny's haggis. He was a really nice guy underneath his craggy exterior, and my first mentor. He did not suffer fools gladly, and it was always better to heed his advice. Of course, the incident took place many years ago when I was a fledgling shooter, probably at the tender age of ten or eleven. Andy's words must be indelibly etched into my hard drive. I sometimes hear his booming voice and think about him even now when I go bird hunting. He was right, of course. When we shoot moving targets with a shotgun, we are never, ever shooting *at* any of them; we are attempting to place the charge of shot into the anticipated flight path of the target. It sounds easy enough, but apparently it isn't; otherwise, I would be out of business, and there would be no need to publish books of this sort. Very few people are blessed with a natural ability to accurately calculate the amount of forward allowance needed to hit a moving target; the infinite combinations of speed and distance are too complex.

Several decades later, the parameters are still the same, and these days when I shoot, I always attempt to do exactly what Andy suggested. What has changed significantly is the fact that now, with another forty years under my (rather more prominent) belt, I am more successful when I bird hunt because over the last twenty-five years or so I have given a great deal of conscious thought to the science of shotgunning. I have learned to decipher the variables of moving targets and to apply visual logic to them, and I often manage to hit the things that I intend to hit. I have learned to read the line and feel the lead of any target, and when necessary, I have practiced to make it all come together. However, I don't delude myself into thinking it all happens instinctively or that I have progressed to this higher level by some sort of inherent natural ability. I realized long ago that successful target evaluation isn't an inherent trait—it is a skill. We must learn how to do it like any other skill that uses basic hand-eye coordination. My ability to hit the targets successfully today is the result of an intuitive learning process and practice. So here's an inspiring bit of information for you. The *only* reason we miss moving targets with a shotgun is because the barrels are pointing in the wrong place as the shot is triggered. Understanding exactly where we need to point the barrels is the difficult part.

Anyone with a normal physique, good eyesight, and reasonable coordination skills can learn to become a good shot, but to become an *expert* shot requires something more. Elevation to this higher level requires systematic study, and ultimately, our success with a shotgun will depend on our ability to decipher all the variables involved and apply them to each target. What I am suggesting is that natural ability takes us only so far, and this applies to every sport that relies on hand-eye coordination.

How often do we see this with shotgunning? Someone tries his hand at it for the first time and is instantly hailed as a "natural." He applies absolutely no visual logic, he happily swings the gun with gay abandon, and the targets are pulverized, to the amazement of the open-mouthed onlookers. He is blissfully unaware of such mundane things as lead, gun fit, and shot patterns. Then, after this initial success and for no apparent reason, the targets begin to sail by untouched. Frustration kicks in. No matter how hard he tries now, he cannot repeat the performance, and in fact, the harder he does try, the more he misses. The early success was short-lived; in other words, it was little more than beginner's luck.

I have witnessed this scenario hundreds of times in the last twenty years or so. So what now? This is where the "natural" has to think. He needs to achieve mechanical excellence with a gun that fits. He needs to decipher the variables of moving targets, apply a large dose of confidence, and focus mentally. Then he needs to practice to make it all come together. I am sure that golf ace Tiger Woods, tennis star Pete Sampras, skeet champion Robert Paxton, and even the legendary Lord Ripon would all agree with that statement. Don't get me wrong, I'm not suggesting for one moment that for a few there is not some degree of natural ability involved; some people find it easy to point and swing a shotgun, just as some people can hit a baseball or play golf or tennis better than others. The key words here are *few* and *some*. Unfortunately, most of us—myself included—do not fit into that category. I was never one of those guys, and mastery of the shotgun, and my ability to consistently hit targets, was sometimes a difficult, arduous journey. Like losing weight or kicking a bad habit, most of us expect instant gratification—maximum results with minimum effort—and most of us would prefer to believe that there is an easy way to shotgun perfection.

INSTINCT OR INTUITION?

Some people believe that with sporting clays and wingshooting, we should always shoot "instinctively," with no conscious application of lead. For some of the targets, some of the time? Possibly. But for most of the targets, most of the time? I don't agree. However, before all the "instinctive" hunters out there blow a fuse, let me explain. To do something instinctively or subconsciously means to do it *without* the aid of conscious thought. *Webster's Dictionary* defines *instinct* as "a strong impulse or motivation, a natural capability or aptitude." As an example of this, you're having fun playing with the kids in the yard, and suddenly, when you least expect it, one of them throws you a tennis ball. Your hand comes up and you catch it perfectly. Or you're sitting outside and a mosquito lands on your leg. You whack the mosquito without thinking about it. Both were instinctive, reflexive actions, triggered by visual information.

There was absolutely no thought process involved with either movement to enable you to perform them. Even if there were, chances are the action would not be quite as spontaneous, you would not be quite as successful, and the mosquito would live to see another day. By catching the ball and swatting the insect, you are using nothing more than basic faculties provided by nature. This is why we are sometimes successful with a shot at the twenty-yard dove that appears suddenly from behind the tree, or the rabbit target that hops unexpectedly on the sporting clays course.

Unfortunately, this is not what most shotgun shooting is about. Consistent shotgunning is a combination of subconscious, repetitive, athletic motion and accurate computation of visual logic. That's a mouthful, but let me explain. Our mount and swing, for example, should be practiced repetitively, like any new motor skill, until we have acquired muscle memory and can do it spontaneously without thinking. But the application of lead is not a motor skill, and the variables that we encounter when shooting moving targets are so infinitely complex that subconscious application is impossible if we are to be consistent.

Ask any bird hunter what he would like to achieve, and the answer is always consistency. Final answer? Absolutely. It is the same with the sporting clays shot. With sporting clays, high scores, which we strive for when we shoot in competition, are the product of consistency. However, if you are convinced that you always shoot instinctively, and more importantly, if you are happy with your shooting ability and stroke birds out of the sky with a confident flourish, maybe the remainder of this chapter isn't for you. However, if you *really* want to improve your average at sporting clays and wingshooting, read on.

THE LOGICAL SOLUTION

The laws of physics dictate that in order to hit any moving target, we must direct the shot charge in front of it. Over the decades that I have been a shooting instructor, I have become increasingly amazed by the number of people who are convinced that there is a simple, foolproof way to use a shotgun and apply lead to a moving target without any conscious consideration for the variables involved. Some of these people also believe that shooting requires no formal training to become accomplished. After all, grandpappy was a good shot, so why should I need lessons? Most adult males who shoot, or *think* they can shoot, suffer from a form of neurosis when it comes to taking instruction and conveniently forget some of the key issues. Don't forget that grandpappy often succeeded out of necessity and that most valuable commodity—experience. A McDonald's or a suitable convenience store wasn't around the next corner when the grumbling in his belly reached the serious level.

As I said at the start of this book, the so-called natural shot is a mythical beast. Just like the unicorn, there is no such animal. Everyone can learn to become a better shot with quality instruction, but some guys try hard to convince themselves that they do not care. These same guys, after a disastrous day pursuing the gray speedsters, trudge wearily back to the truck like condemned men, tired, despondent, with hardly enough energy to put one foot in front of the other. You would hardly recognize the same guys after a good day when they have shot their limit. There is a spring in their step and their chests are puffed out like a rutting rooster pheasant for a week. So who's kidding whom?

The thing that defeats more shotgunners than any other is how much lead or forward allowance we must give a moving target. I have had too many conversations over the years with too many clients who insist that they never see lead—they always shoot right at the bird, clay target, or whatever. Now, with over twenty-four years as a shooting instructor under my belt—older and wiser, perhaps—I don't rise to the bait. Why? Sometimes these conversations are frustrating and futile for me because I have no idea what people see as they trigger a shot; only they know.

Our ability to successfully intercept moving targets is dependent on accurate evaluation of all the variables involved. Think about a quarterback who is making a running pass to a receiver. Does he throw the ball at the receiver? Of course not. He directs his throw in front of the receiver so that it can be collected smoothly. Before he throws the ball, he evaluates the variables of angle, speed, and distance. The visual stimuli (ocular information) that his brain has received is rapidly converted into physical effort to place the ball into the correct place in front of the receiver, so that the pass can be collected smoothly. His ability to place the ball accurately is based mainly on what he has learned in the past and on practice.

It is the same in hunting situations with a shotgun. The specialist dove or duck hunter triggers his shot when it *looks right to him.* The decision to do this at exactly the right moment is based on an accumulation of knowledge, which in turn is based on an accumulation of data that he has retrieved from the depths of his memory bank. The only difference between the quarterback and the guy with the gun is the use of the gun as an intermediary and the necessary adjustment of timing. The visual logic that both need to apply is similar. With the quarterback, however, his teammate can either slow down or speed up to synchronize the move. Unfortunately, clay targets and flying birds do not allow us such a luxury, so we need to get it right the first time.

Now, this next part may surprise you. The most ridiculous advice that I have seen in how-to articles is that we should always look at the leading edge of the target or the beak of the bird. I read it all the time in magazines and books. The writers suggest that we should concentrate 100 percent on the target (they often say with a hard focus on the target) *as the shot is triggered,* because our subconscious mind is actually deciphering all the variables so that we "instinctively" put the shot column precisely where it needs to go. These same writers suggest that even when the lead requirement is several feet or more, the eyes should remain focused on the target. Really? Well I for one do not do that; neither do many of the experts that I talk to. In many shooting situations, this advice is misleading and has about as much relevance as keeping your eye on the ball has to do with flower arranging or needlework.

These same people will then engage in lengthy discussions on the importance of gun-mounting procedure and good gun fit, and tell us that if the gun fits, it will shoot where we look. Correct. Very few of us would have a problem with that statement. So if, as we trigger the shot, we are looking at the leading edge of the target, or the beak of the bird, or whatever, where does the lead bit come in? By magic? By devine intervention? We are never, in any situation, shooting at the target, and I never encourage my students to apply this sort of illogical visual approach. Even the straightaway trapshot is rising and then falling, and each target requires a different sight picture.

I know that in some cases our shot pattern is wide enough to compensate and save the day, but this "look right at the bird" approach is misleading and will always result in a lot of missed targets. Even worse is the fact that some devotees of "instinctive" shooting take this approach a step further and suggest that if the intrepid bird hunter dares to even *think* about applying visual logic and lead, he has committed one of the cardinal sins and will miss. They say that we should not only focus on the target, but also *shoot* right at it. I know a lot of these guys. They say convincingly: "If I don't think, I hit; if I do think, I miss."

Everyone out there has their favorite story about old Instinctive Harry, who is an incredible shot, always strokes birds out of the sky, never misses and never thinks. Over the last twenty-five years or so I have shot with lots of these guys (who have never had a lesson in their lives) many times. The strange thing is that they always seem to have a bad day when I'm around. It's the shells, the gun, the weather, or the sausages they had for breakfast, and after they are in the bar at night and have had a few beers, they always seem to remember that they hit more birds that day. It's a bit like the gambling man. Everyone knows when he is on a winning streak, but nobody hears about his losses.

Some of these "instinctive" clients that come to see me are reasonable shots. Unfortunately, none of them are expert wingshooters or world-class competition shots, because they are never consistent and their success with a shotgun is patchy. There is the difference. Some of these same guys will also (often proudly) tell me that they *never* see their barrels as they trigger the shot, as though it is strictly taboo to do so. Later, when enjoying a beer at the gun club or during a lull in the activity in the duck blind, these same guys will engage in lengthy discussions on the visual merits of this rib or that rib, sighting planes, and the like.

Years ago, with clients who would tell me that they never see their gun as they shoot, I would ask them to focus on a distant object, a tree or cloud, for example. Then, while maintaining this focus on the object, I would ask them to mount their gun and ask them again what they see. Obviously, the answer should be the object in focus and the barrels in their peripheral vision. Some of them would still swear that even though the barrels of their gun were central to their line of vision, they would not see them as they triggered a shot.

To me, this was amazing, because I am always aware of my barrels as I shoot. I also know this: the only way we can be consistently successful at shooting moving targets is to have a good realization of where our barrels are, using our *peripheral* vision, as we trigger the shot. Otherwise, how can we direct them onto the target line? There is no doubt in my mind that the best shots see a perfect target-barrel relationship every time they pull the trigger, and it does not matter if the target is a dove, duck, pheasant, or goose in the field or a clay pigeon on a sporting clays course or skeet field.

Many attempts have been made to rationalize ways to apply lead, and over many decades, countless pages have been written on the subject. Sustained lead, swing-through, and pull-away are the main contenders. These three all require a visual awareness of the target-barrel relationship as the shot is taken. Probably the man who came closest to convincing everyone that there really was one foolproof method of applying lead that would triumph over all the others was Robert Churchill. His method was the famous English or "instinctive" shooting method, and for many years it was the preferred one (sometimes the only one) taught at the majority of the shooting schools in England. Bird hunters sometimes use this shooting method today. The success of the method depends entirely on basic hand-eye coordination and a smooth follow through; the speed of the gun builds in the necessary lead. Does it work? Sometimes. According to Churchill, his method was so superior to every other that there was never the slightest hint of a suggestion of lead or forward allowance necessary, and it all happened magically, but just how effective was it? We shall see.

Several decades ago, I read Churchill's book *How To Shoot* and Churchill and McDonald Hastings's *Game Shooting*. In those days, driven pheasants were unattainable for me, driven grouse even more so, and most of what I read was decidedly vague and more than slightly confusing. Recently and quite by chance, in a used book store, I came across a copy of *The Shotgun,* by McDonald Hastings (Robert Churchill's biographer), and I welcomed the chance to read once again the theory of allowance by eye and the instinctive shooting method. In chapter 14, entitled "The Shooting School," I was once again inextricably caught up in the many inconsistencies of the method, and although I dissected each section slowly, paragraph by paragraph and then sentence by sentence, I was still baffled; the only result for me was bloodshot eyes and a headache. I am not alone with my observations. Over the years, Churchill's theory of allowance by eye has often been a source of bitter controversy among shooters.

Churchill's method was an integrated system of gun mounting, or drills, as he called them. He maintained that with the swing of the gun and total concentration on the target, the brain would rapidly compute all the necessary variables and that it was capable of doing all this *subconsciously:* "Allowance is needed, but it is no business of your brain. The secret is to regularize your movements and mount the gun properly to your shoulder so that hands and eye coordinate. Apparently you will be shooting straight at the bird but unconsciously your brain will be making all the necessary forward allowance." (*The Shotgun,* David & Charles, 1983, p. 176).

I agree with the bit about mounting the gun properly to your shoulder, but I'm afraid that is all. The rest is hard to swallow and as full of holes as Swiss cheese. According to Churchill, the gun should be mounted at a speed equal to that of the bird, and if the bird is a slow incomer, the forward allowance would be slight. With a fast crossing shot, and the gun moving in unison with the bird once again, the speed of swing would be increased and the amount of lead proportionately greater. The shot is triggered as the gun comes into the face. Regardless of the speed of the bird and, more importantly, the *range* of the bird, the shot should be taken when the barrels are pointing *at the bird,* and Churchill was quite clear about this; there should never be any conscious application of forward allowance.

Also in the book is a section explaining how important it is for the shooter to diagnose where the shot charge went so that it could be rectified on the next shot, if the first was unsuccessful. In other words, if the miss were behind, some sort of remedial action should be taken to shoot farther in front. Subconsciously. Now, maybe I'm missing the point, but if the shooter has no conscious indication of how much lead he sees as he triggers the shot, how does he know where he missed? There is also a section in the book on calculating range. Why would this be important if the shooter should be doing everything subconsciously? There are many more astonishing inconsistencies.

I have no idea why so many hunters worship at the altar of this so-called "easy to apply" method, or why they have as much credulity on the subject as they do. Even now, I suspect that there is an army of devoted Churchill followers out there who are baying for my blood and insisting that when they hunt, no matter how fast the birds are or how far they are, they always shoot right at them and down they come. So, are there actually intelligent people out there who are gullible enough to believe that it is possible to shoot a moving target with the barrels pointed right at it and a gun speed that is equal to the speed of the target and still hit it? Apparently so. These same people will probably suggest that I am mistaken, that I (and many others before me) have misinterpreted the basic fundamentals of the method.

One of these "instinctive" shooters came to see me recently. He was a prominent businessman in the Dallas area, and he had recently returned from a disastrous driven pheasant shoot in the United Kingdom where he had trouble with long crossing targets. When I asked him to shoot a few off the high tower, he was well behind all of them. The conversation went something like this:

"You're a long way behind these. When you shoot the next one, double your lead."

"Lead? Oh, I never see lead! I just swing the gun and pull the trigger; I manage to hit some of 'em. I always shoot *instinctively*," he said proudly. But he was missing the targets, so we had a problem. I tried again.

"OK, how about instinctively shooting a bit farther in front of the next one?" The only response to this remark was a blank expression. Joking aside, it isn't easy to double the lead if you never saw it in the first place.

On high driven birds and long crossing shots, the lead requirement does not happen instinctively or subconsciously. The only way we can apply the correct amount is by using the bird as a moving reference point and seeing some daylight as we trigger the shot. Don't confuse this with "measuring," which it isn't. It is just a way of indicating to the shooter where his shot charge needs to go. The eyes, if your gun fits you, should do all the work and put the pattern where you look. Need more lead? Look farther in front. How far in front? That's the problem. At long ranges, a conscious gap needs to be established. Over the last twenty years or so, I have had to deal with clients who take a lot of convincing as to just how far in front they need to be, until I get them to stand behind me on a long-range, full-crossing shot and show them. They just cannot believe how much is needed. The difference between the lead on a forty-yard shot and that on a fifty-yard shot is mind-boggling, and with any target that is at the edge of this range, the shooter needs to initially mentally override his computer until he becomes more familiar with the amount needed. Most experienced wing hunters and, without doubt, all experienced clay target tournament shooters must cultivate this awareness of where their barrel needs to be pointing in relation to the target as they trigger the shot; and it does not happen subconsciously if they are to be successful.

So just why did the instinctive method command such a following? I believe Churchill succeeded largely because of aggressive marketing and the publication of a small book written by him in the 1920s. There is no doubt that when push comes to shove, there was absolutely no scientific knowledge or application of the laws of physics attached in any way to his method. The only reason that the Churchill method succeeds sometimes on some targets is because of the application of one of the laws of kinetics—momentum.

In fact, you might like to try this simple experiment. The next time you are near an expanse of shootable water, throw something out at a distance of about twenty yards. A stick is ideal. Next, swing your gun along an imaginary line through the floating stick, and pull the trigger as you come up to it, in other words, when the muzzles of the gun are pointing straight at it. Due to something called shooter reaction time (which is the combination of neurological, physical, mechanical, and ballistic periods), the bulk of the shot charge will hit the water past the stick.

Shooter reaction time is simply the time it takes the brain to process the neurological/optical information it receives signaling that the time has come to pull the trigger, the time it takes the signal to get from the brain to the finger instructing it to pull the trigger, and the time it takes the muscles of the trigger finger to react and pull the trigger. There is additional delay because the trigger must then disengage the sear and allow the hammer to fall, which in turn strikes the detonator (these together being known as lock time), which in turn ignites the main charge. The propellant then explodes, and the resulting buildup of gas pushes the shot charge out of the barrel. The combined time for all this (shooter reaction time, lock time, and the time it takes the gasses to expand enough to push the load out of the barrel) may be only one-twentieth of a second, but in that time, the barrel will move forward and no longer be pointing at the stick.

Since the barrel's point of aim is moving and the floating stick is not, in that one-twentieth of a second, the point of aim will move past the target. The faster you swing, the farther past the stick the shot will hit, even though you perceive yourself as firing when the barrel is pointed directly at the stick each time. This is where the built-in forward allowance comes from. Swing the gun fast, and you have more built-in lead. Swing the gun slow, and you have less built-in lead.

However, if a certain amount of forward allowance can be established on a *stationary* object by relying on speed of swing and shooter reaction time, than on a *moving* target, the gun *must* do one of two things:

1. Move considerably faster than the target to establish any forward allowance at all (in other words, the Churchill swing-through method).

2. Keep pace with the target and be held out in front of it by a predetermined amount until the shot has left the barrels (in other words, the sustained lead technique).

Churchill realized that the hand is quicker than the eye and that acceleration in the final stage of the mount and shooter reaction time do the rest. The success of the method is totally dependent on these two things, and the inconsistencies are explained in more detail in Chapter 8.

This is why the Churchill method works for some shooters, sometimes, and why it is often the preferred method for some people when hunting in the field—the sudden appearance of the bird triggers the reaction to it, and the resultant rapid gun speed and momentum of the barrels do the rest. There are two main drawbacks, however: first, as I have already mentioned, birds (or clay targets) do not always fly in straight lines; second, the human body tends to move the easiest way. Produce too much momentum in the barrels, and you will be committed to a specific line. If the target is not flying on that line, you have problems. You can often see this happen clearly with a late shot at the second target of the double from station 6 (the high-house target) on a skeet field. If the first target (low house) beats the shooter and this target is shot late, there will be rapid acceleration in the muzzles of the gun in an attempt to catch up to the second target. This will in effect produce the equivalent of a pure Churchill move. There will be no choice but to attempt to shoot this second target well past its transitional phase (where it is dropping slightly), and the shot will often pass harmlessly over the top.

The second problem is that at extended ranges, where there is a progressive slowing down of the shot charge after it has left the gun, the method will favor the guy with the slow reaction. The person with lightning reflexes will shoot behind every target unless he can dramatically increase his gun speed. Although the Churchill method can be used with great success in some wingshooting situations, in competition it is hopelessly inconsistent, because of the difficulty in producing the exact speed of swing on two identical shots. Perception of lead varies as gun speed varies.

About now you might assume that I am completely opposed to any form of instinctive shooting, but you would be wrong. The basic principles of the Churchill method work well in certain circumstances, and it can often be applied successfully at ranges out to twenty-five yards, particularly situations which require reflexive, spontaneous shooting. Quail hunting is a good example of this, and in these situations, a conscious application of forward allowance is usually unnecessary.

The scene is a group of quail hunters in a mesquite-filled gully somewhere in western Texas. Suddenly, with a whir of startled pinions, a covey of bobs explodes like a Thanksgiving firework. As they enter the peripheral vision of Mr. Reasonably Competent Shotgunner, he decides that they are fair game, and the gun comes up and two of the birds drop out of the sky with puffs of feathers. His reaction to the appearance of the quail was a spontaneous one, and the shots were made apparently without the aid of conscious thought. Mr. RCS had no idea why he hit the birds, how much lead he gave them, or even exactly where they were when he pulled the trigger. Sound familiar? The gun seems to have a mind of its own, reacting independently from the man who carries it. Quiet confidence trickles over Mr. RCS like warm maple syrup over an IHOP pancake, and at the end of the day, he puts more birds in the bag than his buddies. The successful shots he made were surprisingly uncomplicated and, dare we say it, almost easy? But most quail are shot at fairly close range and are not traveling nearly as fast as the illusion of their rapid wing beats gives. The sudden appearance of the bird in the peripheral vision is enough to trigger a response to push the muzzles in the direction of it; the momentum of the gun and follow-through do the rest. With shots like these—narrow flight angles, a fast-handling gun, and a wide shot pattern—the circumstances are very forgiving, usually enough to produce the desired outcome and save our bacon. This is the essence of the Churchill shooting method.

But hold on a minute. Didn't Churchill suggest that the success of his method depended on the purchase of one of his fast-handling twenty-five-inch-barreled guns? Yes, and he sold more than a few of them. Did they work? A fast-moving gun was certainly an advantage to the success of the method, and there is no doubt that by the law of averages, some people could use one with success some of the time. While we are on the subject of fast-handling guns, didn't the inspiration for the Churchill XXV actually come from the United States? Absolutely. The first short-barreled guns that Churchill's company produced were never intended for the U.K. market but were shipped to the United States in the 1890s for use on bobwhites in the Deep South. So we have established that at modest range and narrow angles the Churchill method should work.

Now let us return to Mr. RCS. He is elevated, from that day forth, to the ranks of a great "natural" shot. He is the guy with superior hand-and-eye coordination skills, the guy that all the wingshooters talk about in hushed whispers and throw admiring glances at when he walks into the room. However, sometime later Mr. RCS and his buddies are duck hunting. As a flock of teal comes screaming over the bayou mudflats like skirmishing Mig fighters, the gun comes up, but this time the outcome is different. Three shots, no teal down, and throughout the day Mr. RCS often fails to connect. He blames his failure on thinking too much.

I have witnessed this scenario hundreds of times over the last twenty years or so. It is one of the main reasons why wingshooters who are normally reasonable shots at *short range* game birds show only moderate success when first introduced to birds at any sort of extended ranges. The explanation is simple. Some people have a natural ability to point a shotgun better than others, in exactly the same way that some of us can hit a baseball, or play tennis or golf better than others. For these so-called natural shots, reliance on instinct may come very easily, and they succeed because of this and nothing more. Eventually, however, any natural ability we have takes us only so far, and then we need to harness it so that we can use it to our best advantage. I know lots of guys who have never had a lesson in their lives, and they are excellent shots on some things, but fail miserably on others. A snap shot at a quail, for example, can be instinctive. Pass-shooting high geese is not and needs a more conscious approach.

Think about the lumbering Canada goose that looks as big as a plane and seems to be hardly moving. His methodical wing beats give us the illusion that he is slow, but he can bowl along all day at forty-five miles per hour, and he is even faster with a strong tailwind. He will need a lot of lead, make no mistake. What about the white-wing dove that cruises the hot thermals of a Texas breeze at forty yards plus? He might be doing in excess of fifty miles per hour and need nine to ten feet of lead. Then there is the canvasback duck that tops the cypress trees and comes plummeting into the bayou like a Harrier jump jet. He could be touching sixty miles per hour and need even more lead.

All these shots are very different from shooting pointed quail. At extended ranges, I can assure you that it is impossible to swing the muzzles from behind the bird fast enough to give enough forward allowance and remain in control. Even if we could, this huge amount of momentum in the barrels would produce muzzle movement in a straight line, and birds do not always fly in straight lines.

To illustrate this point better, a mile down the road from where I lived in Scotland was Westerhall Estate and some of the best driven pheasant shooting in the world, and I would sometimes load for the visiting guns. Many of them, very familiar with the instinctive method (the only method taught at the shooting schools of the south of England at one time) would find the birds impossible to hit until I explained that they should see a lot more daylight as they pulled the trigger, especially on the crossing birds. Just exactly how much daylight? Well, a quick calculation reveals that if the pheasant was flying at forty miles per hour and was forty yards away, the lead requirement would be at least seven to eight feet. Extend the range to the maximum, about fifty to fifty-five yards, and we need at least fourteen to fifteen feet.

Many of the shooters who had been taught the instinctive method, finding their performance hopelessly inadequate at these long-range pheasants, would resort to a quick "flick" of the gun at the end of their swing in a desperate attempt to put the gun farther in front of the bird. Unfortunately this "flick" would often pull the gun off-line, and a miss either to the left or right of the overhead bird would be the result. Try it for yourself if you like, but I can assure you that it is impossible, with a bird doing this speed and at this range, to move the gun fast enough (and remain in control), pull the trigger as the muzzles point straight at it, and still connect. Also, don't forget that at extended ranges we must build in extra angular lead to compensate for the progressive slowing down of the shot charge. With this type of shot, we need to develop a conscious awareness of the lead requirement if we are to connect.

Still don't believe me? Well, let's forget about the Pinnochio factor for a minute and ask for hands up by all the guys out there who have given the leading drake in a flock of mallards a barrel, only to see the third bird in line fold as neatly as a Scotsman's wallet? See what I mean? This type of shot requires a conscious application of lead, and people who tell you otherwise are mistaken.

Long before Churchill, the physiology of shooting was accurately stated by Dr. W. J. Fleming in a letter to *The Field* on February 19, 1887. There were two shooting methods in those days—holding on, which was basically swinging the gun and shooting right at the bird; and holding ahead, which was sustained lead. Dr. Fleming concluded that holding ahead was without a doubt the more consistent of the two methods. There have been many others since then who would agree with him, among them Major Sir Gerald Burrard and Gough Thomas. I am decidedly in Fleming's camp.

Churchill promoted his method so adroitly that even today there are people out there who are completely convinced of its unquestionable success, regardless of the evidence to the contrary. Unfortunately, there are still people who try to cash in on the success of the method as though it is infallible, and even more unfortunately, there are people out there who are gullible enough to part with huge sums of money to learn to shoot using it. I often see shooting schools and instructors advertising "English instinctive method taught" and "Churchill method taught" as if the method is the Holy Grail of wingshooting. Well, it certainly is not infallible, or even the best way to intercept moving targets with a shotgun, although as I have said, it is useful in *certain* situations in the field. One indication of the method's limitations is that none of the top competition shooters use a Churchill move in any way, shape, or form to shoot skeet, trap, sporting clays, or anything else.

Over the years, I have been in the privileged position to be able to talk to thousands of people who are superb shots, both world-class competition shots and accomplished bird hunters. Do they shoot without consciously seeing the lead? Absolutely not, and I never do. So unless the pure Churchill-style shooter is content with being restricted to shots that require little or no lead, sooner or later he must be prepared to develop a personal awareness of how much forward allowance he needs on every target. I have no doubt that he will connect with more birds as a result.

THE EYE OF THE BEHOLDER

The last century or so has seen the invention of many gimmicks, gadgets, gizmos, and spurious claims from self-professed shooting experts that, if we are gullible enough to believe them, will give all shotgunners an easy, quick way to become accomplished shots, painlessly and with minimal effort. Even as I write this chapter, I see that there is another so-called shooting instructor who has come up with a "magic sight" in the shape of a small orange clay target, which slides in and out and fixes on the side of the shotgun. The idea is to line the sight up with the moving target at a predetermined range, trigger the shot, and pulverize the target, and shooter instantly becomes a skeet champion.

There was a similar device on sale in the United Kingdom many years ago that consisted of a small wire ring that attached to the side of the gun. All you had to do was estimate the range, put the pheasant or duck or whatever in the center of the ring, and pull the trigger. Ingenious! I even remember one of my shooting friends turning up at a shoot with one. By lunch time, it was relegated to the bottom of a muddy ditch, but not before the rest of us had almost died of laughter. So let's spell it out: these gimmicks, all of which are guaranteed to give instant results and gratification, have been around for years and bob to the surface like a cork in a barrel occasionally, but unfortunately, none of them work. There is no easy way. Lead or forward allowance is in the eye of the beholder, and no two people see it the same. The ability to trigger the shot at just the right time, regardless of the shooting method used, only comes with practice. For those of you who shoot sporting clays, if a shooter does well on a station that his buddies had a problem with, what is the first thing his buddies ask as soon as he steps out of the cage? You guessed it—how much lead did he see? Unfortunately, relying on others is not the answer, but how often do we see this happen at a sporting clays tournament? Plenty of times, I bet. I guarantee that you will not hear many top shooters ask anyone how much lead they saw. Alternatively, you are sitting in a ditch pass-shooting high speckle-bellies, and the successful guy in the next blind shouts over, "Lead 'em by a suburban." Of course you don't need his advice (you're just as good a shot as he is), but you try extending your lead by a couple of barrel lengths just in case, and guess what? Down comes a fat white-fronted goose. In just the same way, there are always plenty of guys with shooting instructor syndrome who are willing to volunteer free advice, you know, the "you're over it," "you're under it," "give it three feet,"or "you're in front" guys who mean well but usually don't help. I call this the woodpecker complex. Absolutely the last thing you need when you are missing targets is some guy pecking away at your eardrums offering you his free advice.

Pretty ladies are always magnets for woodpeckers. A fellow is hunting ruffed grouse deep in the forests of New England. As he strolls along, enjoying the scenic solitude of his surroundings, he spies a very attractive female hunter coming the other way. Birds are scarce, and as they stop to exchange pleasantries, the lady notices that the hunter has a large compass dangling from his belt.

"What's the compass for?" she asks.

The intrepid hunter explains that once, after a long walk and as nightfall approached, he became hopelessly lost. The compass was a safeguard to prevent this from happening again.

"Don't you ever worry about getting lost?" he asks the lady.

"Oh no!" she replies. "If I *do* manage to get lost all I have to do is fire a couple of shots in the air, and as if by magic, guys appear from behind the trees saying, 'You're behind it!' 'You're over it!' 'You're under it!' It works every time."

Individual target analysis through experience is the only way. You will get out of this game no more than what you are prepared to put in. Moving targets are, well, *moving*. Don't get me wrong—the ability to calculate the amount needed for successful interception is lacking for everyone at some point in their shotgunning career, even good shots. But make no mistake, the person who takes the time to *learn* to decipher all the variables and evaluate targets correctly is the one who will eventually develop into the best shot.

Many people are hopelessly inconsistent in the field because they cannot apply specific leads. For example, take the guys who insist that they must use a rapid swing-through method in wingshooting. I have no idea why they do this, and when I see it with my own eyes in the field, it always puzzles me. When a bird presents itself from a distance, they let it come, pass them, and then swing the gun rapidly through it in a desperate attempt to connect with it. Why? I have no idea. If the bird in question is a white-wing dove or something else speedy, the amount of gun movement required to catch up is considerable. Instead of a swing, they take a "slash" at the target, and in most cases the shot will be a miss.

These guys are one variant of what I call poke-and-hope shotgunners. They have no idea how much lead they need or roughly how far away the bird is, and they are content with a ragged poke in the hope that they will connect. It is never easy to hit fast incomers, but it can certainly be made a whole lot easier if we try to cultivate a mental awareness of how much forward allowance is needed to connect when the bird is still well out in front, instead of trying to take it as it passes at full throttle.

Of course, in many situations in the field we have no choice—we must swing through from behind the bird. This swing-through gun movement will give some built-in lead that is often an advantage, because of our tendency to underestimate lead, but it must be *controlled* swing-through, not an erratic slash through the target. Why? So that we remain on the target line. Lose the line, and we might as well forget the lead. Sometimes these poke-and-hopers hit, and sometimes they miss, but there is no doubt in my mind that most of them are hopelessly inconsistent. That is why some of them eventually come to me for shooting lessons. Some of these guys, when I suggest that they should have a more logical approach to reading moving targets, object at first, as if the application of basic physics will destroy their inherent ability to stroke birds from the sky. After their first postinstruction dove- or duck-hunting trip, most change their minds and come back for more, ecstatic with the improvement. I love it when that happens.

TARGET EVALUATION

So, is there a way to learn to read all the variables and apply the requisite amount of lead to a moving target? Of course. There is a way to apply lead to targets, a logical and effective way that does not try to circumvent the laws of physics by using erratic gun speed. The late Nash Buckingham called it the moving-spot technique, and many top shooters use it today. Used properly, it will teach a shooter to cultivate a mental awareness of what lead he needs on any moving target, and an understanding of how to apply that lead to each target regardless of the shooting method used. It is an intuitive, systematic technique that has been in existence for hundreds of years, since the days of the flintlock. Remember that the fashionable art of shooting flying birds has been in existence since the restoration of the monarchy in 1660, when King Charles II returned to England from exile in France. In those days, due to the variable lock times of the primitive firearms and also the doubtful quality of the powder, it was important to keep the gun pointing ahead of the bird until the shot had left the barrels. It was the only way they could be successful.

But here is the bad news. This method, once mastered, can be applied successfully to all moving targets, but do not think of this as an easy option. Complete understanding of how to use this method is not easy, and there is some work involved. What about the good news? There is no mystery involved. The reason the technique works so well is because it is based on pure logic and a systematic breakdown of all the variables. This is exactly how the experts shoot. Over a period of time, they build up a personal mental repertoire of sight pictures, which they can eventually successfully apply to each target. They have the ability to see a subtle but consequential target-barrel relationship on every shot and to adjust it to each shooting situation based on all the variables involved. Once learned, these visual cues confirm correct muzzle placement on the target line, and the correct lead requirement as the shot is triggered.

Recently, I watched the great Robert Paxton, who is a member of the Dallas Gun Club, a thirty-two-time all-American, and one of the best skeet shooters in the world, deep in concentration, systematically pulverizing target after target. He shot with absolute precision; there was no guesswork involved—he new exactly where the target was and exactly where his barrel was each time he pulled the trigger.

"Aha!" I can hear you say. "He was shooting *skeet,* and that's different. I'm a bird hunter. This doesn't apply to me, does it?" Well, if you would like to take a bigger proportion of birds, then yes, it does. Before I coach anyone at sporting clays, I insist that they start on a skeet field. Sometimes these clients object, but they should not. Don't forget that two enterprising hunters invented the game of skeet as a way to hone their bird-hunting skills, and the skeet field is an ideal medium to learn how to accurately interpret all the angles. Skeet also teaches you to stay mentally focused. Many years ago, most skeet targets were shot with the swing-through method, and although it was reasonably successful, it turned out not to be the best way to notch up big scores. Skeet is the game of perfection, and high scores are the product of consistency. Today 99.9 percent of the serious skeet shooters and, without a doubt, *all* the world champions use some form of maintained lead for shooting their targets.

I have often heard bird hunters say, "I don't shoot sporting clays because it ruins my wing shooting." Really? I have no idea where this ridiculous myth came from. Sporting clays refines and hones your ability to successfully hit a variety of moving targets with a shotgun. It, too, was originally designed to replicate hunting situations in the field. The things we learn on a sporting clays course can be applied to live birds. But then cynicism kicks in again. With sporting clays, we get a chance to evaluate the target before we shoot it, and when we bird hunt, that does not happen. I would agree. But what about FITASC? We don't know *exactly* where the targets are coming from, and the gun-hold position is mandatory low gun. Sound familiar? And isn't FITASC considered to be the epitome of practice for wingshooting skills? Absolutely. Successful wingshooting is the ability to hit varying moving targets with a shotgun. Skeet, sporting clays, and trap are (surprise, surprise) the ability to hit varying moving targets with a shotgun. Moving targets are *moving* targets, and it

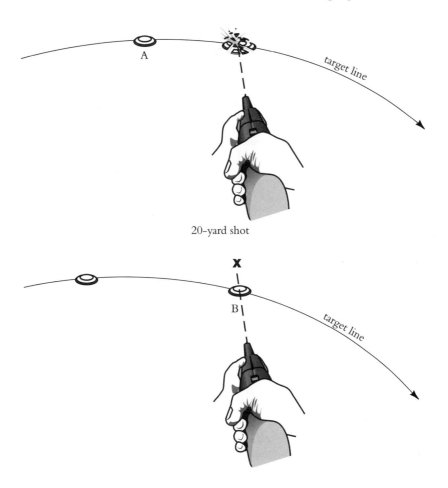

20-yard shot

40-yard shot

Target line, or trajectory, is far more important then lead. Targets rise, there is a period of transition, then they fall. We must also know exactly where we intend to shoot them on this line, and this is directly proportional to the range of the target. A standard, 1,200 feet per second shell will take approximately 0.06 of a second to travel 20 yards, 0.097 to travel 30 yards, and 0.139 second to travel 40 yards. At 40 yards the shot column will have a remaining velocity of only 660 feet per second. Target A is shot at the top of its trajectory at twenty yards. If this same target is then shot at forty yards, visually, its trajectory may still be reasonably horizontal. However, the target will be dropping and in position B by the time the shot pattern reaches it. The shot column will pass harmlessly over the top of the target. This is why range is so important. We need to develop a mental awareness of what the target is doing by the time the shot pattern reaches it, not what it's doing as we trigger the shot.

doesn't matter if it's a skeet target, sporting clays target, or a dove cruising the breeze on the Texas panhandle. The fundamentals apply to all of them.

Our success at intercepting moving targets with any degree of repeatable success hinges largely on two things: the ability to read the line, or trajectory, and the ability to apply the requisite amount of lead or forward allowance once we have done this. There are five variables that we must consider before we shoot any moving target:

1. The trajectory (deviation from the horizontal line) of the target
2. Where we decide to shoot the target on this trajectory
3. The angle of the target
4. The speed of the target
5. The distance to the target, or range

Developing the Line

There is no doubt that of these five variables, the most important one to consider is the line. Unfortunately for most of us, this is where our troubles begin. Line is more important than lead. Lead is more difficult to evaluate because it is determined by three factors: angle, speed, and range. Line is merely the two-dimensional segment we perceive the target to be traveling along relative to the position of our eyes. Providing we have the appropriate coordination skills to move the gun, line should be as easy to develop as it is to point a finger, but shooters routinely get this wrong. Develop the line correctly and we have a greatly improved chance of hitting the target because we have eliminated two of the variables—we cannot miss above or below the target.

Let's look at the trajectory of the clay target first. Clay targets do not fly in straight lines—the target rises, there is a period of transition, and then it falls. We must decide *exactly* where we intend to intercept the target on this line. Our foot positions are dependent on this and so is our timing, especially on pairs. Like a game of pool, you should always make sure that the cue ball, in this case your gun, is in position for the second shot. This is an individual thing. Nobody shoots a target in the same place as the next guy, and yet each may be shooting it at the proper time for himself.

Logically, there are only four ways to miss a moving target with a shotgun—above, below, in front, and behind. Factor forward allowance out, as with slow, close targets, and we should have no problems, right? So why do so many of us often miss such easy targets even when we got the lead right? Quite simply, sloppy visual information—we just don't make *enough* visual sense of the target line. The omission of this simple initial step, known as developing the line, results in far more missed targets than any other. This is especially true with targets that are in transition because of the time lapse between the visual stimuli that our brain receives and the shot column reaching the target.

What do I mean by this? Consider a forty-yard, full-crossing target as an example. We decide where we intend to shoot the target on its trajectory, carefully set ourselves up for the shot, call for the target, see what we think is the required sight picture, and trigger the shot, but the target does not break. What went wrong? We triggered the shot as the target was in the transitional phase, and by the time the shot column reached it, energy was bleeding off and it was already dropping. Our shot column went harmlessly over the top. It happens far more than you think, even on apparently easy targets. On long crossing shots, the problem is magnified because the shot column takes so much longer to reach the target. The solution is to take the target before it transitions, or if that is not an option, to anticipate the transition and allow for it.

With sporting clays presentations, once we have decided exactly where we will shoot the target on the trajectory, we can apply the clock-face system. Let's say we intend to shoot a full, left-to-right crossing shot at twenty yards, just as the target reaches the highest point on its trajectory. Imagine that the target is in the center of the clock face. We will shoot the target at three o'clock with a perceived lead of approximately three feet. If we then shoot the target later on the trajectory, as it starts to drop, we may shoot it at four o'clock, with slightly less perceived lead. Why less lead? Because the target has already gone past the 90-degree, full-crossing position. The angle is developing into a *closing* angle, and the target is also bleeding off energy and slowing down. Shoot the target later still, and we may need five o'clock and even less perceived lead. The pictures in the skeet section, Chapter 19, depict this. All these sight pictures can be applied to live birds in the field.

Now what about wingshooting situations? Usually, there is more time to develop the line than we think. Bird hunting is exciting, exhilarating stuff. We see the bird flush, experience the inevitable adrenaline rush, and give the bird a barrel as it passes, but do we really take the time to mentally evaluate the line properly? Most of us do not. It is poke-and-hope shotgunning at its best. Live birds curl, jink, twist, and take whatever evasive action they consider necessary, especially if they are being shot at. We fail to see the subtle curve in the flight of the cackling cock pheasant as he twists over the mighty English oaks. We hurriedly

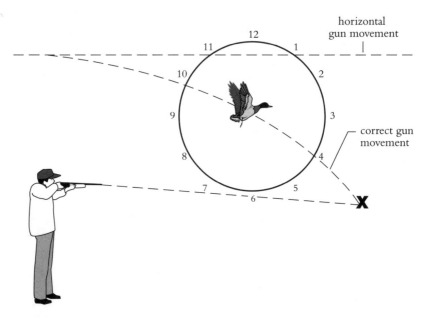

In bird-hunting situations, it is better to develop the line with a combination of arms and body movement. Why? Putting the gun in your shoulder too early will result in all the movement in the final stage of the mount being produced with body movement. The upper torso pivots easily on a horizontal plane. If the gun isn't doing what the bird is doing as it decides to do it, it doesn't matter how much lead you give the target, you will miss. Visualizing a clock face is often helpful. Too much gun movement and a fast uncontrolled swing on a duck that is dropping into the decoys will produce horizontal movement, and this is one of the reasons why most of us shoot over the top of them. Visualizing the clock face as the gun comes into the shoulder should result in success. This duck will be shot at 4 o'clock.

poke at the mourning dove as he breaks across an opening in the tree line. Our futile salvo spurs him on as he deploys the afterburners and vanishes like a gray ghost on the warm Texas breeze. We miss the almost imperceptible nuance in the flight of the red grouse as he lifts from the purple heather and curves swiftly away on the wings of wind, but see it we must if we are to come to terms with him. We watch the flock of greenheads dropping into the decoys, but somehow we still manage to shoot over the top of them.

In many wingshooting situations, unlike clay target shooting, there is also the (often exasperating) task of trying to decide what a bird will do and when it will do it, necessary to give the hunter a reasonable chance of successful interception. Simply put, you need to know (or make a pretty good guess at) where the birds are going to be by the time the shot charge reaches them. Most hunters who come to see me are poke-and-hopers—they see a bird coming, throw a wildly flailing gun up to their face, and shoulder and hope for the best. A huge amount of gun movement and a ragged poke in the general direction of the bird are the best they can manage.

Excessive gun movement produces excessive momentum in the barrels, and usually this results in gun movement that is more or less in a straight line. Most birds do not fly in straight lines, at least not most of the ones I have shot at. If the gun barrels are not doing what the bird is doing as it decides to do it, you have got problems, and that is exactly the reason why we shoot over ducks so often. "Dropping in" to the decoys should give us a clue, but it does not always. Remember also that wing beats signify acceleration. A pheasant that comes over the oak trees will be rising if he's still flapping. Once he sets his wings, he is losing height.

The rooster pheasant that lifts with rapid wing beats from the Kansas cornfield will be rising, but how many of us still manage to shoot underneath him? Why? Because we just do not make enough visual sense of the bird. We are all guilty of it at some time or other. Don't do it. Take the time to consciously evaluate all the variables; your brain is capable of doing just that in the time between seeing the bird and completing the mount. The difference between a poke-and-hope shot and what I call an intuitive, educated shot may be only a small fraction of a second, but it can make all the difference in the world to the final outcome.

Feeling the Lead

Provided we have a gun that fits and reasonable coordination skills, the gun will respond to our normal pointing attitude; all we need to do is point it in the right place and we will stroke birds from the sky with quiet confidence. So now let's imagine that our gun fits us like a glove, our mechanics are excellent, our footwork is the envy of Rudolf Nureyev, and we can make a pretty good attempt at developing the line of any moving target. The next thing we need to consider is the amount of forward allowance needed.

We are told that if our gun fits and we learn to mount it correctly, it will shoot where we look, right? Absolutely. Once we can accurately evaluate this amount, all we need to do is look out in front of the target—the eyes will follow the gun—and trigger the shot. The problem is, how do we know exactly *where* to look?

A true driven pheasant will be a straight on shot at 12 o'clock. Unfortunately, high-driven birds are usually not as predictable as this and are seldom perpendicular relative to our shooting positions. The clock-face approach works well on driven birds. Birds curling to the right and left of the straight-on shot will be shot at 1 o'clock and 11 o'clock respectively. This bird should be shot at 11 o' clock. Birds that are lower will be shot at 10 o'clock and 2 o'clock.

The second most common way for a shooter to miss a moving target with a shotgun is by missing behind because of a miscalculation of the amount of forward allowance needed. Think about the new shooter for a moment. There is always a look of amazement on a his face when, after repeatedly shooting behind a target, his coach tells him to miss the next one by three feet in front and at last he connects with it. By the same rule, anyone who has taught others to shoot will know that one of the problems is explaining to shooters exactly how to quickly evaluate the target and how much lead or forward allowance they actually need; in fact, I would say that there are two questions that are asked more than any other by would-be proficient shotgunners: How much lead does this target need? What exactly does this look like over the gun? In other words, *at the target end*.

Angle of the Target: The Geometric Solution

We have already determined that lead requirement is dependent on three variables—angle, speed, and range. Let's look at angles first. Shooting is a game of trigonometry. The guys who are the most successful and impressive shots in the field, and the guys who win sporting clays and skeet tournaments, know this. They are the ones who are better at applying basic trigonometry than the rest of us. Inability to read the angles correctly is what defeats most people. So what's the best way to do this? Well, without a doubt, the most convenient way is on a skeet field, and whenever possible, this is where I start my clients. Most of the instructors I know in the United Kingdom do the same. Many top sporting clays shooters initially develop their skills on the skeet field, and George Digweed is a prime example. Five-time world sporting clays champion George Digweed? That's right. George shot competitive skeet for many years and is the current record holder in the United Kingdom—475 straight.

In the United States, former Olympic shooter and frequent major tournament winner Dan Carlisle is another excellent example of a cream-of-the-crop skeet shooter who excels on the sporting clays circuit, and there are just too many others to mention. If we go back to the old chestnut about skeet and sporting clays, "spoiling your wingshooting ability" for a moment, anyone who has seen a five-time world sporting clays champion shoot driven pheasants or pigeons would soon be persuaded to change his mind and start feeling sorry for the birds.

You say there is no skeet layout at your club? No problem. Failing access to a skeet field, I start clients on a reasonably fast outgoing target and move them around in a semicircle at a *measured* distance, about twenty yards. I say a measured distance for a good reason, and I will explain why later. As the student moves around, he progressively increases the lead, and before long, he is breaking full a 90-degree crossing target. Obviously, the maximum lead requirement we need on any target is when we are 90 degrees to it. At first, a student moving from station to station needs to think carefully about the lead requirement before he calls for the target. After an hour or so, he gains confidence and begins to pull the trigger when the target-barrel relationship looks right to him.

And that brings us to the difference between *perceived* lead and *actual* lead. Actual lead is the required amount that shot has to be directed in front of the target to score a hit, as calculated by using the laws of geometry and physics. Apparent or perceived lead is the amount the shooter's brain thinks is necessary from the optical information it receives. Perceived lead is equal to actual lead only on a full 90-degree crossing shot. With all other (angular) shots, the actual lead is the same as this amount, but the perceived lead, depending on the angle, is not.

One of the best demonstrations of how the perception of lead changes as the angle changes is accomplished by using a piece of 2 × 4 about four feet long and placed on the center stake on a skeet field, directly under the flight line of the target. The length of the 2 × 4 represents the lead requirement that the laws of physics dictate we need on a full 90-degree crossing shot at twenty yards if shot with the sustained lead method. We can do the calculations as follows: a standard skeet target is traveling at about 50 miles per hour (50 miles per hour = 73 feet per second). A standard shotshell velocity for the purpose of our calculations is about 1,200 feet per second. Forty yards is 120 feet, and this means that the shot column would take $1/10$ second to go 40 yards, or half this ($1/20$ second) to travel 20 yards; therefore, the target would travel approximately 3 feet 8 inches in this time interval.

If the piece of 2 × 4 is placed directly beneath the flight line of the low-house target, looking at the piece of 2 × 4 from skeet station one, the perception is that it is about a foot long, so the lead on low-house station 1 looks like about one foot. The lead on low-house station 2 looks like about 2 feet. As the student moves around in a semicircle, the piece of wood gives him the lead. Simple, isn't it? The pictures in Chapter 19 illustrate this. The actual lead is the same every time; it is the perception of lead that changes. This demonstration serves its purpose as a visual evaluation of the lead requirement on each target as the angle

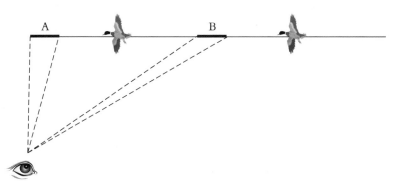

Opening-angle target. The maximum lead requirement we need on any target is when we are at 90 degrees to the target line. With any target that is coming toward the shooter, the angle of the target relative to the shooter is increasing all the time. The perception of lead will increase accordingly as the target gets closer to this 90-degree maximum. The perception of lead as the dove gets to position A will be more than the perception of lead at position B.

changes. Unfortunately, I cannot claim the credit for inventing this demonstration—a famous shooting instructor in the United Kingdom showed it to me many years ago. Of course, it is not foolproof, but it certainly makes the light come on a lot quicker for a lot of shooters.

Everything the student learns by shooting the targets in this way can easily be applied to the sporting clays course and eventually to wing-shooting. All these angles can be broken down into component parts: narrow-angle crossing shots, wide-angle crossing shots, and full-crossing shots. All quartering targets can in turn be divided into two other categories, either incoming or outgoing. I call the outgoing targets closing-angle shots (reducing angle in relation to the shooter), requiring progressively less lead, and the incoming targets are opening-angle shots (increasing angle in relation to the shooter), requiring progressively more. Incoming targets always need more apparent lead than outgoing targets. Gun movement is also directly proportional to target angle: straightaway target, minimum gun movement; full-crossing shot, maximum gun movement. Obviously, targets requiring compound leads are the hardest to read, but with all of them, it is just a matter of deciding into which category the target fits before you try to shoot it.

One of the most commonly missed shots is the overhead quartering-away target, which is at an acute angle to our line of sight, making it seem much faster than it really is. Most people will give this narrow-angle target a huge amount of gun movement and lead, missing in front. As the distance to the target is increasing, the angle of the target relative

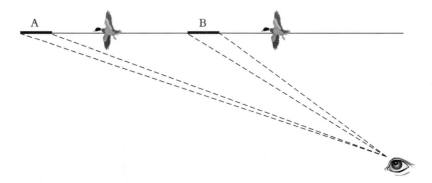

With a target that is going away from the shooter, the angle is decreasing. The perception of lead on the duck at position A will be less than it is at position B, even though the duck is farther away.

to the shooter is decreasing and the target is also slowing down, so the *perceived* lead on the target is actually *less* as the range increases. A narrow-angle quartering shot that requires only a small amount of perceived lead at twenty yards does not need any more at forty yards. The exact opposite is true of opening-angle quartering in shots. The *perceived* lead on a quartering in target may be considerably more as it gets closer, because the angle of the target in relation to the shooter is increasing all the time up to the maximum lead requirement when the target is at 90 degrees to the shooter.

Speed of the Target
This is the final piece if the puzzle. Luckily for us, speed of the target isn't the most critical part of the equation. Accurate computation of the angle and the range has a far bigger influence on successful shooting. First, we've already calculated the lead on a fifty-mile-per-hour target. Now what about a forty-mile-per-hour target? forty miles per hour = 58.66 feet per second, which means that at 20 yards this target needs 2.93 feet of lead. The difference between the fifty-mile-per-hour target and the forty-mile-per-hour target is only about eight inches, easily enough margin of error for our shot pattern to compensate if we get it wrong. As luck would have it, sporting clays target speeds usually fall somewhere between thirty-five and fifty miles per hour. And guess what? Also luckily for us, lots of birds fall well within these parameters, from white-wing doves to Canada geese. The only time speed is deceptive is when targets, either clays or live birds, are high in the air. This is

Quail hunting must be one of the most exciting (and sometimes nerve-wracking!) shooting situations there is. Quail aren't traveling as fast as you think—their rapid wing beats are an illusion. In most situations, narrow angles, a fast-handling gun, and wide shot pattern will save the day and result in success.

easily explained. Take two driven pheasants, for example, both flying at forty miles per hour. One is twenty yards high, and the other is forty yards high. Both are flying toward the waiting gun, at an angle of approximately 45 degrees. The low bird will cover the distance to the gun twice as fast as the high bird, giving the illusion that the high bird is moving slower. He isn't. Speed is much easier to judge if you make a conscious evaluation of range. This effect is explained in more detail in Chapter 18, in the "Tall Towers, Short Answers" section. This is exactly the reason why pass-shooting geese is difficult; they look almost as if they are motionless. Don't be fooled. Geese at forty yards plus need lots of lead.

After two or three lessons, depending on the progress of the student, I am ready to go to the sporting clays course. I always ask my clients to evaluate each target before they shoot it. The position of the trap is often a good clue to the nature of the target. Is it a narrow-angle shot, wide-angle shot, or full-crossing shot? In the place where they intend to shoot it, is it rising or falling? Is it more than twenty yards, or less? How fast is it? Why did I say earlier that initially it's always best to shoot all the targets at a known distance? Because now the shooter has something to relate to without guessing. He has a visual reference to the lead he sees on a narrow-angle shot, wide-angle shot, and full-crossing shot at twenty yards. What his eye perceives to be the correct amount of lead can now be applied to other targets. One shot, for example, which gives most people a headache, is the long 90-degree crossing target that always requires more lead than it seems, and we always shoot behind it. But if a shooter is familiar with the amount of forward allowance he thinks he needs on a full-crossing shot at twenty yards, logically he must need at least twice that at thirty yards, three times at forty yards. What does this look like over the barrels of the gun? Once again, there is a way to do this, and the chapter on range describes one of the ways. Eventually, anyone can learn to develop the ability to feel the lead on each target, but don't expect it to happen overnight, because it won't. These are things that are only learned by practice and experience. The brain is an incredibly complex organ, more than capable of computing all the variables of a moving target, and eventually any shooter can learn to read targets, and when he can, he will develop what I call muzzle and trigger patience and give his targets the correct amount of lead regardless of the method he uses to shoot them. This is an intuitive process; he won't be doing everything by instinct because it was necessary for him to learn it, but every time he pulls the trigger, the light will be getting brighter, whether he hits the target or not. Everything the student learns on the skeet field and the sporting clays course can then be applied to actual hunting situations in the field. Of course eventually he needs to trust this accumulation of knowledge, apply it to each target, and more importantly, *pull the trigger when the picture looks right to him.*

Finally, as a parting shot, remember what Annie Oakley said to the reporter of the *New York Sun* in 1892? "The ability to trigger the shot at just the right time is a feeling." Then she added, "But practice and experience helps."

THE IMAGINARY MOVING-SPOT TECHNIQUE APPLIED

I could detect the urgency in the client's voice at the other end of the phone. "I've been shooting sporting clays for years now, and I just can't seem to get above 70 percent." How many times have I heard that before? "I'm coming to the Dallas area on business, and I thought you might be able to help."

We then engaged in a lengthy discussion on this client's particular problem targets, but smoothing out bumps in the road over the phone is not exactly my strong suit, so I said I thought I could help, and we arranged a time and a date to meet. The day came and "Fred," as I will call him (as they always say at the beginning of *The Untouchables* episodes, the names have been changed to protect the innocent), explained that he had already taken lots of lessons. We started, as I always do with a new client, on one of the skeet fields.

Now, Fred was a decent fellow who lost no time in making it clear to me that he took his shooting seriously. It was obvious that he had a strong desire to succeed on the sporting clays course. Quartering shots were powdered with an aggressive precision, so no problems there, but as we progressed to the center station, on a full-crossing shot with maximum lead requirement, his success was "patchy."

"What do you see with this target as you trigger the shot?" I asked him. Fred looked surprised. "What do you mean?" he asked. "I'm not looking at the bead, I'm looking at the target and trusting my instincts—that's the right way to do this, isn't it?"

"Nope," I replied. "You're only half right—the bit about not looking at the bead—but the bit about looking at the target as you trigger the shot? I never do that, and it isn't what any of the top guys do," I continued. "If your gun fits you, it will shoot where you look, right? If you're looking at the target as you trigger the shot and the target's moving, you're going to hit exactly what you were looking at—the space where the target was when you pulled the trigger. Besides, if it *was* the right way to do this, the target would be breaking, wouldn't it?"

Fred looked puzzled and shook his head in disbelief, as most of my clients do when I tell them this. I explained to him that with narrow angles and trap-type targets he could get away with looking at the target as he triggered the shot. On targets of this sort, minimum angle and a wide shot pattern is usually enough to save the day, and that is why he had been successful with the quartering targets. But with full-crossing shots, extended range targets, and compound leads, he would need to apply something more specific if he was to improve his 70 percent average. So we continued the lesson.

On the center stake of the skeet field I have my piece of two-by-four that is painted white, which I use as a visual aid for students. I pointed it out to Fred. "See that piece of two-by-four over there?" Fred nodded. "How long do you think it is?"

Fred carefully scrutinized the piece of wood, thought for a moment, and then said, "about four feet."

"Exactly, now shoot this target again," I said, "but before you do, mount your gun on the end of the piece of wood. The lead you need is the length of that two-by-four. Try to imagine that the piece of wood is between the target and the barrel when you trigger the shot and see what happens; in other words, look out in front of the target about the same distance as that piece of wood and pull the trigger."

Fred still couldn't believe his ears. "You mean I shouldn't be looking at the target when I trigger the shot?"

"Nope, not if you want to hit it," I said. "If you want to hit it, you'll be looking at the space in front of the target where it is going to be when your shot arrives. Try it and see."

Bang! Dead bird. Bang! Dead bird. Bang! Dead bird. Suddenly, the targets were breaking with almost monotonous consistency. Fred, for the first time in his shooting career, was learning to be more precise but without unnecessarily tracking the target. His gun hold-point, insertion point, gun speed, and rhythm were the same each time, and the targets were breaking in the same place as a result, consistently. The look on Fred's face said it all. "This all seems too easy but isn't what I'm doing called 'measuring'? I've been told that to reach full potential with a shotgun I have to shoot instinctively. Doing it this way, I'm looking for a specific sight picture."

"But the target's breaking now, isn't it?" I replied. Fred nodded in agreement. "And I don't agree that it's 'measuring;' it's just a way that I use to indicate to you how much lead you need to see on that particular target. It seems to work, doesn't it?" I asked. Fred nodded his agreement.

Now as luck would have it, that morning I had received my December 2001 copy of *Sporting Clays* magazine. Inside was an excellent shooter profile of Jon Kruger by Katy Skahill, which I had been reading during my lunch break. On page 10, Jon says, "I don't really believe much in instinctive clay shooting." I retrieved the magazine from my office and pointed this part out to Fred. So far so good. There it was in black and white: Jon Kruger, who has won the U.S. Open in 2001 and 2002 and is without a doubt one of the best shots of all time, doesn't shoot clay targets instinctively. Fred was noticeably impressed.

"When you shoot in competition, you need to be aware of a specific sight picture as you trigger the shot. That's what you have to do to make sure you can repeat the shot," I continued.

"Are you sure this is what the top guys do? It's not what I've been told before," said Fred.

"Absolutely. There is no other way if you want to be consistent," I replied, but I sensed that Fred wasn't 100 percent convinced, not just yet anyway.

I taught Fred, over the next two hours or so, a logical way to apply lead and how to read targets. The next day was Sunday and Fred had booked another three hours. As we progressed around the sporting clays course, I would ask him at each station to carefully evaluate each target with consideration for angle, distance, speed, and trajectory and to decide where along the trajectory he intended to shoot each target. I would ask him, on report pairs, to consider where he expected his gun to be as he started to shoot the second target of the pair. This bit is important. As with the cue ball in a game of pool, you must plan and execute so that your gun will be in the optimum position for the second shot.

By station 15, it was obvious to both of us that the light was getting brighter and Fred was breaking more targets than ever before. Then we arrived at the high tower. At the Dallas Gun Club we have an excellent, 120-foot tower, and on one of the shots, at the request of some of the members who would be going to the Nationals, we had a long crosser and I do mean *long*—over seventy yards. Fred, as I pulled a target, looked at the speck that appeared over the trees with dismay. "Is that a midi?" he groaned.

"Nope." I shook my head. "It's a standard, but you can still hit it from here." The look told me that Fred was skeptical. "Just lock onto the target and make sure you develop the line correctly; then look out ahead to where you think the target will be when the shot charge gets there and trigger the shot."

Fred carefully positioned himself for the shot. I was more nervous than he was, silently hoping he would hit the target. "Pull!" The target appeared above the trees and seemed to remain in view forever. Fred smoothly inserted on the line in front of the target, stayed with it for a heartbeat, and (I was peering down the barrel over his shoulder) at exactly the right time in my mind, he fired. There was a noticeable delay between the report of the gun and the shot column reaching the target, but the target broke. The look on Fred's face was a picture, and he came out with a few choice adjectives that I had never heard before in Scotland.

"Were you looking at the target as you pulled the trigger?" I asked Fred.

"No, I was looking out in front, just like you said I should," he replied. I then went into a lengthy explanation about central and peripheral vision and how the "imaginary spot" technique of applying lead works.

"Do you remember what your visual perception of the distance in front of the target was?" I asked Fred. Fred nodded. "See if you can do it again." Fred proceeded to do just that, several times. He shot the rest of the course as if he was floating on air, but my story does not end there. The next week I heard from him again. He excitedly explained that his shooting had dramatically improved, but there was another reason for the call.

"Remember what you said about primary concentration on the target and then looking at a space in front of the target as you trigger the shot?" he asked. "Well, I found another article about Jon Kruger and guess what? He says the same as you! I'll fax you a copy." I thanked Fred and said that I would like to read the article.

Sure enough, on page 50 in the December 1998 issue of *Sporting Clays* magazine, there was an excellent article by Nick Sisley entitled "Stellar Star of the Game." I quote from the article: "You've heard the axiom over and over, 'Look at the target, look at the target.' Again, surprisingly, this isn't what Kruger does. Instead, he's trying to focus on a spot somewhere out ahead of the target. Why? *Because that's where his shot-string has to go.* Once he—or any of us—pulls the trigger, there's a time lapse between then and when the shot charge gets to the bird. This is why lead is essential. Of course, target speed and distance govern how far ahead of the target Kruger will be trying to focus."

There it is, the shooting man's elixir of life, the illusive secret of successful shotgunning! Jon's advice was the same as Andy McCloud's all those years ago. It has also worked for Nash Buckingham and a lot of other top shooters. Of course, you still have to learn exactly *how far* in front to look, and you still have to have a smooth swing and a gun that fits, but with practice, you will learn the required leads. With good coaching, you will learn them quickly.

CHAPTER 16

Evaluating Range

Walk around any sporting clays course during a tournament and my guess is that at every station there will be a group of guys feverishly changing chokes to give themselves maximum pattern density to break the targets at a calculated range. They all know that a close target calls for an open choke, and a distant target a tight choke. But before they know which choke will be right for the job at hand, they must calculate the range at which they will attempt to break the target. The next weekend some of these same clay-busters decide to go duck or dove hunting, and as the birds run the gauntlet of the hunters, hardly any of them connect. Why? Failure to calculate range, because often in wing-shooting situations people do not bother, instead just expecting it all to miraculously come together. Most often, it does not. Even if we are conscious of the need, the ability to judge range, for most of us, does not come naturally. We have to work at it.

Most wingshooters, if they are honest with themselves, regardless of the quarry species, often react with a naively optimistic attitude when presented with a shot that may not reoccur. You get the picture. You have been sitting in the duck blind since long before dawn, and you have forgotten where your butt's supposed to be. The ducks are about as scarce as rocking horse droppings. As you give the dog a nudge to make sure it hasn't died from boredom, you hear the faint whistle of approaching pinions and . . . yes! Here they come! As you stagger to a shaky attention, the first teal spots the movement and flares. Too far, you think, but you give him the first barrel anyway. Then you give a straggler the other one as a parting shot. Just in case. A couple of rump feathers drift down in the chill morning air, and as the feeling of guilt trickles over you like syrup over an IHOP pancake, you begin to regret that you shot. Most of us have been in this situation at some time or other, and hopefully we learn from it. The wingshooter owes it to his quarry to make a conscious evaluation of the distance involved to give him the best possible chance of making a clean kill. By paying attention to range, he avoids shooting targets that are too close and blowing them to pieces, and shooting at birds out of range. Just as importantly, he uses the range to know how much lead to put on the birds that are within his range.

Obviously, this is always more difficult to do in the field on live targets because more often than not, we have no idea where the birds are coming from or where they are going, unlike clay targets, which we can always evaluate before taking the shot. Still, the effort must be made in whatever time the bird allows us, if we are to optimize our wing-shooting effectiveness.

Surprisingly, the importance of evaluating range is often neglected even at shooting schools, and although I always cover this subject with my clients, many instructors do not bother. The shotgun, at close range, is an incredibly powerful weapon, easily capable of inflicting massive damage on body tissue. Anyone who has read the stories of Jim Corbett, who protected the tea plantation workers in India at the turn of the century from marauding leopards, will know that a 12 gauge loaded with buckshot was often his choice of weapon for dealing with these big cats in thick cover at close range. However, the energy of the shot charge dissipates quickly at ranges of ten yards and more.

This loss of energy is directly proportional to shot size and distance, reducing the effective killing range rapidly as the range extends and the shot size decreases, for two reasons. The first is the loss of energy per pellet, and the second is the loss of pellets that actually strike their target due to spread and pellet dispersal. In choosing a suitable shot size, a balance must be found where there are enough pellets to strike the target, but where each pellet retains enough energy to penetrate the quarry and reach a vital organ. If one of these criteria is not met or, even worse, if neither is met, wounded birds will be the result. If the shot size is too large, a clean kill will depend on luck. Too small, and even the best shooter will fail to kill *cleanly* because of the lack of penetrative power. There is no point, as an example of this, in using a cartridge with shot size 8, which would be perfectly acceptable for dove hunting at thirty- to thirty-five-yard ranges, for duck hunting at forty yards plus. There simply would not be enough energy to penetrate through the thick

The piece of two-by-four in the foreground is two feet long and ten yards away, the next piece is four feet long and twenty yards away, the third is six feet long and thirty yards away. Visually they all look similar, and if the shot charge was constant over these distances, lead would be easier to apply. Unfortunately for us, it isn't, due to the deceleration of the shot column.

feathers and then the flesh of the bird and strike one of the vital organs with enough force to kill.

By the same rule, on the sporting clays course, skeet chokes and no. 9 shots may be the perfect medicine for the twenty-yard crossing midi, and no. 9 shot is the most popular size for short-range targets like skeet, where the longest shot is only about twenty-five yards. The same pellet size would be inadequate on forty-yard-plus trap targets or long-range sporting clay targets, and the result would be a lost bird in many cases. Also, the direction of the target (both feathered and clay) affects penetration due to something known as synergism. The literal translation of synergism means the action of two forces of energy working together to produce a combined force. With any target that is coming toward the gun, the combined force of the energy (of the target and the shot column) increases the striking energy, and therefore the penetration, accordingly. With a trap-type target (or a bird that is flying directly away), there is no synergistic boost, and the penetration and energy with which the pellets strike are reduced.

When I lived in Scotland, I was close to the Solway Firth, which offered some of the best public-area duck and goose hunting in the

United Kingdom. I thought it was fun in those days to sit in a mud-filled ditch half the night, freezing to death with only a shivering Labrador for company. I found out the hard way that the fat barnacle goose that looked as big as a house and hardly seemed to be moving at all was actually pushing near to the limit for the range of my magnum 12 gauge. In the half light of the freezing dawn, range was especially difficult to judge.

Overoptimism was a prevalent problem among the duck and goose hunters that shot over these coastal mudflats, and unfortunately, it was infectious. Many of the hunters were so trigger-happy and desperate to get off a shot at anything that approached "within range" (which was often nearer to one hundred yards than fifty), that often nobody was lucky enough to bring anything down. Every season there must have been thousands of ducks and geese that were pricked and sentenced to die a slow and agonizing death as a result of some of these eager and (unfortunately for the geese) impatient "sportsmen."

Now, I know that there are a lot of people out there who make a lot of claims about dropping geese as dead as a doornail at eighty-five yards and more. I owned a gun shop for many years, and it was my frequent duty to listen with wide-eyed astonishment to such stories. Some of these goose hunters would pace off the distance to the bird as "proof" and produce witnesses who were willing to nod approvingly and testify to the authenticity of the claims. Of course they may get away with such tales in the bar at night when the bullwhip is ankle deep, but in reality, I don't believe any of it. These guys always seem to omit the important bits like (1) how far the bird traveled after it was killed cleanly, (2) Pythagorean theorem, and (3) how many bottles of beer they had consumed at the time. You don't believe me? Well try throwing a magnum load of $1\frac{1}{2}$ ounce of shot through a full-choke barrel at a pattern board at a *measured* eighty-five yards and tell me you are still not convinced. The pattern, at this range, will cover a barn door, and there will be holes in it that a steer could slip through. At extended ranges—sixty-five yards or more—a goose would have to be very unlucky indeed to be hit by a pellet or two that would kill it *cleanly.*

So just how can we learn to develop a mental awareness of range? There is a way. Successful shotgunning is often an accumulation of knowledge based on real shooting situations in the field, and my experience with the geese on the Solway surfaced again in later years when my wife and I managed a shooting complex in the south of England.

The facility was in North Devon, less than ten miles from the west coast of England and in an area frequented by an abundance of Canada geese. Canada geese have toxic droppings, and huge flocks of them would fly in from the coastal mudflats to use some of the trout lakes in the area as an overnight roost. As an attraction for the vast hordes of holidaymakers who descended on the west coast each holiday season, these lakes were stocked with farm-raised rainbow trout that unfortunately could not distinguish the difference between food pellets and goose droppings.

At first the effects of these nocturnal visitors were not obvious, but after several successive nights, with exposure to the overnight ablutions of several hundred birds, the trout would become sick and eventually die. Steps were taken to expose the culprits, and eventually, accusing fingers pointed at the geese. By popular demand (and with full approval from the local authorities), the fishery owners declared war on the geese. As luck would have it, the shooting complex we managed was right on the main flight path between the Tamar Lakes and the Clovelly Country Club. As a bit of extra sport for the guests, we would lie in wait and ambush the geese as they came in at dusk. It was all great fun, but unfortunately, it soon became obvious to me that even the experienced shots were struggling to connect with the geese because of a miscalculation of range.

The point I make is that at fifty yards, a Canada goose looks big, but he is easily within range of your gun. At eighty-five yards, he still looks big, but he is not within range. His slow, methodical wing beats make him appear to be sitting on the end of your muzzles, but anything short of a lucky shot with an elephant gun won't bring him down. Many geese were blasted by the guests at ranges that were impossible, so in true sportsmanlike fashion, I devised a plan. I made a life-size plywood cutout of a Canada goose, gave it a realistic coat of paint, and each week, when the new guests arrived, I would test their range-finding capabilities. This Canada goose replica worked amazingly well. Within a short space of time, clients could guestimate the yardage to the plywood goose reasonably accurately, in some cases to within a few yards. The guests were politely asked not to blaze away at anything that was more than forty to fifty yards away, and they brought more geese down as a result. It was a sort of "don't shoot till you see the whites of their eyes, lads" thing, as the cavalry officers used to tell their men.

The importance of calculating range was recognized long ago. Sir Ralph Payne-Gallwey, who was a great experimentalist, in his book published in 1913, *High Pheasants in Theory and Practice,* describes an experiment where he suspended dead pheasants from a kite forty yards

The distance to the target can have a dramatic effect on the lead requirement, and all shooters must develop some sort of mental awareness for the amount needed. A standard shot load takes approximately $1/20$ second to travel 20 yards, $2/20$ second to travel 30 yards, and $3/20$ second to travel 40 yards. A bird or clay target traveling at approximately forty miles per hour will travel three feet, six feet, and nine feet in the same time periods. A skeet field is forty yards long. The piece of 2 X 4 in the foreground is three feet long and twenty yards away, the second is six feet long and thirty yards away, the third is nine feet long and forty yards away. These pieces of 2 X 4 represent the lead requirements at these distances at the target end. Of course it isn't foolproof, because the distance to the target and the speed of the target isn't constant, but it certainly helps. The perceived lead requirement on a sixty yard shot may be almost twice the requirement on a forty yard shot due to the progressive deceleration of the shot charge.

off the ground. He then proceeded to shoot at each dead pheasant, twenty shots per bird. Remarkably, one would think that after twenty shots each, the birds would be blown to pieces, but on postmortem examination, according to Sir Ralph, there were few potentially fatal wounds on any of the carcasses. There is no doubt that dead flesh is more resistant to penetration than a live bird, but nevertheless, what conclusions can we come to with this experiment? Apart from the obvious one that Sir Ralph must have been a really bad shot (which was not the case), the only one I can come up with is the fact that the maximum potential of a 12-gauge shotgun using no. 6 shot in those days was somewhere around forty yards. Sir Ralph went too far and suggested that some pheasants (which were shot normally in the field, i.e., not kite suspended) were dead in the air but on postmortem showed no marks on their carcasses where shot had penetrated. His theory to explain this was that the shot blast destroyed the air pockets that supported them on the wing, and that these pheasants either died of shock or were so traumatized by the experience that they plummeted earthward in a trance-like state and were killed by the impact force of hitting the ground!

This I cannot agree with. Birds are killed quickly by pellets that find their way to a vital organ, the heart or brain, for example. They do not usually die quickly from shock. Wounded birds that do not receive a lethal dose of pellets immediately often find their way into thick cover to die later from either loss of blood or, in many cases, asphyxia caused by a lung shot. At extended range, in some of the birds I shot, a single pellet, sometimes two (these were extremely difficult to find), had penetrated the head and neck area. These isolated pellets, I believe, were quite capable of stunning the bird, and the fall to the ground from forty yards plus did the rest.

Sir Ralph also noticed (as most shooters eventually do) that there is an increased difficulty in evaluating range when the targets are overhead, and this applies to both live birds and clay targets. The simple explanation is that this phenomenon is a true optical illusion. As an experiment,

At extended distances, perspective is important. Range is always difficult to evaluate with any target against the open sky because of the absence of familiar objects, trees, or landscape images with which to compare the targets or birds. On the sporting clays course, with a high crossing shot off a tower, there is also an optical illusion, and the target always appears to be moving much slower than it really is. Clay targets or high birds always appear to be smaller than when seen at the same distance horizontally.

in an effort to explain this, place two objects (two sticks will do) a few feet apart at a distance of perhaps twenty to thirty yards, and ask several people to guess how far apart they are. You will get wildly conflicting answers. Then do the same again but ask one of the people to stand next to the sticks, and the answers will be much more accurate, the reason being that there is now something of a known size with which they can make a more accurate comparison. With birds high up in the air, or clay pigeons thrown from a high tower, there are no trees or landscape features with which they can be compared. Consequently, they appear to be about half the size that they would if they were seen at the same distance horizontally, and because of this illusion, they also appear to be moving slower—exactly the reason why many people miss high birds (or clay targets) behind, and exactly the same reason why people blast away at ducks and geese at extended ranges. This type of long shot will defeat even the expert at some time or another, because the ocular stimuli the brain receives just are not convincing enough on these targets. Misses will predominate until the mental computer learns to override the eyes and put the shot charge farther in front. On the sporting clays course, orange or white targets against a dark background are frustratingly misleading and always seem to be closer than they are.

Based on my own experience, I would agree with the first part of Sir Ralph's experiment. Good sporting birds such as driven pheasants are a valuable commodity in Scotland, and there has never been a shortage of wealthy takers. The distance at which some of these "experienced" shots would attempt to shoot birds was often ridiculous. On some of the drives, especially late in the season when they had been shot at a few times, the birds would be coming over *in excess* of seventy yards high, hopelessly out of range. Many of the "guns," having paid in advance for a certain quota of pheasants, would attempt these shots in an effort to make the bag limit. How do I know this? Before I came to the United States, I was lucky enough to have, right on my doorstep, some of the best driven pheasant shooting in the world. I lived a mile from Westerhall Estate in southwest Scotland, and often, as we waited for the birds to flush, I would make a conscious estimate of the distance of the birds as they flew over. We have steep-sided valleys in Scotland, and on some of the drives, lines of utility poles ran down these. Utility poles in the United Kingdom have the length stamped on the side, and from this, it was easy to make a fairly precise calculation using basic trigonometry of just how high the birds were. I often shot birds that by my estimation were inside this fifty-yard limit, and some of them were clearly hard hit but not cleanly killed. The ones that did come down would set their wings and often glide for well over half a mile. I made a habit of marking these down so that I could examine them later. Some were later determined to have several pellets in them, but the penetration of the pellets was so reduced that it was luck, not my shooting skill, that brought the birds down. It certainly was not an exhibition of good sportsmanship on my part, I regret to say. There must have been many pricked birds that found their way into thick cover to die days or even weeks later. In fact, the dogs would often find them on the next weekend's drives. Piners, we would call them. The true sportsman, when faced with a bird that he estimates is at the limit of his range, should not shoot, in fairness to the birds.

Lead or forward allowance is directly proportional to range, and if the velocity of a shot charge were constant over these distances, it would be easier to calculate. If we shoot at a crossing target at twenty yards and it needs three feet of lead, does the same target require twice as much (i.e., six feet) lead if we back up to forty yards? I'm afraid not. In 1926 Major Hugh B. C. Pollard, in his book, *The History of Firearms,* pointed out that a charge of shot takes 0.05 of a second to travel 20 yards, 0.1 of a second to travel 30 yards, and 0.1429 of a second to travel 40 yards. The major, who was a renowned scientist as well as a ballistician, also pointed out that a bird traveling at forty miles per hour would travel *approximately* three, six, and nine feet in the same time intervals. What this meant was that due to the deceleration of the shot charge, the angular lead must be increased in proportion to the distance, and the twenty-yard shot that *may visually appear* to need three feet, may also *visually* appear to need approximately twice as much (six feet) at thirty yards and nine feet at forty yards to compensate for the deceleration.

We know today, in ballistic terms, that this was incorrect, but it was pretty close. The actual time it would take a load of shot with a muzzle velocity of 1,200 feet per second to travel 20 yards would be approximately 0.06 of a second; 30 yards, approximately 0.097 of a second; and 40 yards, approximately 0.139 of a second. The actual amounts of lead that the laws of physics dictate we need on 20-, 30-, and 40-yard full-crossing, forty-mile-per-hour targets would thus be 3.52, 5.69, and 8.15 feet. Those are also the leads you would need to see if you shoot with the sustained lead method. Swing-through shooters would need to see less because of the extra gun movement they produce. However, the visual *perception* of nine feet of lead at forty yards usually works very well, because most of us have a tendency to underestimate lead requirement at extended range. With live quarry at extended ranges, it is always better to err on the forward side; then at least we have a chance of a head shot and a clean kill.

Of course, in the past, attempts to rationalize lead requirements at extended ranges have often been dismissed. In fact, Robert Churchill said in his book *Game Shooting,* "It is hopeless to try to calculate this." Why? We do it all the time with other sports that depend on hand-eye coordination. Why should shotgunning be any different? In the heat of the moment, we will not always get it *exactly* right, but there is no reason why we cannot make a pretty good stab at developing *some* sort of mental awareness. In any case, in most wingshooting situations, the calculations that our brain must hastily make as it receives ocular stimuli do not usually need to be exact—our shot pattern and (on rare occasions) shot-string will often save the day.

Now what about targets on the sporting clays course? The most frequently asked question (especially on a full-crossing shot) is "How much lead do I need?" The second question is "What exactly does this look like over the end of the gun?" So, is there a way in which we can learn to make an evaluation of this lead requirement before attempting to shoot the target? Not precisely, but make no mistake, the best shots always attempt to make a conscious evaluation of range so that they can step up their angular lead accordingly. How do they do it? Usually by shooting thousands of targets to build up a mental repertoire, but there is a shortcut that I use with my students, which seems to work.

I use three pieces of 2 × 4 board, which I have painted white. The first is three feet long, the second six feet, and the third nine feet. First I place the three-foot length under the flight line of a suitable forty-mile-per-hour full-crossing target and move the student back until he is twenty yards away from the approximate breakpoint. Of course target speed is not constant; faster targets require more lead and slower targets require less, but let's not split hairs at this stage. If the student then mounts his gun on one end of the length of wood, the amount of lead he needs is when the target is at the other end of the board, if he shoots the target with the sustained lead method.

The six-foot length of wood is then substituted, the student is backed up to thirty yards, and the process is repeated; then again from forty yards with the nine-foot piece. This demonstration helps the shooter to develop a mental awareness of how much lead he needs *at the target end*. Simple, isn't it? But don't forget this applies only to full, 90-degree crossing shots—the angles are more complicated. At ranges in excess of this, the angular lead must be increased proportionately to compensate for the shot charge slowing down. The difference in the perception of lead required between a forty-yard shot and a sixty-yard crossing shot looks to be a ridiculous amount, almost double. Some of my students think I am exaggerating until I get them to stand behind me as I demonstrate. Then they try it for themselves and the target breaks.

The shooting method used is one of the other variables that must come into the equation. On a controlled swing-through shot, for example, just how far do you swing-through before you trigger the shot? What about pull-away? Pull away how far? It depends on the personal visual perception of the shooter, and lead is in the eye of the beholder. Question a group of guys on a sporting clays course. On the same target, one man may say he needs to lead the target by three feet and the next guy may think he needs four, and the next may think he needs six. It does not matter that they see the same lead differently. These leads, if they can all break the target, are obviously what work for them. All these guys have developed a personal awareness of how much is needed *for them,* and that is what is important. Regardless of the shooting method we prefer, we still need to develop this mental awareness. My method with the lengths of wood gives a student a reasonable, personal indication of how much he needs. Though it is not foolproof (nothing is in this game), it certainly beats guessing, and I guarantee that all this visual logic at clay targets can eventually be successfully applied to live quarry.

In hunting situations, of course, birds often appear from nowhere quickly, but there are still some things we can do that will alleviate at least some of the guesswork. Take duck hunting over decoys as an example. As you set the decoys out in front of the blind, put the farthest decoy out at a roughly paced forty yards. Any birds that come within this range are game. Or poke a couple of sticks in the mud to the right and left of the blind, once again at a roughly paced forty yards, ideally with empty, yellow 20-gauge shells stuck on the ends, as these show up quite well. This is a useful thing to do even for the expert duck hunter with the full choked gun, who has the skill to attempt shots at extended range. The same applies to driven bird shooting. If the birds are appearing over the trees in front, make a guestimate of the height. The size of the birds as they come over these trees will be a good indication of their range. We always flatter ourselves, but most good tall pheasants will be coming over at about forty yards. At fifty yards plus, clean kills are a fluke, and at this range it is head, neck, or nothing when it comes to bringing the birds down.

20 yards   30 yards   40 yards

20 yards   30 yards   40 yards

20 yards   30 yards   40 yards

The sizes of birds at various ranges in the field.

Often, the man behind the gun is the determinant of the upper limits of a 12-gauge shotgun, rather than the size of the shot load and the amount of choke in the gun. It is possible that a good shot will cleanly kill his birds at up to fifty yards, but beyond that, more birds will be crippled than killed cleanly. We may fool ourselves into thinking that so-and-so can shoot pheasants at excessive ranges, but in reality, this is not the case, and although at times a true "cloud scraper" will be brought down at fifty yards plus with a lucky shot, we owe it to the birds to leave them alone when they are obviously in excess of this. Even with tight chokes and powerful loads, at these excessive ranges clean kills are unlikely, and the following story is an example.

During a lull in the activity at a pheasant shoot on the duke of Buccleuch's estate as we were picking the birds, I had the misfortune to come across two splendidly dressed "sportsmen" who were discussing the pleasures of driven pheasant shooting. I say misfortune for good reason. One of these gentlemen, obviously not short of a bob or two, was using an exquisite pair of 20-gauge English sidelocks. Most of the pheasants this guy would be shooting at throughout the day would be at ranges in excess of forty to fifty yards, and that was the reason he was here in the first place—high-quality birds. The discussion between the two (this subject has a habit of bubbling to the surface from time to time) was on the merits of the 20 gauge versus the 12 gauge. The conversation went something like this: "Oh, I have a pair of 12 gauges, but I prefer to use these. Lighter, you know. Still pull the old long-tails down just as well. Half and full choke, you see, just as good as the 12," said one of the sports.

Over the next several minutes, the conversation between the three of us continued, and it became obvious to me that despite all the ballistic evidence I had injected into the conversation, this gentleman had absolutely no intention of using anything other than his 20 gauge loaded with $7/8$ ounce of shot for birds that would be stretching the limits of a 12 gauge loaded with $1\frac{1}{8}$ ounces. As a "parting shot," as the three of us stood next to a dry-stane dyke (stone wall), I removed two of the stones, one noticeably larger than the other, and asked, "If I dropped one of these on your foot, which one would you prefer it to be?"

Point made, I continued on my way, but I observed that the gentleman hit several splendid cocks later in the day, which we never found. The sad thing is that some people really believe it is better to kill birds with a small gauge and small shot, and when bird hunters get together in the lounge bar and share stories, there is always some egotist present who declares that he considers it to be more "sporting" to do this. Some of them even believe that a 20 will kill *more* efficiently than a 12. Presumably, these people still believe in fairies, that babies actually are found under gooseberry bushes, or that black is really white and vice versa. Don't get me wrong, 20 gauges have a place, but forty-yard-plus driven pheasants, ducks, or similar-size birds shot at extended ranges are not it.

Pheasants, especially, are big birds and as tough as old boots. They can carry a lot of shot, and even when they hit the rock-hard, frozen ground from forty yards up, if there is a spark of life left in them, they will soon be sprinting for cover with the staying power of a marathon runner. This is reason enough for using a 12 gauge firing $1\frac{1}{8}$ ounces. At ranges up to thirty-five yards, the 20 gauge may be adequate, but more than this, and it isn't. At forty yards plus, the effectiveness of the 20 gauge drops dramatically, and even high-velocity shells add only slight improvement.

Unfortunately, the story does not end here. Some time later, another "sportsman" arrived at the estate to shoot driven pheasants, this time armed with a .410 that was pushing out a $\frac{1}{2}$ ounce of lead. This sportsman proudly announced in his booming voice that the gun was bored full and full, and that he had returned from a successful driven partridge hunt in Spain. Driven partridges in Spain, unfortunately, do not compare in any way to stratospheric Scottish pheasants that have three times the body weight and twice the height. Much to my disgust (and that of the head keeper), he was allowed to use the gun, having paid for the privilege. I often wondered just how many of those splendid sporting birds crawled off to die under a bush from peritonitis. Very sad, and I hope that one day that sportsman reads these words and recognizes himself. Undergunning is by no means anything to be proud of.

So why do so many shooters do it? I have no idea. Perhaps they consider it to be more sporting to attempt to kill more birds cleanly by using not enough shot. The shooting world is full of these guys, and when I lived in the United Kingdom, I met many of them. Shooting at live quarry imposes on us the necessity to make sure that we make the best possible attempt to kill our quarry as quickly and cleanly as humanely possible. We owe it to the birds.

I saw lots of strange things over the years at the shoots, not all bad and often very amusing. Scotland has a lot of colorful history, and people visited there from around the world, not just for the superb grouse and pheasant shooting, but also for the single malts and all the pomp and ceremony that went with it. Most of the time, they were out for the best possible time they could have, and who could blame them? Unfortunately, with some of the visitors, there was a language barrier. Some jovial French gentlemen, fitted out in all the appropriate attire—Barbour jackets, tweeds, and gaiters—attended one of the shoots at Westerhall Estate. All of them were exuding elegance as convincingly as the English sidelocks that accompanied them. As the head keeper briefed the guns and gave his customary safety talk—don't shoot low birds, don't shoot into the trees, don't shoot the dogs, certainly don't shoot the beaters, and absolutely don't shoot after the whistle—one of these fellows (we will call him Maurice) was muttering *oui* or *non* and shaking or nodding his head approvingly. The guns drew their pegs, the beaters lined quietly out, and the drive began. Suddenly, a shot rang out from the other side of a small line of conifers, which was a couple of hundred yards in front of me. I had not heard the rattle of the pheasant pinions as the birds lifted off, or even seen any birds flush, which was unusual so early in the drive. Then there was another shot and yet another. By this time, some of the birds had started to flush, and the steady popping of the guns signaled that the drive proper was progressing nicely. Later, as the whistle signaled the end of the drive, I walked around the line of conifers, where the early shots had been, and found Maurice, surprised by my sudden appearance, red in the face and obviously very pleased with himself. He was standing ankle deep in dead pheasants. I congratulated him on his shooting, and he replied with a grin as big as the channel tunnel, "Ah oui, monsieur, zeeze pheasants zey run so *fast!*"

I soon learned from someone who had witnessed the very unsporting display from a distance exactly what had ensued. Maurice, who had never shot at anything in excess of twenty yards in his life, was hopelessly out of his depth on the tall pheasants at forty yards plus and, try as he might, could not connect with them. To save face, in desperation, he had decided that anything that managed to creep through the fence ahead of the beaters was fair game, airborne or not! I hastily explained in my limited French vocabulary that it might be better if he allowed the birds the luxury of getting off the ground before he shot them, and he slipped me a 20 pound note at the end of the day. Very generous, the French.

Finally, while we are on the subject of shotgun range, for all the competition shooters out there, just what is the effective range of a 12-gauge shotgun on a standard clay target? As amazing as it may seem, it is possible to chip a *visible* piece off a standard 110-mm clay target at approximately 85 to 90 yards with a standard 1,350-feet-per-second $7\frac{1}{2}$ shot size shell.

Many years ago, I watched four-time world sporting clay champion George Digweed do just that at a shooting ground in the south of England, and he did it again in front of an audience at the World English in San Antonio in May 2001.

There were many skeptics after this remarkable shooting exhibition, some of them claiming that they had since "proved" that the feat was impossible by shooting at a stationary clay target that was suspended off the ground. Unfortunately, this test is inconclusive. Shoot at a stationary standard 110-mm target (with the concave side toward the shooter) with a standard-velocity shell of somewhere in the region of 1,350 feet per second, 7½ shot size, and a full choke barrel, and you will be lucky to chip a visible piece off at 70 yards. Why? As a clay target comes off the throwing plate of an automatic target launcher, it is spinning like a Frisbee in the initial stage of its flight. If a pellet or two in this early stage of its flight strikes it, it is possible to break it convincingly because the effects of centrifugal force on the spinning targets will force it apart. I have done it myself at a measured eighty-five yards, though achieving *consistent* breaks at this range was impossible for me (due, I believe, to my own inability to center the pattern on the target every time), and I could only break an average of one in five targets.

If we return to the exhibition by the great man himself for a moment, I have no idea what choke was in George's gun at the time, but in any case, at these sort of ranges, I would have thought it would be a fluke to break the target, but George could, and did, in front of an audience, and he did it with mind-boggling consistency. It proves something that I have already said earlier—sometimes success depends upon the shooter, not the shotgun.

CHAPTER 17

Cleaning and Maintenance

Do you ever bother to make a calculation of what it costs you to shoot birds? First there is all the travel involved—the airfare, rental vehicles, 4 × 4 truck, trailer, and Kawasaki mule to get you to the duck blind. Then there is the expensive quail lease in south Texas, duck-hunting trips to Paraguay, the German pointer and the black Labrador, food and vet bills for the dogs, hunting licenses, ammunition—the list is endless. Then there are the guns. The Benelli autoloader for the ducks and geese, the Beretta 20 gauges for the dove trips to Argentina, the pair of Arietta side-by-sides for the occasional trip to the United Kingdom for grouse and pheasant hunts. Finally, there are the Damascus-barreled English sidelocks that cost you substantially more than a messy divorce (and probably very nearly caused one!), just because you have to have them.

Then there is the maintenance of the guns and the regular visits to the reputable gunsmith, just to make sure that when that cloud-scraping cock pheasant rattles over the mighty English oak trees, there is no nauseating click as the gun fails to do its duty and detonate the charge at the right time. What's that? You always have your guns serviced regularly, regardless of whether they need it or not? Certainly you do, and I bet you *always* religiously clean your gun after every outing, don't you? Now without cheating, cast your mind back and consider exactly what you mean by "regularly serviced." See what I mean?

I am always amazed that to some people "regularly serviced" means every twenty years or so, and usually then only when the gun malfunctions for some reason. When a shotgun malfunctions, it is usually because there has been a gradual buildup of minor problems that are ignored over a period of time. Lack of lubrication in the right areas and

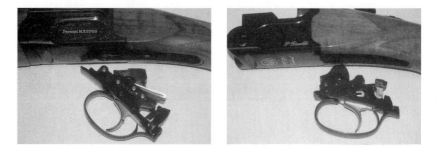

Many quality competition guns, like the Perazzi MX 2000 (left) and Beretta Trident (right), now come with detachable locks. This is a huge advantage with cleaning and maintenance and also security. The lock can simply be removed and stored separately from the gun.

buildup of dirt and debris in others will eventually put more stress than necessary on some of the intricate components of the mechanism. This is why preventive maintenance is important—the problem should be solved before it can happen. Preventive maintenance is a huge gray area for many shotgunners, but the eventual goal of all shotgunners is trouble-free performance with their guns, isn't it?

Most gun owners will shower affection and vast quantities of money on their cherished automobiles and have them regularly serviced, but they begrudge spending a small amount on their beloved shotgun, even when their values may be very similar. Wingshooters are notorious for neglecting their shotguns, and after a season of faithful, flawless service, their favorite piece is usually treated to the luxury of a quick squirt of gun oil and then bundled into an inconspicuous corner until next season. Shooters often shower verbal abuse on their guns when they fail,

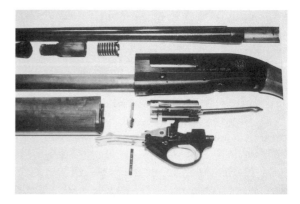

The semiautomatic is comparatively easy to strip down for cleaning. Most of these increasingly popular guns come in parts, with an instructional manual for assembly.

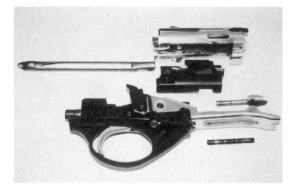

The trigger assembly on this Beretta 391 can be removed easily for cleaning by removing the bolt handle and pushing out the pin shown at the bottom left of the picture.

and the number of times customers would come into my gun shop in Scotland with the remark "Can't understand it! Worked okay last season and now there's something wrong with the damned thing!"—as if it were the gun's fault—would always bring a smile to my face. Shotguns as a whole are remarkably reliable and can often stand years of neglect and abuse. A gun that is in good, working order will serve you faithfully for many years, but it cannot be expected to perform flawlessly ad infinitum, and it usually will not without proper care and attention, but what exactly is proper care and attention?

Side-by-side game guns are usually more vulnerable to abuse than the more rugged over-and-under. This is because they are traditionally made primarily for wingshooting rather than targets, and everything is lighter as a result. If you are lucky enough to own a best English gun, chances are that it was made between 1900 and 1950—the golden era of the true classics. Many best English guns can give reliable service for well over one hundred years, so normal wear and tear is to be expected. The ribs on a best English gun are attached to the barrels with solder instead of brazing to keep the heat down during this jointing process and prevent distortion of the tubes. The loop where the splinter fore-end attaches is also soft-soldered into the space between the barrels. This soft-solder is very strong, but in time, the loop may start to lift.

An early indication of this is a gun that suddenly becomes "loose" and one or both of the ejectors fail to operate properly. The rib, over a period of time, may also become loose. It is easy to check for this, and in fact, anyone who is thinking of buying a used English sidelock should first try this simple test to give a clear indication of the status of the rib. The barrels should be removed from the gun and hung from the forefinger by the hook. The end of the muzzles should then be flicked

Detatchable lock from a
Holland & Holland over-
and-under.

with the thumbnail of the other hand. This should result in a clear, ring-ing sound, indicating that the jointing solder is still intact. Any pair of barrels that has a dull sound should be avoided—it means the rib is loose.

Examination will sometimes reveal a noticeable gap between the rib and barrels, and if this situation has existed for any time, there is a chance that moisture has penetrated into the rib cavity. The rib will have to be removed and resoldered and the external pitting investigated. Although it takes a long time for this external pitting to become severe, I have seen guns that needed to be scrapped on occasion. Professional

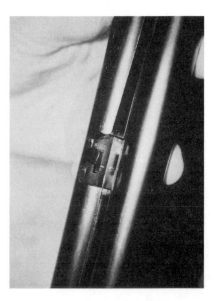

The splinter fore-end attaches to the barrels of a side-by-side by the front loop, which is soft-soldered into the space between the barrels. With a modern gun, this soft solder is very strong, but with some older guns (usually pre-1890s) this solder was considerably softer and in time, the loop may start to lift. An early indi-cation of this is a gun that suddenly becomes loose and one or both of the ejectors fail to operate properly.

examination on a regular basis is the best preventative. Sometimes as the barrels are handled on an old gun it is possible to hear something loose that rattles up and down in the rib cavity. This is usually a small blob of solder (known as a dead man in the gun trade) and is usually the result of the front loop being replaced at some time. Usually, this is nothing to worry about and is not noticed during normal use.

Barrels are blacked to protect them from rust, but this wears off through normal use. Normally, this is not a problem so long as the gun is cleaned and oiled regularly. Owning a gun shop for many years, I would have to display constant vigilance and make sure that the guns in the rack were wiped down after anyone handled them. Ridiculous as it may seem, in warm weather, barrels will start to rust *in an hour or two* after being handled by a prospective customer with sweaty hands. Never place a gun cabinet on the outside wall of a house or in a garage, because the cold can penetrate the outside wall and trigger the rusting process.

A gun brought into a warm cabin or vehicle from use in cold temperatures will be immediately covered with condensation and should therefore be allowed to warm to room temperature and dry for an hour or so before finally being cleaned and returned to the cabinet. If possible, seal the cold (but dry) gun inside a dry case before bringing it inside, as that will keep most condensation off of it while it warms up, but do not

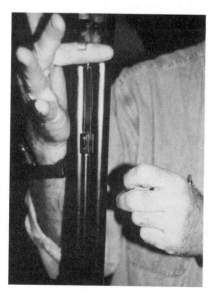

Anyone who is considering the purchase of a quality English sidelock should try this simple test. The barrels are jointed to the rib with solder that is fairly soft. The barrels should be removed from the gun and hung from the forefinger by the hook as shown. The barrels should then be flicked with the thumbnail or finger of the other hand. You should hear a clear ringing sound, indicating that the jointing solder is still intact. Any set of barrels that has a dull sound should be avoided; it means that the rib is loose. If the rib has been loose for some time, it usually means that over a period (this may be several decades), moisture will penetrate the cavity between the rib and the barrels. Although the barrels may look sound on the outside, they may be badly corroded on the inside, underneath the rib. A new set of barrels may cost more than the gun is worth.

leave it in the case for more than an hour or so before removing and cleaning and oiling it. Never store a gun in a case. If the gun is wet, bring it in, take it apart, and carefully dry it off and out. If it was cold when you brought it in, you will have to dry it repeatedly until it warms up to room temperature.

Always make a thorough visual check for bulges and dents in the barrels. A bulge can occur when someone sticks the end of his gun in the mud or snow without realizing it. Surely no one is *that* stupid are they? That is basic safety stuff, isn't it? It is, but I assure you it happens, because almost every season in my gun shop in Scotland there would be someone who came into the shop with a mysterious bulge in a barrel that "just appeared," or a dent in their best English sidelock barrels that magically manifested itself and "wasn't there last time I used it." The careless hop across a water-filled ditch to intercept the rising mallard or the hurried clamber through the fence on the quail lease can do it. You vaguely remember hearing a clunk as something hit the steel-straining pole, but you didn't think it was that bad at the time.

Any dent that occurs in a barrel as a result of an accidental knock should be examined by an expert gunsmith before the gun is used again. Old Harry down at the gun club may be a real nice guy and may know all about guns, but don't risk it—take the gun to a professional. Dents can be raised by using a special tool—a tightly fitting plug that is slid inside the barrel to be used as an anvil. Any residual blemishes can then be "lapped" out. A lapping tool is made from lead cast onto a steel rod and rotated inside the barrel. The lap is coated with fine emery powder and cutting oil. Don't put sentiment before safety and fire the gun until this is done. Usually, a good gunsmith, who will also have a barrel thickness gauge to see that the barrels are still within the proof measurements, can remove small dents easily. After the dent is removed, if he thinks it should be reproofed, that's fine; it would be much better for the gun to fail under controlled conditions than to blow up in the user's face during normal use. Remember (I do not mean to sound as though I am scaremongering), guns can be replaced, eyes and fingers cannot.

Cultivate the habit of cleaning the barrels after every shooting trip. This is much easier today than it used to be. When I was a youth, the propellant in many cartridges was corrosive, and after a hard day's use, it was advisable to flush them out with boiling water before oiling to make sure there was no corrosive residue remaining. The propellant of modern cartridges is not corrosive, but after a busy day, when several hundred shells

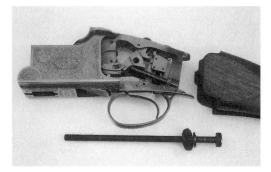

Most over-and-unders are attached to the stock with a long stock bolt. Removing the butt pad will reveal the bolt-hole, and the bolt can then easily be removed from the stock with either a socket wrench or large screwdriver.

have been fired, there will be plastic and lead deposits in the barrels. These must be removed because it is possible to trap microscopic amounts of moisture between this fouling and the steel of the barrel. Today, there are several cleaning products on the market, and perhaps the most popular is Quick Scrub III, an amazing, all-purpose cleaner and degreaser. It comes in an aerosol can and is environmentally friendly, nonflammable and non-water-based. Who could ask for more? It can be sprayed directly down barrels of shotguns and rifles. Simply remove the barrels and blast all the buildup of residue away. Do this after each time the gun is used; then at the end of each season, remove the stock of your breaking gun and clean the whole action with it. Removing the stock bolt (or nut), which is found in the hole under the butt pad, will expose the actions of most over-and-unders and side-by-sides. The competent do-it-yourselfer can attempt this, but the emphasis is on *competent*. If in doubt, have your gunsmith do it. Never let any liquid soak into the wood stock or fore-end.

The side plates of a sidelock must be removed to expose the action. These side plates should be a very tight fit to prevent moisture and dust from entering the action, and I would recommend that their removal be left to the expert or a competent gunsmith. The actions of pumps and autoloaders can be flushed out in the same way. All that must be done then is to relubricate all the action parts. I prefer hydroscopic gun oil because this will lift the water off the metal and form a moisture-impervious barrier. Something like WD-40 is good for cleaning metal parts and can be used to dispel moisture, but it is not suitable as a gun oil. Aerosol sprays of any sort, although convenient, encourage a too liberal application, which over a period of time can seep through the lock mechanism and into the wood at the head where the action fits and soften it. Squirting

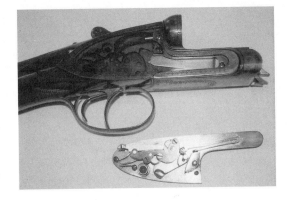

Boxlocks usually have a floor plate, which can be removed for servicing. In the sidelock, the lock assembly is attached to the side plate. Removal of this is best left to the expert, but it can be removed by first taking out the retaining screws and tapping the front of the action smartly onto a piece of hardwood. If this doesn't work, leave it to the expert.

copious amounts of oil through the firing-pin holes and into the trigger mechanism will serve no useful purpose, and most of it will drain through the lock work and into the head of the stock. The cost of replacing a premium-grade stock because of this will often leave the owner reaching for the whiskey bottle! Quality guns (especially older ones) should be stored in the gun cabinet with the barrels pointing down so that any surplus oil can drain away from the woodwork, which brings us to maintenance of the wood.

Most standard field-grade guns have low-grade woodwork and a polyurethane finish, which requires very little maintenance. Mud and dirt that gets engrained in the checkering from a day at the duck blind is best removed by allowing it to dry and then brushing it out with a fine-bristled brush. A toothbrush is ideal. Any chips and knocks can be revarnished to prevent moisture entry.

Top-quality side-by-sides and over-and-unders will have the luxury of walnut woodwork. Quality guns are works of art; and these guns will have ornate designs and exquisite engraving. Over the years, the skill of the modern engraver has been elevated to a higher level, and to enhance the beauty of the engraving, only the finest, well-figured walnut is used. Why walnut? Although other types of wood have often been tried, walnut has for centuries been the main choice for gun stocks for several reasons other than its pleasing-to-the-eye aesthetics.

Although walnut grows in many countries around the world, French walnut is the ideal strength and density. It is the most sought after, but nowadays it is hard to find and prohibitively expensive. The colors in the grain come from the minerals in the soil as the tree slowly matures, and the climate and soil conditions in the Mediterranean countries provide ideal growing conditions. Many gun makers now use Turkish and American walnut as a substitute. The entire tree can be used, but the base of the trunk and the top of the root system produce the best grain figuration. The mature tree is cut carefully by experts to maximize the number of blanks that can be obtained. These blanks are sealed at each end with beeswax and then allowed to dry for up to ten years. Throughout this seasoning process, many blanks will be rejected, but when the moisture content has been reduced sufficiently, the resulting blanks will be stable enough to be carved into stocks and fore-ends. This workability is another excellent quality of walnut. The stocker can work the wood with precision and remove only the minimum necessary to permit the lock to be seated and its components to function correctly.

The grip must then be checkered so that it will present a nonslip surface to the user's hand during handling. The finished stock is then sealed with an oil finish that is hand rubbed in and allowed to dry over several weeks. This will not only enhance the beauty of the grain, but also make the stock durable. All this will take an experienced stocker at least 150 to 200 hours on a best side-lock. Add to this the price of the blank, and you could be looking at $5,000 to $6,000. Minor blemishes can be restored easily with the application of a small amount of boiled

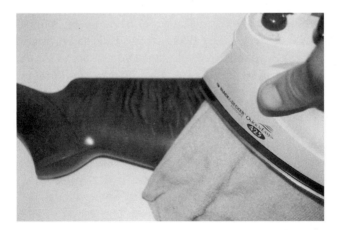

Minor dents can be removed by steaming, which will raise the fibers of the wood so that they return to their original state. To do this, two or three folds of cotton material (an old bed sheet is ideal) should be soaked in water, placed over the dent, and firmly pressed with a hot domestic iron. With oil-finished stocks, any milky appearance that this leaves can be removed with the application of a small amount of warm walnut oil.

232 • *Successful Shotgunning*

linseed oil. During use in wet weather, a stock with an oil finish will develop a cloudy or milky appearance. This is caused by the vegetable oils used to finish the stock emulsifying with the water. This will vanish if the stock is dried out and a little stock oil rubbed into it. Minor dents in the stock and fore-end can be removed easily by steaming. A damp piece of toweling is placed over the dent, and heat is then applied with an ordinary domestic iron. The steam produced will swell the fibers of the wood, and the dent will *usually* disappear. If it does not, there is another way, which involves the application of more intense heat by igniting a small drop of methylated spirit that is applied to the dent. For obvious reasons, this second method is best left to the expert.

A trigger that becomes increasingly stiff or heavy or acquires any noticeable difference in the pull should be investigated as soon as possible, never ignored in the hope that it will correct itself in time. A shotgun trigger is a precise mechanical device of careful design and should never be adjusted or altered by anyone except a competent gunsmith. Ejector problems are common and can be due to several things. With over-and-unders, the usual problem is a simple one of a buildup of dirt or rust in the chamber. In an old gun, wear around the head of the ejector will allow the neck of the cartridge case to swell and expand into it as the gun is fired, trapping the cartridge in the chamber as the gun is opened.

Misfires are occasionally due to a worn, broken, or fouled firing pin, but they can also be caused by a weak or cracked mainspring in the side-by-side or a weak coil spring in the over-and-under. Actions should be completely stripped on a regular basis. Springs and lock parts (especially sidelock sear springs and mainsprings), which work under severe shock and stress loadings, can often develop a hairline fracture that is apparent to the trained eye. A good gunsmith will notice and replace these before they fail completely. A shotgun, with care, will last many years, certainly fifty or more. Doesn't it make sense to give it some regular attention? Finally, a shooter's reaction to a gun malfunction can be a mixed one of surprise, frustration, and in some cases, extreme anger. Here is a story about one of those people—the wrong sort.

I used to load for the double-gunners on the Earl of Dalkeith's grouse moors above Langholm. One of the clients that I loaded for was obviously a very wealthy man, and during a lull in activity one day, as we were waiting for the birds, this fellow bragged incessantly about the fact that he was one of the leading producers of a certain brand of frozen foods in the United Kingdom. I found out later that the business had been established by his father, and during the course of the conversation, I realized that I knew his father and had loaded for him several times in the past. He had recently passed away, I was saddened to hear, as he was a gentleman—always polite, always amusing, and never arrogant in any way. Unfortunately, the son had not inherited all of his father's good traits. It was obvious to me that the fellow had no real interest in grouse shooting, his form was terrible, and there was a continual barrage of obscenities when he missed. He shot with an exquisite matched pair of Joseph Lang sidelocks that he had inherited from his father, and it was apparent that both guns were suffering from neglect, with noticeable rust marks on the outside of the barrels and an obvious lack of lubrication—they had a gritty feel when I opened them.

This became increasingly worse, until halfway through the morning, when the gun was ejecting badly and then refused to open at all. The malfunction came as no surprise to the client, whose reply was, "Yes, the damn thing sometimes does that. Give it here, I know how to fix it." He proceeded to attempt to force the gun open by banging it across his knee. After several attempts, the force he applied was so great that he smashed the wrist of the stock. As if this were not enough, in disgust, he then threw the two halves into the corner of the grouse butt. It was very sad to see; it could all have been prevented with a little routine maintenance.

CHAPTER 18

Sporting Clays

Sporting clays, or English sporting, to give it its proper name, originated in the United Kingdom many years ago. It is still by far the fastest-growing shotgun discipline in the United States at present, and it appears that this trend will continue for quite a while. In the United Kingdom, game shooting was very fashionable in the late 1800s, and by the end of the nineteenth century, each of the English gun-making firms had its own shooting school offering simulated game shooting to encourage the Victorian sportsmen and -women to improve their marksmanship. The gun-making firm of Charles Lancaster, Coach and Horse Yard, Great Titchfield Street, London, was reputedly one of the first, and in 1889, Lancaster wrote a book called *The Art of Shooting*. The book has an illustration showing America's legendary "Little Miss Sure-shot" herself, Annie Oakley, receiving instruction from Lancaster when she visited England in 1887 with Buffalo Bill's Wild West Show. As early as 1888, sporting clays targets were shot at Cogswell and Harrison's shooting ground at Colnbrook, near London, but serious tournaments did not take place until after the end of World War I.

The first English Open sporting clays competition was held in 1925, but the sport did not really take off until the 1970s. Here in the United States, Remington introduced sporting clays, and a simplified version was shot at Remington Farms in the late 1960s. Shooting hall of famer Bob Brister was a prominent figure in the development of sporting on this side of the pond.

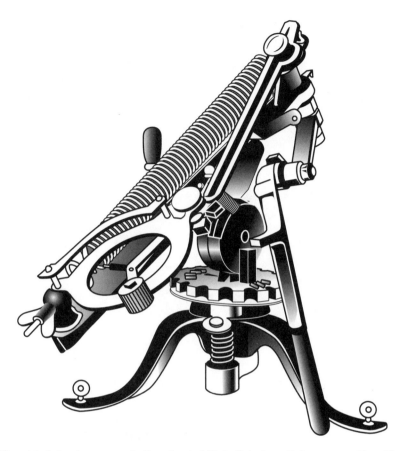

The original clay pigeon was actually a glass ball filled with feathers. Various means of launching these inanimate targets were tried, including this one, a Swiftsure launcher manufactured in England in the 1890s.

Sporting was originally intended to replicate the types of shots we would experience while hunting in the field, but today it has progressed far beyond that. Apart from the standard (110 mm) targets, there are also specialty targets. These are midis (90 mm), minis (60 mm), and battues, which are 110 mm in diameter but half the thickness of standard targets, rabbits, which either roll along the ground or can be thrown as loopers, or chandelles, to give them their correct name. Layouts are not standardized and are changed periodically to respond to the insatiable appetites of the shooters for new challenges. Each target requires a special approach.

A variety of targets is found on the testing sporting clays course.

A good course needs to be changed regularly, so machines need to be reasonably mobile. This machine is mounted on a trailer and is powered by a 12-volt battery that is topped up with a solar panel charger.

TALL TARGETS, SHORT ANSWERS: HIGH TOWER TARGETS AND TALL PHEASANTS

Organized driven pheasant shoots, where beaters would tap their way through the woodlands of the great sporting estates and flush hundreds of birds over the waiting guns, originated in England in East Anglia around 1875. The idea was to encourage the birds to fly high and fast

Sporting clays were originally intended to replicate the targets found in actual bird-hunting situations in the field. Here the participants in a tournament try their luck on the 120-foot "Duck Tower" at the Dallas Gun Club.

over the shooters to test their marksmanship. There were many attempts, even in those days, to rationalize the theories of shotgun shooting and explain the skills of the sport. Which shots do you think would give these Victorian sportsmen their biggest headache? The high birds and long crossing shots, of course, and consequently, many books were written on the subject. One was written in about 1925 by the Victorian naturalist Sir Ralph Payne-Gallwey, *High Pheasants in Theory and Practice.* Later, as a result of the challenges presented in this type of shooting, shooting schools, notably the Holland & Holland and the West London, evolved. They became popular as the sportsmen and -women of this era sought to improve their marksmanship, and each shooting grounds had its own high tower to simulate these difficult targets.

So here we are in the twenty-first century, and things have not changed much. The sight of a high tower poking ominously above the tree line as we walk around a shooting grounds is usually enough to send shivers down our spine. Make no mistake, the high tower is a formidable opponent and the nemesis of many a good shooter. Sporting clays tournaments are won or lost at the high tower, and anyone who has journeyed to England to shoot driven pheasants will know just how difficult the real thing is.

I was lucky. For many years I lived in the heart of some of the best driven pheasant shooting in the world. It was my job to make sure that the visiting "guns" could manage to hit a few. A fifty-yard-high hen pheasant screaming down the side of a Scottish mountain with a stiff tailwind behind it makes a clay target with its predictable trajectory seem a lot easier. Notice that I said *easier,* not easy. High birds are anything but easy, but with a *systematic* approach, they can be beaten. High tower shots can either be straight driven or driven away (where they come directly toward or away from you), or crossing to the left or right. Each requires a different technique, as those that work at closer ranges fail on the high tower because the margin for error is much less. There is a lot of sky around a target when it is forty yards or more off the ground! We will deal with the crossing birds first.

The Secret Is in the Stance
Good foot positions are the key for success at tower clays on the shooting ground and at driven birds in the field. It is very difficult to move the gun accurately on the same trajectory as a high crosser if your stance is wrong. The proper stance on a high crossing shot should be with the

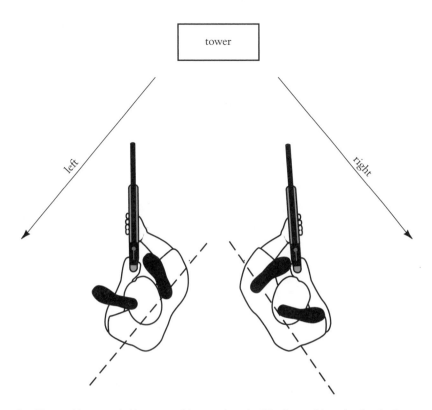

Good foot positions are vital for successful tower shots. It will be impossible to develop the line of the target properly if your stance is wrong. The shoulders should be parallel to the flight line of the target, and by doing this, the shoulders will remain level as the shot is taken. Most high crossing targets are missed off-line than any other way.

shoulders approximately parallel to the target's line of flight. The shoulders should remain level as the shot is taken. This will ensure that there is plenty of room for a smooth and assertive swing well past the intended breakpoint of the target. I say "assertive" because slowing or stopping the gun on a long crossing shot is inviting a miss. Failure to set yourself up correctly for this type of shot will cause you to run out of swing and, in an attempt to keep the gun moving, drop a shoulder and "rainbow" under the line of the target. This is known as dropping off the line. Many high crossers are missed below for this reason.

The longer the gun is in your shoulder, the more conscious you become of it. Therefore, attempting to shoot high crossing birds with a premounted gun is a mistake. The barrels, if you do this, become a distraction because they are central to your line of vision. This makes reading the line of the target difficult, and this is even more the case with a live bird. The *majority* of crossing targets, if we think about it, both on a sporting clays course and birds in the field, require a fairly horizontal gun movement. The human body pivots easily on a horizontal plane, but now we are called upon to produce a gun movement that is neither horizontal nor vertical, but somewhere in between. This is a difficult movement for most people to make, and to move an eight-pound gun *smoothly* above your head to intercept the target takes lots of practice. Put the gun in your shoulder too early, and the muzzles will almost certainly try to move horizontally. If the target is not moving in a horizontal direction relative to you, then you've got a problem. The secret is to use your *arms* to produce most of the movement. A smoothly engineered movement along the line of the target (known as developing the line) is essential for success on this type of shot, and if the gun is not moving accurately along the same line, it does not matter how perfectly you lead the target, you will miss. More shots on high driven pheasants, or on the high tower at the shooting grounds, are missed off-line than most people realize.

So assuming we get our foot positions right and we can successfully move the gun on the same line of the target, the only way we can miss is in front or behind. It is not very likely that we will miss in front, so why do most people miss behind? Three main reasons:

1. The lead requirement on a high crossing shot deceives everyone initially, and a more conscious approach is necessary. My clients are always amazed at how much daylight they need to see to break a long, fast crosser off a high tower. Instinctive shooting is one thing and is easily applied to closer targets where speed assessment is simpler. With a high crossing shot, there is an optical illusion, and the target appears to be moving much slower than it really is. If your club has a high tower that elevates to different levels, you might like to try the following experiment. Shoot a driven target at its lowest setting, coming over you at perhaps twenty feet like a driven grouse. Then elevate the tower to its highest setting and do the same thing again. See how much slower the target appears to be? Obviously it cannot be, as the targets are coming off the trap arm at the same speed, but that is what it seems like. That is the main reason why many people miss high targets behind. The brain refuses to accept the ocular stimuli it receives and gives the order to fire,

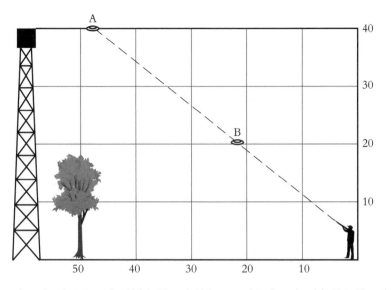

On an incoming shot, target B, which is 20 yards high, comes into view when it is 20 to 30 yards from the shooter. Target A comes into view when it is still 60 yards away. The lower target will be over the gun almost three times faster than the higher target, which will make target A seem much slower. It isn't. Speed and distance are deceptive on high tower shots and high birds. Because of the angle of the bird relative to the shooter's position, the *perception* of lead on target A (even though it is farther away) will be less than when it is directly over the gun, where it will be at 90 degrees to the shooter's position.

unfortunately usually when the amount of forward allowance is about half what is needed.

2. Anyone who shoots skeet will be familiar with the lead requirement on a station 4 target. If we apply basic physics to this, a target that is moving at approximately forty miles per hour and passing over the center stake at twenty-one yards requires approximately three to four feet lead if shot with the maintained lead method. Logically, a target at thirty yards requires at least twice this lead, and at forty yards three times as much, because of the progressive slowing down of the shot charge. Distance to the target makes it necessary to increase the angular lead even *farther* to compensate for this. At ranges of fifty yards and above, this deceleration is even more pronounced, and the lead on a sixty-yard shot may be as much as fifteen feet. That is the second reason why people miss behind—miscalculation. Don't confuse this more calculating approach with measuring. It isn't. It merely gives the shooter a clearer indication of what is needed.

3. To most of us, the clay targets coming off a high tower look to be about the size of a pinhead. Likewise with a true tall pheasant. The lead requirement is so much on some of them that as the gun pushes ahead to establish lead, the target is fast fading into our peripheral vision. So now what do we do? Look at the gun, of course, to "measure" the lead. Human eyes cannot focus on two things at the same time, so guess what happens next? We stop the gun, don't we? That is the third reason we miss behind.

So now let us imagine that you have read this and you are ready to take your next high crossing shot off the tower. Decide where on the target's trajectory you will shoot it, and in most cases, this will be where it is nearest to you. Set yourself up correctly. Concentrate *mainly* on developing the line, and as soon as see what you perceive is the correct amount of forward allowance, take the shot. Because we can see most high tower shots for a long time, it is easy to become mesmerized by them. If you are not careful this will lead to tracking, i.e., following the target with a mounted gun. Don't do it. *Preferably shoot as soon as the gun hits your shoulder to complete the mount.* The amount of perceived lead depends on the individual and his or her preferred method for shooting the target. The swing-through shooter, for example, will see less lead than the pull-away or sustained lead shooter, due to the variation in the amount of gun speed. If you miss, and you *know* you were on-line, then the problem must be the amount of forward allowance you gave the target. Increase your lead, as it is unusual to see someone miss a fast, high bird in front.

So much for the high crossing shots. Now we will look at the best way to tackle the straight incoming driven pheasant and driven away shots. The technique is completely different. Low driven targets, like driven grouse, should be taken well out in front with the weight over the leading leg. This is because the oblique angle makes them the vertical equivalent of a narrow-angle quartering target, and the lead requirement is minimal. A truly high bird of forty yards or more is nearest to you when it is directly overhead, so logically this is the best place to shoot it. This means that we must be able to move the gun in some cases past the vertical. Unfortunately, this is just where most of us run out of swing—the gun stops and we miss behind. On a high driven target, the lead requirement is considerable, and so a smooth swing is essential for good results. Also, when we shoot any moving target, we must put the shot charge into the *anticipated* flight path of the target, which means that a high driven bird will vanish behind the gun as we pull the trigger. Then what happens? Usually, we lift our head to look for the target, and once again, the gun stops and we miss behind.

So how do we maintain visual contact with the target as it vanishes behind the gun? There are two ways we can do this. One is to learn to look "through" and beyond the barrels with the other eye. In the case of a right-shouldered shooter, this is the left eye. With a side-by-side, this is difficult to do, and for this reason, many driven pheasant side-by-side devotees utilize the second method of maintaining visual contact—they have their guns stocked high so that there is built-in lead on the high birds. Incidentally, this is the reason why most driven bird specialists are changing to the over-and-under—the narrow sighting plane means that this "transparent barrels" technique is easier to apply.

With practice, the correct amount of lead can be established accurately each time as the gun overtakes the target. Notice I said *with practice,* because some of my clients, when they try this for the first time, have not the foggiest idea what I am talking about and continue shooting high driven birds by guessing where the target is as they pull the trigger. Persevere; with practice, the "looking through the gun" technique works extremely well on driven tower shots. This technique also works on long springing teal and some trap-type shots. For shooters with a master eye problem, the trick is to close the eye that is *not* above the rib until the line is established and then open it to establish lead. The second way we can maintain visual contact with the target is to turn sideways and take the target as a high crosser.

So how do we make sure that we can produce a smooth, accurate swing up to and beyond the vertical? The secret is to transfer the weight to the *back* foot by raising the heel of the *front* leg (assuming a right-shouldered shooter) slightly as the mount is completed. You might like to try this at home. Keep both feet firmly on the ground and move your gun to the vertical position at an imaginary target. Raise your front heel *slightly* while in this position. See what I mean? As the heel is raised, the hips push forward and the upper torso moves back. You should now be able to swing well past the vertical. This is a progressive, smooth movement that takes place just as the gun is coming into the shoulder, not a sudden lift of the heel. Just as with long crossing shots, most of the movement on the target line should be made with the arms.

Since you would shoot a high driven bird with the weight on the back foot, doesn't it make sense to shoot an outgoing overhead target

Left: A true driven bird will be nearest when it is directly overhead. If the gun is mounted too early, with the weight over the front foot, you will tend to slow or stop the swing as the bird approaches the vertical position.

Right: The arms should move the gun on the line of the target, and as the gun comes into the shoulder pocket, the heel of the leading leg should be raised slightly. By doing this, weight will be transferred to the back foot, the hips will push forward, and the upper torso will move back. This will help to produce a smooth, assertive swing well past the vertical.

with the weight on the *front* foot? Of course. A much smoother, progressive swing in the same direction as the target will be produced if you do this. The best medicine for this target is sustained lead or pull-away. Why? Well if you try to swing through this target from behind, you will find that it takes a bit of catching. Instead of a smooth, precise movement, you will probably end up with a hurried poke. Every millisecond you delay pulling the trigger on this target will make it more difficult to break.

To set yourself up for this shot, put your weight onto your back foot and look back for the target so that you will have good visual contact as soon as possible. Keep your gun fairly high, but not so far back that the barrels are out of your peripheral vision. Be prepared to move the gun on the flash of the target, or the built-in lead allowance you have will quickly evaporate and you will end up chasing the target. As you call for

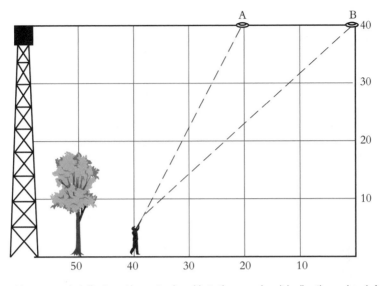

On a driven-away shot, the target is most vulnerable to the gun when it is directly overhead. Any delay with triggering the shot will mean that the target is more difficult to break. Many shooters let this type of target get too far out before firing, which is a mistake.

the target and begin to move the gun, allow your weight to transfer to the *front* leg. Once again, this type of target is best shot where it is most vulnerable to your gun, as near to you as possible. This is where the target is presenting its most vulnerable concave underside. Don't forget that the lead requirement will be just as much as that for an incoming driven bird. Once again, the optical information you transmit to your brain will suggest that the target is moving slowly. It isn't. If the speed is the same and the distance to the target is the same, then logically the lead must be the same. For some reason, most shooters think they can give an outgoing bird less lead than they would give a similar incoming shot.

When a high incomer is approaching dead-on, with no sideways deviation to the left or right, it is difficult to swing smoothly through the target without a slight drift to the left (right-handed shooter), due to muscle tension in the extended left arm and upper body as the gun hits the shoulder. The muzzles will drag off-line and prescribe an arc, and a miss down the side of the target will be the result. To compensate, move your grip on the fore-end back slightly. This will also help to produce maximum swing past vertical because there is now slightly more weight forward of the leading hand than normal, resulting in slightly more momentum in the barrels. This will help to produce a good, continuous, *smooth* swing as the shot is taken.

With a pair of driven targets off high tower, or any driven pair for that matter, which one do we take first? Provided that they are both coming toward you at the same speed, the answer for a right-shouldered shooter is the *right* one. By doing this, we will keep the gun pushed into our face as we move to the second target. Try it the other way around, and we will probably push the gun away from our face and shoot down the side of the target. The foot positions for a pair of driven targets are exactly the same as the ones I recommended for shooting high driven live birds. Stand facing squarely to the tower, feet *approximately* shoulder-width apart. Any wider will restrict your movement. As the right-hand bird is taken, the *left* heel should be raised slightly to give a more flowing movement to the right, and then the *right* heel is raised as the bird on the left is taken. This will ensure that the shoulders remain level throughout the swing.

Finally, because we have absolutely no visual reference to anything as we shoot these high birds—just an empty expanse of sky—it is easy to

Left: With a bird that flies to the right, the left heel should be raised.
Right: With a bird that flies to the left, the right heel should be raised to allow the swing to develop and prevent slowing or stopping the gun.

become disorientated. Good timing, perfect foot positions, and perfect balance are more important on these high crossing shots than on almost any other shot. For many years, I had the pleasure of witnessing some of the best high pheasant shots in the world. The ease and unhurried elegance with which some of these guys could stroke a really high bird out of the sky was incredible, *but it only comes with practice.*

Driven to Distraction?

The growing trend in the United States at the present time seems to be a passion for sexy-looking, exquisitely engraved English sidelocks. Of course, once you have finished salivating over the gun of your dreams and have actually plucked up the courage to pay for it, you need some European-style driven pheasant, grouse, and partridge shooting to go with it. I am all for it. An injection of atavism to prop up the U.K. economy can't be such a bad thing. There is only one thing that does cause me slight concern. There are a lot of successful guys in the United States who fail to realize that driven birds are a different style of shooting than that which they have grown accustomed to, and I don't mean all the pomp and ceremony that is thrown in. Most of them have no idea what to expect.

Driven pheasants, the epitome of game shooting.

Take driven pheasants as an example. It is not dove hunting in Lubbock, it certainly does not equate to quail hunting in south Texas, and it is nothing like ruffed grouse shooting in Pennsylvania. Driven pheasant shooting in England or Scotland is a different ball game altogether, and for the uninitiated, hitting them is hard. The sight of a grown man, after having parted with his hard-earned dollar, almost reduced to tears by lunchtime as the wheels come off on a driven pheasant shoot is not pretty. *Really* tall pheasant shooting is specialist shotgunning, and Churchill's theory of allowance by eye and "bum, belly, beak, bang" aren't going to help you much. A more conscious approach is necessary if you mean business.

One of these guys who was considering a trip across the pond called me recently and asked, "Have you ever shot driven grouse?" The voice at the other end of the line had a Texas drawl as thick as a slice of my mother's fruitcake. I confirmed that I had often been lucky enough to "pop a few caps" from the inside of a grouse butt.

"What about driven pheasants?" the voice continued. "Have you done that too?"

"You mean those much sought after, quality high birds?" I confirmed that I had indeed done that too. A lot of it. Westerhall Estate in the Scottish Borders has some of the best tall pheasants in the world, and this estate, along with some others, was less than a mile from where I had lived. The gentleman at the other end of the line then excitedly explained that at last, to fulfill a lifelong ambition, he was going to Scotland, the land of his forefathers, for a shooting vacation. The first leg of the visit would be to shoot driven grouse and later, driven partridge and pheasants.

"Exactly when are you thinking of going?" I inquired.

"In about a week," came the reply. "So I guess we'd better book some shooting lessons."

The reply surprised me in some ways, but then on reflection, nowadays no one gives a second thought to jumping on a plane to go shooting on the other side of the world for a couple of days. The world is shrinking, so I suppose I will have to get used to it. I agreed that it would definitely make perfect sense to book some lessons, and we did. Now, a couple of quick lessons was not going to give me much time to straighten out the bumps in the road with this client's shooting form, but every bit helps, and Scotland is a long way to fly just to bag sky.

When this client arrived, he was a nice, affable, unassuming sort of guy, and we established a rapport quickly. Unfortunately, it was also abundantly clear that he knew very little about driven birds, which of course was understandable. He took his shooting seriously and particularly wanted to do well on the pheasant drives. At the Dallas Gun Club we have an excellent 120-foot high tower with two machines on it that will throw a pretty good pair of simulated tall pheasants. This client quickly proved that he was no slouch with a shotgun, and after a few hours of concentrated coaching, he was breaking birds with quiet confidence in good style. I congratulated him on his shooting, and in turn, he confided during the course of the lessons that although he had in the past read articles about driven pheasant shooting, he had absolutely no idea what to expect when he arrived in Scotland. Our conversation during the lessons had helped to fill in the finer points and finesse of the game, and he felt much more comfortable as a result. That is why, in a nutshell, I decided to write this section. So for all the folks who have decided to journey across the pond to try driven birds, here is an attempt to fill in some of the gaps before you make the trip.

Picture the scene: a November morning, the low winter sun splashing everything with amber and gold, the hoarfrost sparkling the bracken with a myriad of colors like a quality crystal wineglass. It looks almost idyllic, with a flavor of soft surrealism. You have already drawn your peg number, and the time has come at last to put your confidence in Mr. Purdey, Mr. Holland, or Mr. Lang. That fast-handling thoroughbred, that icon of the driven pheasant shoot—the English sidelock—needs to earn its keep. "Easy come, easy go" did not serve as a valid argument at the time you made that self-indulgent purchase, did it?

So, what now? The long walk to your peg, burdened with gun, kit, and cartridges. The keeper signals the way, nodding you toward the steeply descending path. Timber posts have been knocked in at intervals down the side to assist your descent (or demise, should you slip), and you discover that the muddy track you tread meanders along the side of a small, boulder-strewn river. As you reach your peg, blowing out steam into the icy air like an old locomotive, you realize that you are at the bottom of a steep gorge. The thing of beauty that all the guys were drooling over last night in the lounge bar (the *gun,* not the busty blonde barmaid), with the French walnut stock that glows like the cape of a November cock and the exquisitely carved fences, now feels as heavy as a sack of Irish potatoes. In front of you is a high wooded escarpment, behind you, another one. Thirty yards to the left is your neighboring gun, and another gun is thirty yards to your right.

You made it! You open the shooting stick and plonk down on it, grateful for the rest. The gun exudes elegance as you free it from its slip, and as you lovingly run your eyes over its seductive contours, a warm feeling of pride consumes you. Ah yes, it was worth every penny! Better have a few energetic slashes with it at imaginary birds, you think; then there is just time for a quick breather as the beaters line out.

So what exactly is a beater? On the large estates in Scotland, on all driven shoots, the birds are pushed out over the waiting guns by beaters. They are local guys who do it for the love of the game. They usually happen to be (self-professed) experts on such interesting topics as fishing, fighting, ferreting, the consumption of alcoholic beverages, and the anatomy of pretty ladies. They are the backbone of the shoot. The success of the drive and the hard work of the gamekeeper ultimately depend on a good supply of knowledgeable beaters. They line out in a regimented fashion, perhaps thirty yards apart, at the edge of the woods, and then tap their way through with hazel sticks, braving the tangle of undergrowth, inclement weather, hangovers, unruly livestock, and low shooting guns, all to flush the birds. One of them will have a clicker, which he will press every time he hears a shot, so that the keeper knows exactly how many shots have been fired on each drive. Often the beaters will walk ten to fifteen miles during the day over difficult terrain. More often than not, they will do everything they can to ensure success for the guns, and all for the princely sum of about $20 per day. No, that was not a misprint, and I am writing this in 2002. You thought the time of the feudal system, peasantry, and serfdom was over? Apparently it is not, but luckily for the shoot organizers, the money is not the attraction for any of these guys. At the end of the season, the estate holds a keepers' day, where the beaters are invited to shoot for free. I have done it hundreds of times over the last twenty years and thoroughly enjoy it.

There will be twenty to thirty beaters in a line on each drive, and the idea is to keep the birds moving in front of this line at a steady pace, making sure that no one gets too far in front and leaves gaps for the birds to get through. The keeper knows his job perfectly and will be orchestrating the progress of the beaters' line with the aid of a two-way radio. The idea is to hold the birds together as cohesively as possible until the flushing point is reached, which is usually at the top of the hill. The birds (there could be as many as a couple thousand in one drive) will be forced out of the thick cover and over the waiting guns a few at a time, not all at once. You can expect at least five drives per day, on a good day, depending on the quota of birds to be shot. That is a lot of birds!

Your breathing and pulse rate steady just in time, and the tension mounts. The gruff command, "Hold the line, lads," can be heard as someone's young, unruly springer runs ahead. Keeper and beaters push forward in unison, methodically tapping their way, poking the birds out of their hiding places with their hazel sticks.

"Look for 'em, lads," the keeper calls out, knowing that the birds are sitting tight, reluctant to fly. Who can blame them? Pheasants are smart. Some of the wily old cocks let the beating line pass, then try to break back, but they are spotted by a flanker and turned. Flanker? To stop the birds from breaking out and flying the wrong way, flankers are positioned at strategic points. They are simply older beaters, usually past their sell-by date and less energetic than the younger chaps. Each will be equipped with a hazel stick like the rest of the beaters, but with a white plastic fertilizer bag nailed to it so that it can be used as a flag. When birds that are about to fly in the wrong direction are spotted, the flag is waved rapidly. The noise and the flash of white usually turn them.

The "Arc of Fire"

Etiquette plays a big part with driven shoots, not just from the politeness aspect, but also for safety reasons. The subject of gun safety and loading is already covered in this book and should need no further comment, but in the heat of the moment, with so many birds, it is easy to become overexcited and careless. Do not attempt shots that may be marginal, and do not "poach" birds that more rightfully belong to the next gun. As you look to the front, imagine a line straight ahead. All the birds that come over you 45 degrees to the left and right of this are legitimate birds, to the front and rear. In other words, you have a 90-degree "arc of fire" in front of you and the same behind. Do not take birds that are below the tree line, and do not fire a shot after the whistle (or horn or whatever) signals the end of the drive.

The keeper and beaters know their job perfectly, and for the next few minutes after the shoot begins, there will be a steady stream of birds coming over. Anything that looks as though it will fly better for one of your neighboring guns should be left for them, unless of course your neighbor is a good friend and you attempt to "wipe his eye." This is when you shoot a bird that is obviously not yours just as your neighbor tries to get onto it. Eye wiping is "not exactly cricket, old boy." It can be great fun, and a lot of guns do it, but it is rude to poach unless done among friends. After all the drives are finished and the final bag is counted, it is customary to tip the keeper. All the birds that are shot belong to the host and he will usually invite you to choose a brace to take home if you like. That's right, you paid all that money for the right to shoot and do not get to keep the birds!

High Hopes and High Birds

An eerie silence precedes the action and then distant noise—faint, hollow tapping and the rustle of dogs crashing through the bracken—signals the coming of the beaters. Suddenly, there is the metallic alarm call of the first cock bird as his straining pinions lift him skyward through the lattice-work of the spruce branches. The strong desire for freedom spurs him on, and he extricates himself from the tangle. He quickly gathers speed and curls out of sight before you can get on him. The pop of a gun tells you that someone farther down the line has had a crack. Other birds appear quickly, some so high that they are indistinct and nebulous as they sail over the tangled tops of the spruces into the swirling mist of the perfect Scottish morning. Soon the sky seems full, a crisscross of flushing birds. Almost panicking, you wonder which one to take. It is easy to become mesmerized with so many birds. Keep calm. Look through the bouquet, pick your bird, and develop his line. Do not put the gun in your shoulder too early; remember that the easiest way to develop the line of any tall pheasant is with a combination of arms and body movement. The shots should be triggered, ideally, as the gun hits your shoulder, and the longer the gun is in your shoulder, the more conscious you will become of it. Line is more important than lead on these high birds.

Remember also that the perception of lead on the bird that is farther out is less than when he is directly overhead. If possible, for the right-shouldered shooter, take the first bird out in front on the right with your choke barrel, then the next one slightly on the left with your open choke. Why? Do it the other way around, and you will push the gun away from your face and lose the line. It is called a right and left. You need a nice, smooth progressive swing with the gun as you pass through the first bird; then continue the swing and develop the line of the next one. Do not switch from one bird to another, and do not look for the second bird of your right and left until you have killed the first bird. Move your eyes to the second bird, and see its line before you move your gun to it. Have the courage to trigger your shots as you swing through the birds, and they'll fold as quickly as a bad poker hand. They are not folding up, you say, or at least not as often as you would like? You thought you were a decent shot? These high birds are great for the self-esteem, aren't they? Quickly reload and try again—there are plenty more to have a go at.

The beaters are pushing through to the edge of the spruce planta-tion, and the initial rush of birds is over. You hear a shout and, with eyes straining into the pale winter sun, pick out two indistinct shapes lifting out of the distant bracken. One bird has seen it all before, and as he curls back over the beaters, his metallic splutter of a call drifts back to you on the wind. The flankers fail to turn him. The other one is a strong bird, flight muscles well developed, and as he powers upward into the heavens, he catches a stiff breeze, curling ominously over the guns and in your direction. From where you are standing, he is half a mile away and still climbing steeply. Some of the guns have a go at him as he sails over, and you see his tail lift once as one of them gets too close. The beaters have stopped to watch him. He is a real screamer, a true archangel cloud scraper and . . . Oh! Please! Not over me! The stage is set, and he's still coming. Then the next guy swings onto him with the grace and ele-gance of a ballet dancer, and his gun barks, but the cock never falters. Your turn next. The fast-handling, elegant sidelock that you so often swing and point with effortless ease feels like a pig on the end of a shovel. Here he comes, gently does it, and . . . PEEP! The whistle blows, signaling that the drive is over. That's it. Don't shoot after the whistle, however tempting it may seem as that one last cock rattles over you.

Your neighboring gun takes his hat off to salute him; as he has beaten you all and will live to fly another day. Sigh of relief! You look down in disbelief at the pile of spent hulls round your feet. Did you really fire all those for three birds? I'm afraid so, but it is early yet, and there are five more drives to go. A quick swig of coffee to keep the cold out and calm your nerves and then it is off to the next drive. You redeem yourself as the day progresses, and one of the birds you pull down is a real screamer. You will remember it forever. You learn at last how to push through and not rush through, and the birds come down with regularity. Well, not exactly *monotonous* regularity, but you manage to hit more than a few. You begin to realize that it is indeed the line, not the lead, that is most critical.

At the end of each drive, Labradors and springer spaniels, spurred on by their handlers, flit like shadows through the undergrowth and mop up the birds. They do their job well. The game cart is filling up nicely, gathering the birds from the stockpiles at the edge of the rides where the dog handlers drop them. These are all handpicked dogs; only the best are good enough. "Where is it? Seek 'em out then!" The dogs, rudders quivering with excitement and enthusiasm, are a pleasure to behold, and at the end of the day, they (and their handlers) will be exhausted. So there you have it. Driven pheasants are great fun, and at the end of the day the final count is 285 birds bagged: 278 pheasants, 3 woodcock, 1 mallard, and 3 various.

TACKLING THE TEAL

The sporting clays target that routinely gives me more trouble than any other—and I'm glad to say I'm not alone—is the springing teal. These targets are thrown with a special trap so that they go nearly straight up into the air. Usually, they are thrown in true pairs. They command a lot of respect—relax for a second, and the wheels come off very quickly. Next to the high tower, the teal is at the top of the list of problem targets, and many shooters will crash and burn on a tough pair of springers. So let's take a close look at the teal target in all of its many guises.

Sporting clay targets are supposed to be representative of bird-shooting situations in the field, but as the sport has gained in popularity, target presentations have become more complex in an effort to continually challenge the regular shooters. The evolution of the modern springing teal target is no exception, and although wild teal do lift vertically for a second or two as they attempt to become airborne, this vertical acceleration is greatly exaggerated with the clay target version. It is rare to find a pair of predictable teal targets because of the diversity of the presentation. If the targets are launched from a manual machine at a distance, the first will be rising and the second will often be falling in the place you intend to shoot it. With any target, it is essential to get a good read, and in this respect the teal can be tricky, especially the line. This is seldom exactly vertical, and even in the early stages of the trajectory, a teal target that is dropping no longer has the stability of the spin the trap imparts. This makes it much more susceptible to wind interference, which will push this target off a predictable line quicker than almost any other target.

We know that a narrow-angle shot requires minimum lead and that a full 90-degree crossing shot requires maximum lead, but how do we know into which category the teal target fits? From automatic machines, teal targets can be launched at a variety of angles, from a fairly flat angle of 40 to 50 degrees to 90 degrees, or near vertical. Course designers still drop these widely varying targets into the category of springing teal, even though the flatter trajectory teal resembles a trap-type target. A clue to how they should be shot is the amount of face (as opposed to rim) you can see on the targets as they go up. The flatter the profile, or in other words, the more the rim is edge-on to the shooter, the less perceived lead the target requires—it is in effect an elevated trap-type target.

Reading the profile is also important for the choice of shot size: with a full-face target, at moderate range, fairly open chokes are acceptable. The rim of the clay is harder to break on a target with a flatter edge on presentation, and it's getting away faster, which makes it less vulnerable to the gun. Tighter chokes and $7\frac{1}{2}$ shot are the best medicine.

With the vertical or almost vertical teal, you have your choice of taking at least one of them as they are going up, as they stall out at the top and become tantalizingly stationary, or as they cascade back to earth. For most people in most situations, it is best to take the first of a true pair of teal on the way up, just before it peaks, and the second one as quickly thereafter as possible, which is usually just after it has started to fall.

The required sight picture as you trigger the shot on a rising teal target is almost the same as that of the driven target off a high tower. The difference is that the teal rises almost vertically in front of you, instead of coming toward you and passing overhead, as it does with a driven target. The visual perception, however, is very similar.

There are two methods we can use to shoot the teal. The first is to swing through it from behind (underneath), firing as the target is blotted out by the muzzles. The second is to maintain lead, where the gun remains in front of the target at all times. This requires the ability to look

Left: The profile of the target is an indication of the lead requirement. In this picture, the target is showing a flatter profile. The perceived lead on this target will be only a small amount, but the target will be getting away fast because of this flatter angle, more or less like an elevated trap target. It would be best to shoot the flatter target as soon as possible, when it is nearer and more vulnerable to the gun.
Right: Here the target is showing a full face. The perception of lead will be more on this target.

"through" or around the gun with the other eye to maintain visual contact, just as you would do with a high driven target. At extended ranges, the ability to use this method is essential: otherwise, there will be no consistency. With the close teal, especially if the target is a flatter, trap-type teal, the swing-through method works well, because the momentum in the barrels and the delay in triggering the shot due to shooter reaction time will usually be enough to crush the clay, provided you trigger the shot as the muzzles overtake the target. Failure to trigger the shot at the right time will often result in head lifting, and the gun will shoot high. The temptation to do this, combined with the possibility that the target is reaching the peak of its trajectory and starting to slow down, results in many teal being missed over the top.

The lead requirement will be directly proportional to the speed of the target and the range. The position of the machine is a good indication of the range, but keep in mind that a flatter teal will be getting away faster than a more vertical teal. Also remember that wind can have an influence on the predictability of the teal target. Wind variation on a true vertical teal not only influences the line, but also can have a dramatic effect on the range. With a stiff wind from behind the shooter, even an almost vertical teal off a trap positioned twenty yards away, because of the effect of the wind on the full face of the target, can very quickly be pushed out to thirty and even forty yards or more. Because it is still showing its full face, the target often appears much closer, but the lead needs to be increased in proportion because the shot column is taking longer to reach the target.

Holding too low is a common mistake with teal targets. From this address position, with the gun held virtually on the trap, the target will beat me. The rapid acceleration needed to catch the target will result in too much gun speed and momentum in the barrels. The result? Accelerating gun, decelerating target. No prizes for guessing where the shot goes!

This address position is almost as bad. With a gun as high as this, the best I can do is try a ragged poke at the target with a dead gun.

Here I am holding the gun about halfway between the trap and the intended breakpoint. Teal are rarely truly vertical, and I can hold the muzzles to the left or right of the target, keeping it in view all the time. As the target comes past my barrels I can accelerate smoothly after it without the need for erratic gun movement.

The gun insertion point is critical with a teal target, as shown in the photos. In the first picture on page 256, I am holding my gun too low; I will produce too much gun movement, which will in turn produce a huge amount of residual momentum, all on a target that has slowed greatly by the time I am shooting it. The second picture at the top of this page shows a gun-hold position that is too high, which will almost certainly result in a hurried poke with a dead gun. The third picture is about right. I always recommend with any target that line is more important than lead. Teal are so seldom truly vertical. Produce a vertical gun movement on a teal that has a subtle curve right or left at the breakpoint, and you have missed.

BOW TO THE TARGET

Standard target presentations don't give most shooters that much trouble, and they can usually notch up a reasonable score. The best way to tackle a pair of springers, for example, if they are thrown from a manual machine at a reasonable distance, is to shoot the first one on the way up, and spot-shoot underneath the second just as it peaks and begins to fall. Simple, isn't it? But what if they are forty yards away, or the cunning course designer has included a fast quartering-away midi and a springing teal in a true pair presentation, leaving the shooter no alternative but to break the teal target on the way down? A bit trickier, eh?

Now what about battues? As they leave the trap arm, all we see is their razor-thin profiles as they slice through the air. They are usually traveling faster than you think, and the absence of the more concave dome shape of the standard target makes them aerodynamically unstable, which produces the characteristic battue flight.

A lot of shooters struggle with battues, but they are not that difficult if you tackle them at the point where they are at their most pre-dictable—just as they slow down and start to turn to present their full face. This is when they are most vulnerable to the gun. The second target of a true pair of battues, as with the long teal, is tricky, as there is no way to avoid shooting a fast-dropping target. Even though you took the first battue early just as it turned over, the second battue is responding to gravity and dropping. What was a previously a good scorecard can quickly become blemished with a row of doughnuts. Basic shooting fundamentals dictate that we must never slow or stop the swing of the gun on a dropping target because all the forward allowance we have established will evaporate and a miss behind will result. So why do so many of us struggle with dropping targets? The first reason is because we fail to see that many targets are not only dropping but also accelerating, and because of this imperceptible nuance in speed, they require a different approach.

First of all, let's look at exactly which targets drop under power. We know battues do; in fact, we've been told many times, "The battue is the *only* target that accelerates as it drops." Wrong! The next time you see someone miss a springing teal, watch carefully what happens as the target plummets earthward. Skeet targets may float down, but an edge-on teal behaves more like a rock than a Frisbee. There is a degree of acceleration as the target falls, and many shooters fail to see this and try to spot-shoot the target with a dead gun. A miss over the top is the result.

I know there are guys out there who can break droppers with this poking technique, but I doubt they can do it consistently. *All* edge-on targets progressively accelerate as they drop, including on-edge standards, midis, chandelles, rockets, and especially the battue. Standard and midi targets do not accelerate downward as rapidly as battues, rockets, or chandelles, but they do accelerate, and on a long dropping teal, this can be a problem.

The best way to deal with accelerating droppers is to learn to bow to the target. What do I mean by this? Quite simply, with any fast-rising target like teal or any driven target off a high tower, we must produce a smooth, assertive swing through the target. To do this effectively, the hips must push forward and the upper torso must tilt back. Weight is transferred from the front foot to the rear foot. The opposite is true with any dropping target, and the shooter must insert his muzzles under the target and bend forward slightly from the waist, allowing his weight to shift smoothly onto his leading leg (left foot for a right-hander). This forward bend from the waist is extremely important because if the shooter attempts to move the gun on the target line with his arms only, he will usually pull the gun away from his face, causing the gun to shoot high. The bowing motion will ensure that the shooter keeps his head down and "stays in the gun" as he triggers the shot. If you come out of the gun and lift your face off the stock by even a small amount, for example, 1/4 inch at the gun end, then you will shoot two to three feet at thirty yards—even more at extended ranges. Shooting this high isn't much use on a dropping target that might need the shot pattern to go six feet underneath at forty yards to ensure successful interception. The bowing motion will also reduce the tendency to stop or slow the gun and help to produce a progressively accelerating gun movement.

Many of us make a crucial mistake by using the sustained lead method for droppers that are accelerating. The key factor with a sustained lead shot is that gun speed should be synchronized to target speed, but we already know that these targets are accelerating slightly, so we must use pull-away. If the target is accelerating, then logically the gun must be accelerating in harmony with it. Insert under the target line and pull away smoothly. This must be controlled, just slightly faster than the target speed, and all the time the shooter must be looking for the correct sight picture as he triggers the shot. Jerking the gun away erratically is not the answer, because you will never be able to repeat the exact timing of the move from target to target. Dramatically change the speed of the gun each time, and you will change the perception of lead required, which in turn leads to inconsistency.

Just as with standard target presentations, target trajectory or line is the most important thing to consider with dropping targets. It is unusual for a target that is dropping rapidly to produce a truly vertical line—usually there is a slight deviation to the left or right. Failure to see this subtle nuance in the target's trajectory, combined with the added effects of the weight of the gun, often will produce vertical momentum in the barrels as the shot is triggered, and a miss to either side of the target. As the upper torso moves forward with this bowing movement, the arms must guide the gun accurately on the same line as the target. I often tell my students that line is more important than lead because if you get the target line wrong on a dropper, you might as well forget about lead.

Target range and type have a dramatic impact on just how far underneath we need to shoot for successful interception, and this is another area that befuddles many shooters. I often see experienced shooters, faced with a shot at a forty-yard, *decelerating* springing teal, give the target six to eight feet of lead in order to hit it. They will then often shoot a couple of feet underneath a dropping, *accelerating* edge-on teal that is at a similar distance and speed in the area they intend to break it and and expect to hit it. They won't. A rising teal is slowing down, a dropping teal is accelerating. If the course designer gives you no choice but to shoot this target just before it hits the ground, the degree of acceleration may be considerable. And while a forty to fifty yard edge-on dropping teal requires plenty of lead, the physical characteristics and aerodynamic qualities of battue or chandelle targets that are dropping under power are even more demanding and can often require far more lead. Even if we can evaluate the amount of lead needed, this lead requirement will quickly evaporate if we can't apply the corresponding gun movement to complement it; a smooth, progressive follow-through is crucial with this type of presentation.

Edge-on teal, battues, and chandelles require this bowing movement to ensure success, but what about driven-away targets off a high tower? Under normal circumstances these targets will not be accelerating, but if the cunning course designer angles the machine down and throws these under power, they won't be losing much speed, either. Pull-away is the best method for this target. If you try to swing through this target from behind, you will find that it takes a bit of catching. Instead of a smooth, precise movement, you will probably end up with a hurried poke.

Left: With any target that is dropping under power, we must use a pull-away method. As you can see from this picture, as I attempt to keep the gun moving the gun has started to come away from my face. The gun will shoot high as a result.
Right: Here you can clearly see that I have bowed slightly from the waist. By doing this, I will stay in the gun as the shot is triggered.

Just as you would shoot a high driven bird with the weight on the back foot, you shoot an outgoing overhead target with the weight on the front foot. You will have a much smoother, progressive swing in the same direction as the target. Just like the edge-on teal, battues, and chandelles that require a smooth gun movement on the target line, the "bow to the target" approach on targets that are dropping under power from a high tower will ensure that the head stays on the gun. To set yourself up for this shot, put your weight onto your back foot and look back for the target so that you will have good visual contact as soon as possible. Keep your gun fairly high but not so far back that the barrels are out of your peripheral vision. Be prepared to move the gun on the flash of the target, or the built-in lead allowance you have will quickly evaporate and you will end up chasing the target. As you see the target and begin to move the gun, allow your weight to transfer to the front leg and make sure that your upper torso bends forward as the shot is triggered. This type of target is best shot where it is most vulnerable to your gun: as near to you as possible with the vulnerable concave underside showing. Every millisecond you delay pulling the trigger on this target will make it more difficult to break. Many shooters think they can give a high, outgoing bird less lead than they would give a similar incoming shot, but this isn't true.

One final thought: It is easier to go up than down with a shotgun. Our muscular coordination always seems to work better as we lift the gun, rather than lower it. Dropping targets are tough, so don't forget to bow to the target and give them the respect they deserve!

FIRE DOWN BELOW

Many sporting clays enthusiasts would agree that one of the main attractions of the sport is the almost unlimited variety of target presentations they can expect to encounter. But most targets, after we have confidently built up a personal mental repertoire of sight pictures, don't give us that much trouble, do they? You might think that one crossing target is the same as the next one. After months of crushing targets on your home ground with satisfaction, you and your buddies decide you're ready for the big time and plan to visit an unfamiliar course. You've done your homework and put the time in; now let's see if you can put it all together and make that expensive Kreighoff or Perazzi earn its keep.

The day arrives with great weather, great company, and lots of jovial banter as you progress around the course. All is going well and the crosses on your scorecard are adding up nicely. Ah yes, you think, All the hard work was worth it; it's really coming together now. That warm feeling of quiet confidence trickles over—until you walk around the corner and see the next two stations. The first is a left-to-right crossing target followed by a quartering incomer on report. The second is a quartering midi followed by a right-to-left crosser. Unfortunately, they are all at the bottom of a steep ravine about thirty feet below the shooting positions. Low birds, in every sense of the word, can be just as frustrating as the high tower targets and give shooters lots of problems. Your club doesn't have targets like this, but you confidently step into the safety cage. As the targets sail by unscathed and the calls of " lost pair" ring in your ears, a neat row of duck eggs builds up on your previously unblemished scorecard. And as the wheels come off for you and your buddies, there are no more complimentary comments of "Good course!" and "Good targets!" All the praise and words of appreciation for the guy who set the course dry up rapidly, as he is relegated to a position that ranks even lower than the targets that he has cunningly set to destroy you.

But don't be too demoralized. The unfamiliar perspective and misleading angles of shooting targets well below your feet spell trouble for many of us. I'm sure that most of the competitors who attended the 1999 U.S. Open in Polson, Montana, and shot the targets over the tremendously varied topography of steep-sided valleys and hillsides will readily confirm this. Some of the shooters complained that these targets were not really representative of any type of game bird, but a visit to a Scottish grouse moor would soon confirm that some of the grouse butts are positioned so that the birds are skimming the heather well below the guns, and grouse are extremely difficult to pick out against a perfectly matching backdrop of heather. So for all those folks out there who are unfamiliar with this sort of target presentation, here is the best way to tackle it. Make no mistake, all low targets are hard to read, and, just as with the high tower birds, these targets can be crossing, incoming, or outgoing. Let's look at the crossing targets first.

There are two main reasons why low crossing targets give people problems. The first is an incorrect address position. Low targets require a

Top: Any target that is well below the shooter's feet will mean that the butt of the gun is forced down farther than normal in the shoulder pocket, and the cheek is pushed forward along the stock. This will make the gun shoot high. For this reason, it is easy to shoot over the top of low targets if they are addressed with a normal stance.

Bottom: Low targets require a low gun-hold position, well below the target's line. The correct address position is with an exaggerated forward stance, weight well forward over the front foot, and upper torso leaning forward. The feet should be wider apart than normal so that balance and stability are maintained as the shot is taken. By adopting this stance, the shooter will also stay in the gun and reduce the risk of one of the main problems with shooting over the top of low targets . . . head lifting.

low gun-hold position, well below the target's line. The correct address position is with an exaggerated forward stance, weight well forward over the front foot, and upper torso leaning forward. The feet should be wider apart than normal, so that balance and stability are maintained as the shot is taken. By adopting this stance, the shooter will also "stay in the gun" and reduce the risk of head lifting, which is often the reason why rabbit targets are missed over the top. Here we are faced with a target that is not level with your feet but may be over thirty feet below them. With this type of presentation, the target could be either rising or falling in the place you intend to shoot it, but because you are looking down, the visual impression is that it is traveling on a straight course. If you do not give this careful scrutiny, it is likely that you will miss over the top. For this reason, maintained lead is the best method to use, as it lets you keep the bird in clear view at all times.

The second reason low crossing targets are problematic is a poor gun mount. I always teach my pupils to mount the gun smoothly with both hands and arms working in unison. If you don't, your front hand will become a pivot, and as the butt comes into the shoulder, the muzzles will "chop down" on the line of the target. Instead of one smooth muzzle movement, you may pull the muzzles above the line of the target in order to regain control. A smooth lift with both arms is even more crucial with this type of presentation. Even with this perfect gun mount, any target well below the shooter's feet will mean that the butt of the gun is forced down farther than normal in the shoulder pocket, and the cheek is pushed back along the stock. This will make the gun shoot high with another miss over the top.

Now let's look at the outgoing target that appears from below your feet. This is the horizontal equivalent of the springing teal, and there are two methods you can use to shoot it—swing-through or maintained lead. I prefer maintained lead because I look "under" or "through" the gun so that I have visual contact with the target at all times. When shooting swing-through, it is very easy to shoot over the target, because although it may appear to have a flat trajectory, it may be dropping fast. Be careful; otherwise, just as with a springing teal, you may try to shoot a decelerating target with an accelerating gun and miss over the top.

Now, about the incomer: if you think about it, very few targets require a gun movement that is toward the shooter and below his feet. This must be a smooth gun movement; guide the gun, don't fight it. As I suggest in the "Bow to the Target" section, with any shot that requires gun movement with a downward motion, weight must be well over the front foot and the upper torso must move to keep the head on the gun, but this isn't easy and will take a bit of practice. The hold position should be low, about halfway between where the target is seen clearly and where you intend to break it. Don't forget, this target may also be slowing down and dropping in the place where you intend to shoot it, although visually it does not give you this impression. Too much gun speed and you will miss in front.

So there it is—how to tackle low birds. Now you can confidently puff your chest out, ready to meet anything that the cunning course designers throw at you. Well, almost anything.

THOSE ILLUSIVE RABBITS

On the sporting clays course, the infamous, bolting rabbit target is many a shooter's nemesis. Theoretically, this should not be the case; rabbits are usually encountered at reasonably close ranges and are usually the slowest target you'll encounter on the course. The main reason rabbits are missed is that we usually give them too much lead, and they are missed in front. The optical illusion that is transmitted to the shooter does not suggest this, but the explanation is simple. As rabbit targets "run," they come into contact with small stones, bits of broken target, and other debris, and therefore need to be fairly robust, which makes them heavy. Friction as they run along the ground also means that they lose energy quickly. A full-crossing shot at a twenty-yard rabbit requires only a small amount of lead, a fraction of the lead that a similar airborne target requires at the same distance. "Shoot the front feet off" is good advice. The background—bushes, grass, and trees—also give the illusion that these targets are traveling faster than they actually are. Most shooters rush through from behind, establish far too much lead, and shoot in front. Then, as the shot pattern hits the ground in front of the target, the rabbit rolls through the dust cloud that is kicked up. This gives the visual impression that we shot behind, so then we extend our lead and shoot even farther in front of the next one! By the time we realize that this is happening, we've got a neat row of duck eggs on our scorecard.

The second way we miss the rabbit is over the top, and the reason is more complicated than you may think. Try this experiment: Stick a target on the ground at about twenty yards and aim at it like you would with a rifle. My guess is that the bulk of the shot charge will pass over the top of the target because with most sporting clays, guns will throw their pattern above the aiming mark. When shooting at a downward angle, the gun is forced lower into the shoulder, and this will mean that

Correct setup is important on all targets that are at a low angle. In this picture, although it looks as though my muzzles are below the line of the target, as I bring the gun up to my face and shoulder I will lift above the line, which will in turn pivot the gun around my front hand as the stock comes into my face. The muzzles of the gun will drop down, and then it will be necessary to bring them up again to reestablish the line. Chances are the rabbit will be missed over the top.

the cheek is slightly farther back on the stock. When this happens, most shooters will come off the gun slightly and shoot high as a result.

The setup and address position for the target should be well below the line of the rabbit's run. If it is not, as the gun comes into the face and shoulder, the muzzles will be lifted above the line of the target. The muzzles of the gun will prescribe a check mark that will give wasted

By holding the muzzles lower and parallel to my line of sight, I can come smoothly up into the target line. All the unnecessary movement has been eliminated as the shot is taken.

movement. It is always best to deliberately shoot low on rabbits, so that the bulk of the shot charge will be deflected up into the target. Of course, this type of target has a notorious reputation for suddenly bouncing unpredictably, but if your setup is correct, this shouldn't be a problem. Most shooters will react to this bounce by coming off the gun, and they will miss over the top. Correct setup and gun mount are extremely important on any low-angle shot, especially the illusive rabbit.

PRACTICE DOESN'T MAKE PERFECT; PRACTICE MAKES PERMANENT

One of my lady clients was struggling to master some difficult high tower targets and commented that she would like to shoot something easier to boost her confidence. If she had been a novice shooter, I would have agreed immediately, but she was an experienced and accomplished shot, the state champion and a former United States champion. I refused; after all, she was paying for the lesson and there was no point in breaking targets that she was already confident with. Of course, an instructor should always recognize when his methods are not working, especially with a new shooter. But an experienced shooter who is striving for a higher level of performance is different. There is no magic formula, you just need to be motivated to achieve your goals. To continue shooting targets you are comfortable with achieves nothing if you feel the need to take your game to the next level.

A poor performance under tournament conditions is due to a lack of confidence in your ability to hit the target. It may be just one or two problem targets on the whole course that destroy this confidence. You can fail miserably on an easy stand because you are thinking about the difficult springing teal at the next one. You just know you are going to miss before you even get into the cage. Then you experience the inevitable adrenaline rush and the mind goes blank. Most of us have been there at one time or another, a shoot-off situation, for example. Muscles tighten and refuse to respond because they are already tense. The heart races wildly, the mouth goes dry, and the palms sweat. But do your homework, and it is a different story. Targets are quickly pulverized without a second thought. Everyone has problem targets and learning to master them can pay handsome dividends. And remember, a bad score isn't necessarily a bad day if you have learned something from your mistakes.

Shooting a few casual rounds with friends may not be the answer for the guy who is competitive. In a friendly environment he will feel comfortable and completely relaxed. Maybe *too* relaxed to concentrate

100 percent on breaking each target. This is recreation, not practice. Practice is the recognition of weaknesses and the steps we must take to rectify these weaknesses until we feel confident. Successful shotgunning is not an inherent trait—it is a skill that must be learned like anything else. Learning any new skill involves a period of stress as we acclimatize ourselves to the new learning processes, and with shooting, the process is both mental and physical. Don't expect instant results. Until the body adjusts to the extra demands, we go through a period of transition. As it adjusts, we reach a higher level of performance. Sometimes we have to go forward by going backward, or as the saying goes, "things have to get worse before they get better." Remember, "No pain, no gain" applies to psychological training as well as physical. The poke-and-hope shooters who miss a lot of targets with the pretense that it does not bother them are fooling no one but themselves.

"I don't care if I miss; I only shoot for fun" is the usual argument. Surely breaking targets has got to be more fun than missing! "I get enough stress at my day job; I'm only here to relax" is another argument, and I don't believe it. Nobody who shoots a shotgun likes to miss, and it doesn't matter whether the target is clay or the feathered variety.

The strange thing is that so many people are prepared to blame anything but themselves for less-than-perfect scores. At the top of the hit list is their gun. The next scapegoat is the ammo, or the targets, or the weather. Niggling thoughts of self-doubt begin to creep in. It couldn't possibly be you, could it? Were you ever completely confident with that pair of battues and the long crosser followed by the quartering rabbit? And didn't you completely misread the slow incomer? Thought it was a midi until you came out of the cage with a neat row of duck eggs on your scorecard and realized it was a forty-yard standard target.

Once you reach this stage, you should be convinced that there is room for improvement. If your shooting is this erratic there is something wrong. But beware: missing too many targets can generate negative emotions. Frustration kicks in. So now you have a choice. Take up golf or decide that you must improve your game. And *everybody* can improve. The first hurdle is convincing yourself that you can, and when you've made this monumental step, the next one is deciding how to go about making these improvements.

The laws of physics play a huge part in successful shotgunning. If we can evaluate the variables of the target correctly and point the muzzles of the gun in the right direction, the gun goes bang and the target breaks. Reading these variables is the answer, and a systematic approach is the only way. Skillful course designers will try their best to trick and deceive you, but every target can still be scrutinized, broken down into component parts, and divided into specific categories. Failure to recognize these component parts before entering the safety cage on the sporting clays course is a surefire way of ensuring a lot of X's on your scorecard. The thinking should be done *before* entering the stand. We tend to look for the easy way, maximum results with minimum effort, but once you're in the stand, it's too late.

Every step we take to learn anything new involves a certain level of intense concentration, a combination of mental and physical stress until we achieve our objectives and can relax again. I think some people just never have the inclination to do this and avoid stressing themselves to reach the higher level. They avoid taking chances and convince themselves that 50 or 60 percent on the course is all they will ever achieve. Some of these poke-and-hope guys will never be motivated to make changes to improve their game, which is a shame because the feeling of confidence as you enter the safety cage and the feeling of elation as you leave it several minutes later with a neat row of X's are hard to describe but well within everyone's grasp. For everyone out there who would like to jump-start their shooting career and move up to a higher level, here are some suggestions:

1. If possible, seek professional advice. Problem targets will be mastered more quickly under the guidance of a good coach. Of course, the dedicated shotgunner will get there eventually, but a good coach will give you the benefit of his experience.

2. A steady diet of extra shooting is not the answer if you're not breaking the targets! All that happens is that you become frustrated and really good at missing.

3. Limit the number of shells you allow yourself each practice session. It is better to break ten targets correctly than to blast away with gay abandon at hundreds in the hope of miraculously solving the problem. *Quality* practice is better than quantity.

4. Try to imagine that each shell you fire is the last one you have.

5. Take problem targets one at a time. The diversity of targets we encounter on a sporting course is endless, but they can *all* be broken.

6. Every problem has a solution. Sometimes the answer to the problem isn't what we expect and may not be obvious at first.

7. Make sure you have the basics down. This means correct gun fit, good gun mount, and correct dominant-eye diagnosis. I regularly come across clients who have shot for twenty years or so and have never had

their master eye diagnosed correctly who attempt to shoot with cross-dominance and expect good results.

8. Always try to build your score. Don't let one bad stand get to you in the early part of a tournament and ruin the rest of the card.

9. If you've put in the extra work on a specific target and you're confident with it, learn to trust your own judgment.

10. Don't allow yourself to be intimidated by comments from others. Remember, you are there to beat the other guys. Other competitors will talk you out of a target or two if they can.

By the way, the woman I mentioned at the start of this section went on to win her class and no longer fears high tower shots.

CHAPTER 19

Skeet Shooting

THE HISTORY OF SKEET

Skeet. It is a strange name, isn't it? Where did the name come from, and where did skeet shooting originate? Shooting at clay targets as a way to hone bird-hunting skills has been carried out for years on both sides of the Atlantic. In 1920, on the grounds of the Glen Rock Kennels in the small town of Andover, Massachusetts, an enterprising group of bird hunters, C. E. Davies, his son Henry, and William Forster, devised an ingenious way to maximize the various angle presentations but minimize the equipment requirements by using one target launcher.

The original skeet layout was circular, with twelve stations marked on the circumference like the face of a clock and a launcher at 12 o'clock throwing the targets over the 6 o'clock position. A round was shot with two targets from each of the twelve stations, and the last shell in the box was used for an incomer while standing in the center of the circle. Unfortunately, these enterprising bird hunters had a neighbor with a chicken farm on the adjoining land who did not share their enthusiasm and soon put a stop to shooting in that direction.

Not to be outdone, William Forster came up with a simple solution: to divide the field in the middle and use an extra machine. This seemed to be the answer, and the target launcher at 12 o'clock eventually became the high house, and the new launcher at 6 o'clock the low house. The neighbor's chickens did not get peppered with shot anymore, and the three guys could practice their bird-hunting skills. Later, William Forster, who must have been an enterprising sort, was convinced that his new shooting game was so much fun that it should be shared by others. He invented a set of rules that included the doubles and an optional shot.

The Dallas Gun Club in Lewisville, Texas, is recognized by many as one of the premier skeet facilities in the world today.

The complete idea was presented to an eager American shooting public in the 1926 issues of *National Sportsman* and *Hunting and Fishing* magazines. A competition was held with a prize of $100 for an appropriate name for the new sport. Mrs. Gertrude Hurlbutt of Montana won the prize with her suggestion of *skeet,* which came from an old Scandinavian word meaning "shoot." The popularity of the new game grew rapidly over the years, and a governing body, the National Skeet Shooting Association, was formed. Soon after this, the national headquarters was moved to Dallas, but in 1973, the association headquarters was moved to the site of the National Gun Club in San Antonio.

The Dallas Gun Club is still recognized by many as one of the premier skeet facilities in the United States. Until I came here several years

Robert Paxton, thirty-two-time all-American in action.

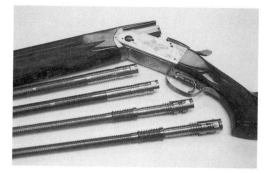

Most quality skeet competition guns come with a tube set in .410, 28 gauge, 20 gauge, and 12 gauge.

ago, my forte as a shooting instructor was wingshooting and sporting clays techniques, and although I had shot English skeet many years before, my involvement with American-style skeet was limited. Although the club has more than its quota of expert skeet shooters, many of the new members here needed skeet instruction, so I took the NSSA instructors' course and brushed up on my own skeet-shooting skills.

Skeet is a game of trigonometry, and everybody (especially a new shooter) has trouble with the lead requirement to give each target. With

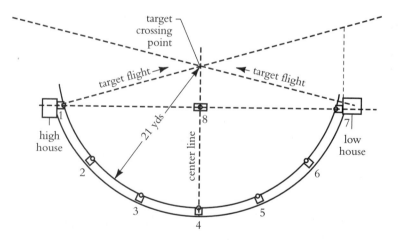

Mechanics of the skeet field. On a skeet field, a target leaves the trap arm at approximately fifty miles per hour. A standard shotshell has a muzzle velocity of approximately 1,200 feet per second, or 800 miles per hour. This is a ratio of 16:1. For every yard the target travels, the shot column will travel sixteen yards in the same time interval. The center stake on a skeet field is 21 yards from the shooting positions, which is approximately 5 feet farther or $1^2/3$ yards. The skeet target will travel approximately $1^1/3$ yards or 4 feet in the same time interval that the shot load takes to reach it.

each round I shot, I began to notice that a pattern was emerging based on my own perception of lead, and I began experimenting over a period of several months. These experiments involved lengths of string, bits of wood, and hundreds of photographs. Because skeet targets have predictable speeds and trajectories, I eventually came up with a formula based on what each individual shooter sees, and by using it, I could easily and repeatedly break twenty-five straights. This formula is both easy to remember and easy to apply. It also enables beginners to enjoy success quickly, which is important. New shooters become demoralized quickly if they can't break their share of targets. I showed the finished method to several experts, including Robert Paxton, Don Snyder, John Shima, and Bob Brister. Their comments were complimentary, so I decided to go a step further and try the method out on my clients. Without exception, everyone who used the method agreed that it works amazingly well, and in most cases, even new students can hit every target on a skeet field within two to three hours.

EASY SKEET: A NEW PERSPECTIVE
FOR THE BEGINNER

Because of the diversity of target presentations associated with wing-shooting and sporting clays, the best shooters use all the shooting methods to be successful. Skeet is different. Provided the targets are regulation targets, they have a predictable speed and trajectory. The method described here works well for skeet and was designed to give beginners a clear and precise way to become a proficient shot at skeet quickly and easily. Although it will also benefit some more experienced skeet shooters, to use it properly would mean a complete overhaul of the methods that they have probably used for years. When used properly, the method described will teach a novice to hit every target on a skeet layout within two or three hours. Doubles should be mastered within two additional hours.

Of course, shooting skeet well is not easy. It involves a complex series of integrated movements that are dependent upon many factors. But in the initial stages of learning, the last thing the beginner needs is a complicated, technical approach. A direct, logical, easy-to-understand, and more importantly, easy-to-remember, system is far better and produces quicker results.

I explain here a new shooting method that works for skeet. Previous chapters provide information on gun fit, type of gun, and eye dominance; however, I would like to make one small point here concerning eye dominance. I believe that in the early days of learning to shoot, many beginners can benefit from closing the left eye (for a right-shoulder, right-master-eyed shooter) just as the gun comes onto the target, even if the test for eye dominance suggests that the right eye is the master eye. Doing this seems to give shooters a clearer sight picture than the normal recommendation to keep both eyes open. This is only a temporary measure; I am not suggesting that the right-shouldered, right-master-eyed shot should always close his left eye as he becomes more experienced and knows which sight picture to look for.

Sometimes the usual method of testing for eye dominance—keep both eyes open, point a finger or line a thumb up with something in the distance, first close one eye and then the other, and the eye that stays in line is the dominant eye—is inconclusive. Of course, it does tell us which eye is dominant, but it doesn't tell us by how much, and it doesn't tell us which eye takes over as the gun comes to point of aim. Although we should never *look* at the barrels or rib when pointing a shotgun, we should always *see* them; they are central to our field of vision. When using an over-and-under shotgun, sometimes the dominant visual impression is the one that the *left* eye receives of the sides of the barrels. This is enough to make the left eye take over occasionally and confuse the beginner. Eye dominance is an incredibly complex subject, so each individual must therefore experiment and find out what works best for him.

There are three basic requirements for shooting skeet targets with any success:

1. A quick, accurate assessment of target behavior. Pointing a shotgun is an instinctive and reflexive act, but if we don't recognize what the target is doing, we can't move the gun on the same line, and therefore we won't hit it. In other words, the ocular information our brain receives must be transformed into physical effort to move the gun on the same line as the target.

2. Good foot positions. There are many weird and wonderful recommendations for the correct stance. These are often accompanied by footprint drawings, like the steps of a new dance routine or lines drawn on the ground at each station. They are so complicated that a new shooter is confused, and he has enough to think about in the early stages of learning to shoot. Because we are all different shapes and sizes, I believe simply that the stance that suits the shooter's personal physical requirements is best. Usually, stocky people adopt a squarer stance and slim people a more angular stance. For the right-handed shooter, the usual recommendation, "belt buckle toward the low house" (high house

for the left-handed) is reasonable and easy to remember. As a shooter's level of ability changes, he will automatically compensate for any shortcomings with this stance until he finds the optimum position at each station that suits his personal physical requirements.

3. Smooth, rhythmical gun movement. Learning to shoot to a rhythm is more important than we think, especially on doubles. Watch a very good skeet shooter. His movements are precise and unhurried. There are no superfluous, erratic movements as he intercepts each target. The barrels of his gun will move inches rather than feet. This is known as economy of movement.

The gun should accelerate *smoothly* onto the line of the target. We always experience forward inertia (resistance to movement) as we accelerate the gun from rest. This is even more noticeable when shooting with a mounted gun. The gun should match the physical capabilities of its user. If the gun is too heavy, it will start with a sudden jerk and be difficult to control. An erratic gun movement is the result.

There are four main reasons why a new shooter experiences difficulty when he uses a shotgun for the first time:

1. Coordination. He has trouble moving the gun *smoothly* on the line of the target.

2. He stops the gun because he is looking at the sight on the end.

3. Apprehension of noise and recoil, which makes him hesitate to pull the trigger.

4. He has absolutely no idea how much lead or forward allowance to give a moving skeet target.

The first three will improve as the shooter acquires some shotgun technique. Every time a new shooter pulls the trigger, he gains experience; it doesn't matter if he breaks the target or not.

Number 4 is the most important. It is probably the single most common reason why people miss skeet targets with a shotgun. Beginners miss more targets behind than any other way; in fact, it is unusual for them to miss in front. As the shot charge leaves the gun barrel, it expands longitudinally and laterally. This is known as shot-string. If a shooter is too far in front of a target, there is a slight chance that the leading edge of the target can fly into the trailing edge of the shot-string. If he is *one-millionth* of an inch behind, he has certainly missed. Skeet is one of the few situations where there may be a *small* advantage with shot-string (Chapter 13 explains why). All shooters experience varying levels of difficulty with mastering the lead requirements on skeet targets. The method explained here makes clear to each student what his personal perception is of the amount of forward allowance he needs to break the target. Also, it gives him an easy way to remember it. Used correctly, this method is an amazingly simple process to learn.

Now let us examine the three main methods of shooting a moving skeet target with a shotgun:

1. *Swing-through.* With this method, the gun is started from behind the target and accelerated through it on the same line. The trigger is pulled when the correct sight picture is seen. There is a split second when the gun will point directly at the target. Shooting with the swing-through method means that it is almost impossible to move the gun at a constant speed at every station. As a result, the sight picture will vary as the speed of the gun changes. Skeet is the game of perfection. Use the swing-through method and you will be inconsistent. Swing-through is more useful for wingshooting and sporting clays than skeet.

2. *Pull-away.* Here the gun is moved onto the target and then moved in front by what the shooter perceives to be the correct amount of lead. For a split second the gun will point directly or slightly in front of the target. The shot is triggered while the barrels are moving much faster than the target is. This method is reasonable, but often the gun speed and target speed are out of synchronization as the gun attempts to move ahead of the target. It is also a slow process because it involves tracking the target for a short time to adjust the target-barrel relationship as the gun moves into the correct position.

3. *Sustained lead.* Here the gun is always in front of the target. The gun-hold point is approximately halfway between where the target is seen clearly and where you would like to break it. This is entirely dependent on the shooter's personal reaction time. Providing the gun insertion point is good, there is no reason why the target should ever be missed behind. With this method, there is a period of time where the gun is too far in front of the target. Sustained lead is one of the oldest ways we know to intercept a moving target with a cloud of shot. Centuries ago, in the days of the flintlock, due to the slow lock times of these guns (and the doubtful efficiency of the gunpowder), the only way to establish lead was to keep the gun moving in front of the target until the shot charge had left the barrels.

The most successful of these methods for shooting skeet targets is without a doubt sustained lead. It is used by more top skeet shooters in the world today than any other method. The reason is that it is quicker, more easily explained, and produces more consistent results. The beauty of the method is that there is too much lead in the early stages of the swing and if the gun-hold position is correct, the target should never beat the gun. If the target and gun are synchronized as the shot is taken, the visual impression will be that the target has slowed down. It also allows a smooth transition to other methods, which will become necessary as we learn to shoot doubles. However, a new shooter should still fully understand the principles of the other two methods. In the early stages of learning to shoot skeet by sustained lead, there will be many times that a target is allowed to pass the gun by mistake. The shooter will now have no choice but to chase the target and shoot it with the swing-through method. Alternatively, the shooter will sometimes allow the target to gain too quickly on the gun, and he will need to use the pull-away method to restore the correct sight picture. With the sustained lead method, I prefer that the shooter breaks the targets *slightly* sooner than is normally recommended.

As a clay target comes off the trap arm, it is spinning like a Frisbee. This gives it stability in the air in the initial stages of its flight path, and it will travel more or less in a straight line. Wind interference on the target is also less when it is spinning. The shooter only has to do two things to hit it—move the gun on the same line as the target and give it lead. As it loses momentum, it also begins to lose height. Now the shooter has three things to do—move the gun on the line, give the target some lead, and shoot underneath it. It is easier to do two things than three. With a standard skeet choke, the effective pattern is approximately twenty-four to thirty inches wide at twenty yards. At ten yards, this is reduced to fifteen to eighteen inches, and at five yards only twelve inches. It would therefore be more logical to shoot the incoming targets at stations 1, 2, 6, and 7 when they are more vulnerable to the gun and slightly nearer to the center stake, than when they are much nearer and already dropping.

All the incoming targets (including stations 1, 2, 6, and 7) should be broken in exactly the same place as if they were doubles. On doubles, to enable us to shoot the second target of a pair nearer to the center stake, we have to shoot the first target quicker. With a proper gun-insertion point, this is easier than you might think. There are only four ways to miss a target—above, below, in front, and behind—and provided that the shooter's gun is moving smoothly along the same line as the target, he can eliminate two of the variables, above and below. Logically, he now has a 50 percent chance of hitting that target. Any miss must be either in front or behind and is primarily determined by gun speed and the amount of perceived lead required.

The only way a skeet target can be given *exactly* the same amount of lead each time is if it is shot on the same part of its trajectory and the gun speed is the same each time. By using the target as an immediate visual reference, it is possible to do this. If the shooter can synchronize the speed of his gun to the speed of the target, he can eliminate another variable. Now we have only one variable left: the amount of *perceived* lead he needs to direct his gun in front of the target as he pulls the trigger. This method will give every shooter a way to calculate this. Please note that gun-hold point and gun-insertion point are different. The gun-hold point is where the gun is as we call for the target. The gun-insertion point is where the gun inserts on the line of the moving target. *Actual* lead is the required distance that shot has to be directed in front of the target to score a hit, which is calculated by using the laws of physics. *Apparent* or *perceived* lead is the distance the shooter's brain thinks is necessary from the optical information it receives. Perceived lead is always more on incoming targets than outgoing targets.

As I have already said, assessing the correct lead requirement is the biggest headache for any shooter, not just the beginner. Lead is a personal perception, and no two people see it the same. You might like to try the following experiment. Knock a couple of posts in the ground about twenty yards away and ask five different people to guess how far apart they are—you will probably get five different answers. Then place a yardstick or a familiar object that you know the dimensions of on top of one of the posts and ask again. The results will be much more accurate because now there is the immediate visual reference of the familiar object. For this reason, it is a waste of time to tell a beginner to lead the next target by three feet. I have some clients who swear that they see six feet lead at station 4 and others who see as little as three feet, even though they are both shooting sustained lead and their gun speeds are similar. Luckily, unlike sporting clays or wingshooting, both of which have diverse target speeds and trajectories, on a skeet layout we know the exact trajectory of each target from each of the shooting stations. We know that the maximum distance from each station to the center stake is twenty-one yards, and we know that the approximate velocity of a standard skeet load is approximately twelve hundred feet per second. The approximate speed of a regulation skeet target is forty-five miles per hour at the center stake, slightly faster for the first ten to fifteen yards or so. From this we can calculate that a target passing over the center stake requires about three to four feet forward allowance. First, though, we need to find out what our personal perception of the lead requirement is for each shooting station. I do this by starting a right-handed shooter on station 1 low house, and a left-handed shooter on station 7 high house. The right-handed shooter will usually move the gun easier from right to left in a pulling motion. Moving the gun from left to right is a push, physically a more difficult movement to make. This is why we put the cart behind the horse instead of in front of it.

LOW-HOUSE TARGETS
Station 1 Low House
I prefer beginners to break the low-house bird *slightly* earlier than is normally recommended, preferably just before the target starts to drop too much. Position your gun just *under* the flight line of the target and approximately halfway between where you see the target *clearly* and where you would like to break it. This is not the normal recommended hold point, and often the new shooter will think there is too much lead in the early stages of his swing. This will help him to develop a personal rhythm and is much better than a hold point that is too far out and results in him chasing the target with an erratic swing. As his confidence improves, so will his speed of swing, and he will find that he can eventually break the targets much earlier than he would have thought possible in the beginning. In the case of a station 1 low house, the breakpoint will be about halfway between where the shooter is standing and the center stake. Call for the target and start to accelerate the gun smoothly toward the line of the target immediately after it appears. In other words, move on the flash of the target, but move smoothly and deliberately. You should be totally committed to start moving the gun as soon as the target is seen. You already have an advantage in that your gun is in front of the target so there is some built-in lead. Any hesitation to move the gun as soon as the target is seen will cause the lead to evaporate and will result in too much gun movement in the later stages of the shot in an attempt to catch up. This doesn't mean that you should anticipate the target and move before you see it. If you do, the gun will arrive at the spot where you want to shoot the target before the target arrives there.

In the early stages of the swing, it is impossible to match the speed of the gun to the speed of the target because the target will be instantly traveling at fifty miles per hour and the gun will be starting from a stationary position. The target will rapidly gain on the gun until the speed of the swing accelerates the gun to match the speed of the target. At the same time, the gun should be moving *smoothly* onto the same line as the target. I call this the area of reducing lead. By using the moving target as a reference point, the gap between the target and gun barrel will close until the speed of the gun and target become synchronized. This is the area of *actual* sustained lead. At this point, the target should be in hard focus. It takes the human eye approximately one-fifth of a second to bring a moving object into hard focus. The gun must appear to be moving at the same speed as the target. In reality, the gun will still be traveling *fractionally* quicker than the target as the trigger is pulled due to the momentum in the barrels, and this will help to produce a smooth follow-through. At this point, we are responding to the visual information that our eyes are receiving, which in turn is transmitted to the brain. There is a chain of events that follows as we receive this information until the split second we pull the trigger. This is known as the shooter's reaction time. With the correct gun-insertion point, this very slight difference in gun speed isn't a problem as long as the trigger is pulled immediately after the correct sight picture is seen. The pattern is wide enough to compensate.

Some slight residual gun speed is also more likely on the narrow-angle targets at stations 2 and 6. Narrow-angle targets appear to be traveling faster than they actually are because they are at an acute angle to our line of sight. The more acute the angle, the faster the target appears. Try to avoid a sudden burst of gun speed on narrow-angle shots, but accelerate as smoothly as possible. As a spontaneous reaction to the sudden appearance of the target, we will always have the tendency to accelerate the gun faster in the initial stages of the swing. It's similar to hunting in the field: miss a dove with your first shot, and the spontaneous reaction to the miss often triggers an increase in gun speed, which results in a hit.

The smoothness of the swing to synchronize the target and gun is crucial to the success of this method. As soon as the target is trailing the gun by what the shooter's brain *perceives* to be the correct amount of lead, he should pull the trigger. If he misses behind, his gun-insertion point should be moved slightly ahead on the target's line for the next shot. This will allow him to adjust the area of synchronization to a point farther ahead of the target, and if the gun speed is the same, he will be able to give the target slightly more lead. If he misses in front, he must move his gun-insertion point farther back on the target line. Where he holds his gun directly influences where he will insert it on the line of the target. With an ideal gun-hold point, it should be easy to the break the target consistently with minimal gun movement. The longer the shooter swings, the more chance there is to make a mistake.

At this stage, remember also that we are trying to break the target about halfway between the center stake and the shooter. Hold position and gun-insertion controls where the target is broken.

If the shooter hits the target, he should repeat the shot until he is confident and can break the target easily in the correct place. He must pull the trigger at the instant the target and gun become synchronized. He should not track the target for more than a millisecond or attempt to increase the lead by suddenly accelerating the gun as you would with pull-away. The gun speed should remain smooth and deliberate, not jerky or erratic. After repeating the shot several times, the shooter's brain should register the specific amount of apparent lead he needs to break the target. This is what I call the shooter's personal lead perception, or PLP. We know that the area where he breaks this target is only about ten to fifteen yards from him. We also know that a standard skeet target is 110 millimeters or just over 4 inches. By using the visual reference of the target (his yardstick), the shooter should be able to make a pretty accurate assessment of how much lead he needs. Remember, lead is a personal perception, no two people see it the same. If the target is broken in the correct place, with the target and gun speeds synchronized, the shooter's perception of lead should be about three target widths, or about one foot. The shooter should now make a mental note of the target-barrel relationship, i.e., how much lead he sees on this station.

The place where this first target is broken is critical. He should shoot this target several times by slightly increasing and decreasing his lead requirement to find out where he can break the target most efficiently. Whatever the shooter's perceived lead requirement is at station 1 will now be used as a measuring unit on all the other stations.

As a general rule, the outgoers should be broken just *before* the center stake and the incomers *after* the center stake in the same place that they would be broken as doubles. Once the shooter can repeatedly hit this target, he has learned the following:

1. He can move the gun accurately on the line of the target.

2. His brain has "locked in" a specified amount of lead to give the target at station 1.

3. Providing there is no noticeable variation in gun speed and his gun insertion and hold points are the same, he can match the speed of the swing to the speed of the target and thus give the target *exactly* the correct amount of lead every time.

4. Lead is established by where the gun is inserted, not the gun speed.

5. Gun-hold point and insertion point are determined by each shooter's individual reaction time. Shooter's reaction time has more influence on gun speed than we realize. Shooters with a slow reaction time and poor muscular coordination can still use this method successfully by adjusting their gun-insertion point.

More importantly, by using this formula, each shooter can calculate exactly the correct amount of perceived lead he needs on every other station.

Station 2 Low House

The shooter now has a predetermined amount of lead to give this target—*double* the lead that he saw at station 1. Once again, the gun-hold point should initially be halfway between the intended breakpoint and where the target is seen clearly. On this station the breakpoint will be at the same place as the low one, because this is where he will shoot it on doubles. If he saw one foot of lead at station 1, he should double it to two feet for station 2. If the target and gun become synchronized *before* the correct amount of lead is seen, i.e., with not enough lead, the gun hold and insertion point should be moved farther out for the next shot. If the synchronization occurs *after* the correct amount of lead is seen, the gun hold and insertion points should be moved back toward the high house. Once again, this is the only adjustment that should be made. There should not be a conscious increase in gun speed. All the stations should now be shot in the same way.

Station 3 Low House

Lead should be doubled again (or four feet).

Station 4 Low House

Lead should be the same as that for station 3 (or four feet) because if you look at the diagram of the skeet field, the flight line of the low-house target is parallel to stations 3 and 4 with the low-house birds and the same for stations 4 and 5 for the high house. Logically, if the distance to the target is the same, the lead requirement must be the same.

Station 5 Low House

Lead should be the same as that for station 2 (or two feet).

Station 6 Low House

Lead should be the same as that for station 1 (or one foot).

Station 7 Low House

No lead. In relation to the shooter, this is a rising target, and therefore the shot should be into the anticipated path of the target, which is slightly above the target. The gun-hold point should be just above the center stake at an angle of approximately 30 degrees. The gun movement should be a gentle lift, and the trigger should be pulled immediately after the target starts to disappear behind the gun.

Station 8 Low House

This is what I consider to be a coordinated ambush or spot shot. The gun-hold point should be well out on the line of the target and directly proportional to the shooter's reaction time. For slow reaction times, the gun should be held farther out; for quick reactions, the hold point should be farther in. The sudden appearance of the target will trigger an immediate and spontaneous response from the shooter, and he must accelerate the gun quickly to intercept the target. The correct sight picture is just before the target vanishes behind the barrel. No conscious effort should be made to synchronize gun and target speed—there isn't time.

Doubles

With a pair of targets, instead of concentrating 50 percent on each of them, concentrate 100 percent on the first until it is shot at, and then immediately focus 100 percent on the second. Doubles are merely two singles.

Don't forget that we are synchronizing the speed of the gun to the speed of the target, so there should be no variation in gun speed from shooter to shooter. Gun speed, shooter's reaction time, and lead assessment are all individual things. This method gives each shooter the opportunity to apply his own personal reaction time and perception of lead required to each target. The only thing that should change is the shooter's gun-hold point. Now we have an easy-to-remember formula to calculate the target lead requirement at each of the stations. The low-house leads are: station 1, 1; station 2, 2; station 3, 4; station 4, 4; station 5, 2; station 6, 1; station 7, 0. All the shooter needs to remember is LOW HOUSE 1244210.

HIGH-HOUSE TARGETS
Station 1 High House

Apparent lead should be nil for station 1 high house. In relation to the shooter, the target is coming down; therefore, he must shoot slightly

Station 1 High House

The *required* forward allowance for a skeet target (which is intercepted over the center stake) will always be approximately four feet if it is shot with the sustained lead method. Where shots are taken at a more acute angle, the *perceived* lead will be different from the *required* lead. In this photograph, taken from station 1 on a skeet field, the piece of white painted two-by-four on the center stake represents the *perceived* forward allowance for the high-house target. Seen over the muzzles of the gun, this appears to be almost zero angular lead from station 1.

underneath it. The gun should first be mounted on the center stake and moved up until it is at an approximate angle of 30 to 40 degrees. This angle is directly proportional to the shooter's reaction time. For slow reactions the angle is less, for quick reactions, more. The shooter's eyes should be looking back for the target but not so far back that he cannot see his barrel in his peripheral vision. His gun should already be on the same line as the target, but he will have time to adjust slightly to compensate for any sideways movement as the target appears. Call for the target, and as soon as it settles on the front bead, pull the trigger. There will be a very slight downward movement with the muzzles, perhaps an inch or two with the beginner. Any more gun movement is unnecessary and will result in a poke at the target. The gun-hold point should be adjusted if there is too much movement. Eventually, as the shooter becomes more proficient, this gun movement will be almost nil. There should be no hesitation as he pulls the trigger.

Remaining High–House Stations

The rest of the high–house targets should be given the following leads:

Station 2 High House
The same target seen
from Station 2. From
here the perceived lead
appears to be about one
foot. This is known as a
narrow-angle shot.

Station 3 High House
Here the angle has
increased. The lead
now appears to be about
two feet. This is a wide-
angle shot.

Station 4 High House
Maximum lead, about
four feet. Actual lead is
only the same as per-
ceived lead on this 90-
degree shot. This is a
full-crossing shot.

Station 5 High House
Still maximum lead, about
four feet because the flight
line of the target is parallel
to the positions of stations
4 and 5.

Station 6 High House
Now the angle to the tar-
get is reducing again from
the maximum. From here
the perceived lead is about
two feet.

Station 7 High House
From here the perceived
lead is about one foot.

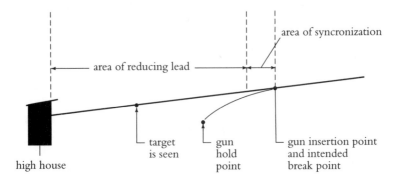

Gun-hold and insertion points for a reducing sustained lead shot.

All the shooter needs to remember for the high-house targets is that they are the exact opposite of the low-house targets: 0124421.

Now we have a formula to apply to each target and a very easy way to remember the leads as we shoot rounds. For example, the incoming targets from stations 2, 4, 5, and 6 all need double the lead requirement of the outgoing targets.

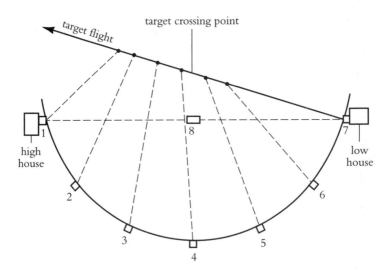

Lead requirements for low house are station 1, 1; station 2, 2; station 3, 4; station 4, 4; station 5, 2; station 6, 1; station 7, 0.

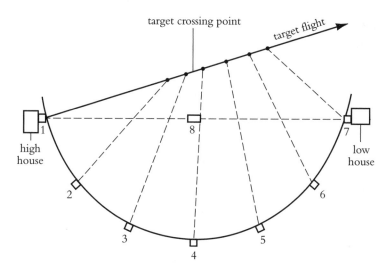

Lead requirements for high house are station 1, 0; station 2, 1; station 3, 2; station 4, 4; station 5, 4; station 6, 2; station 7, 1.

The main points with this method are as follows:

1. There should be no attempt to track the target or to increase or decrease the lead as you would with the pull-away method. If you try to do this, the sight picture will vary as the gun speed varies.

2. When the correct sight picture is seen, the trigger must be pulled the instant the target and gun synchronize.

3. Any adjustment to either where the target is broken or how it is missed in front or behind is made with the gun-hold and insertion points.

4. With correct insertion points at each station and *smooth* acceleration, you will find that the gun-target synchronization point occurs exactly where the correct sight picture at each station is seen.

Of course, to the new shooter, this all seems to happen very fast, and the narrow-angle targets will give him the most trouble. The diagrams on page 290 give the approximate points where the targets should be broken.

Remember that this method was designed primarily to help the beginner. It is easier to teach this method hands-on than it is to explain it in print. All beginners expect good results in the early stages of learning

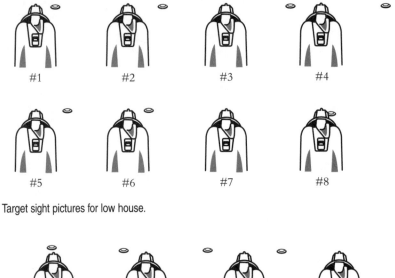

Target sight pictures for low house.

Target sight pictures for high house.

without wading through mountains of technical information. This method has several distinct advantages:

1. It is easy to understand.
2. It is easy to remember.
3. It actually works!

Finally, the only difference between the good skeet shot and the bad skeet shot is practice. Practice doesn't make perfect; practice makes permanent.

CHAPTER 20

Addicted to Dove

It was Monday morning and I was tired; the weekend had been busy at the gun club with a corporate event for 350 shooters. I didn't really need the phone call. "You ever been dove hunting?" Larry asked. "My folks have a farm near Lubbock. Lots of them about this year. You should come." As I hung up the phone, my brain began to absorb the message. Although I had lived in the Lone Star State for over two years, I had not yet had the pleasure of a dove-hunting trip. I didn't need to think twice about it and licked my lips in anticipation.

We drove from Dallas the night before opening day, through the changing countryside until we reached the endless swaying seas of sunflowers, milo, and cotton that surrounded the infant town of Muleshoe. I eagerly scanned each new horizon for the flocks of dove that were supposed to be here, but apart from the odd lonesome one, I was disappointed. As we pulled into the yard, Larry's brother-in-law Gary and an entourage of canine followers greeted us. Susie, a seven-week-old German shorthaired pointer, headed the pack, followed by the appropriately named Milo, a useful-looking Labrador cross; Red, another German pointer; and last but not least, old Shadow, the chocolate Lab long past her sell-by date, but still mobile. Just.

"Howdy! So you're the shooting instructor guy from Scotland. You bring plenty of shells?" Gary's face cracked into a grin. The other guys who were going on the hunt were quick to follow. "Larry told us he was gonna bring you along as his show and tell!" More raucous laughter as I nodded my puzzled response. Show and tell? What exactly was that? These little gray guys couldn't be that difficult to hit, could they?

The adrenalin factor. Dove hunting must be one of the most addictive and exciting forms of bird-hunting there is. (*photo courtesy of Trek International Safaris*)

"You wanna see some doves?" Gary continued, with a drawl as thick as a cup of campfire coffee. Now, I must admit, that did seem like a good idea, not that I was ungrateful for the invitation, but during the 450-mile or so journey I had spotted only three, and by now my genetically engineered cynicism seemed to be taking over. Perhaps "lots of them about" was an exaggeration, and the term wild goose chase came to mind.

We loaded into a truck and were soon bouncing along one of the dusty tracks that bisected the landscape. I soon realized that in the South, dove hunts were social events with groups of amicable, congenial folks, with a few rowdy or different guys thrown in to season the mix. It was obvious that I was the latter, and my accent caused lots of amusement.

As the truck lurched along its erratic way, Gary pointed out groups of trees that were dying for no apparent reason. "Won't be no trees left soon. No one knows why," he spat, as though he would have preferred to blame someone. "It's near impossible to find good dove hunting, but this year's different, there's lots about."

The impact of mechanization over the last few decades had indeed left its mark on west Texas. Small farms had grown into medium-size farms, which had in turn been swallowed up into larger farms, but as always, progress has its price, and the area was not without casualties. Empty shacks, which had once sheltered hardworking but happy families, scarred the landscape, sad reminders of a bygone era. Each house had its attendant stand of elm trees, planted presumably to offer the occupants some respite from the searing heat of the Texas sun. Now the trees had another use. The truck ground to a dusty halt next to an old abandoned schoolhouse, and as we climbed out and slammed the doors, doves spilled from the surrounding trees with their characteristic whistling wing beats. There must have been several dozen. More trees produced even more doves. I was impressed, and Gary's face was a picture of triumphant "I told you so." I looked forward to the morning.

Opening day! After hastily planning our attack over coffee and blueberry muffins, we decided that an undisturbed strip of trees to the west should be the most productive. Four of the guys were placed at strategic intervals at one end, but Gary's son Dustin and I drew the short straws. We were nominated to walk the tree line and flush the birds. A bit like pheasants in Scotland, I thought, except for the heat, cockleburrs, and occasional rattler. As I kicked a dusty path through the field, my mind wandered. I remembered all the times I had spent freezing to death in blizzard conditions with only my dogs for company, sheltering behind a drystane dike waiting for a pheasant drive to start. I know which I prefer.

As we worked our way down the tree line, I could see the doves zipping in and out of the scrubby trees like fleas on a hedgehog's back. An eruption of birds as we came to the end of the tree line would be inevitable. I was using a Winchester model 101 over-and-under 20 gauge with 1-ounce 7½ shells, which I calculated would be adequate. I nervously flicked the safety forward in anticipation, just as the first birds began breaking cover and flying back over us. Take the first one out there with the choke barrel and the second one a bit nearer with the cylinder. That should do it. I lifted onto the first bird and touched the trigger. Unfortunately, by the time the shot arrived at the place where the dove was, he suddenly wasn't there. Repeat high house, I thought, and the same thing happened. Two bangs but no doves. The rest dispersed at speeds that would have made an Exocet missile envious.

Now wait a minute, this wasn't supposed to happen. I have shot wily, heather-hugging driven grouse on some of the best moors in Scotland, have shot stratospheric driven pheasants all over the United Kingdom for over thirty years, and have been a shooting instructor for over

First dove.

twenty-four years. Here I am in Texas shooting at things that just aren't where they're supposed to be when you pull the trigger. What was even more surprising was that this was opening day! These birds had never been shot at before, but the slightest detection of movement in their peripheral vision triggered immediate evasive action, and they would roll and pitch like skirmishing MiG fighters. Milo the dog looked at me in disgust, and I looked for a rattler-free rock to crawl under. Gary appeared from the other side of some mesquite trees. "How many'd you get? I heard a couple of shots." I shook my head, but the look on my face had already told him. I could guess what he was thinking.

But things would get better. The next bird to run the gauntlet curled back and came past me well out into the field of milo. He saw me and turned the afterburners on, but I exaggerated the lead and was relieved to see him crumple and plummet earthward. I marked the spot, walked over to pick him up (Milo had already abandoned me in favor of Gary, no doubt deciding that he would be more productive), and examined the bird closely. The dove looked smaller that it did in flight. The wings were big in relation to the body size, which would account for the rapid acceleration, and the pointed tail was interesting, giving it the appearance of a pigeon-parakeet hybrid. Maybe the tail was the secret of their aerial agility. I have seen hen pheasants coming off the side of a Scottish mountain with a sixty-mile-an-hour gale behind them demonstrate similar maneuvers when they spotted the waiting guns. With pheasants, the secret is to ignore the sideways deviation in the flight pattern and to take the bird well out in front with the choke barrel. This also seems to work with doves, but one thing I noticed as the day progressed was that I was overleading some of the birds. They could accelerate quickly, but because of their small size, they just did not have the momentum of a bird with more body weight and would make heavy going of it when flying into a stiff headwind with a full cargo of sunflower seeds. With a strong tailwind the situation was reversed, and I needed to accelerate the gun well through them. Small birds with rapid wingbeats give the illusion of speed; the reverse of large birds such as geese.

That night, under a perfect Texas sky, we drank cold Texas beer and ate jalapeño-stuffed doves from the barbeque. The taste was superb, and even without the beer, the thrill of it all had intoxicated me. I loved every minute of it; it was certainly as much fun as shooting driven pheasants, but without all the pomp and ceremony. I take my hat off to the little gray ghosts, slicing so easily through the hot Texas air, and I hope I get invited back next year. I wonder if doves are tough enough to live in Scotland. . . .

Index

Page numbers in italics indicates illustrations.